THOMAS HOBBES
AND POLITICAL THEORY

THOMAS HOBBES AND POLITICAL THEORY

Edited by Mary G. Dietz

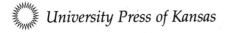 University Press of Kansas

© 1990 by the University Press of Kansas
All rights reserved

Published by the University Press of Kansas (Lawrence, Kansas 66045), which was or-
.ganized by the Kansas Board of Regents and is operated and funded by Emporia
State University, Fort Hays State University, Kansas State University, Pittsburg State
University, the University of Kansas, and Wichita State University

Library of Congress Cataloging-in-Publication Data

Thomas Hobbes and political theory / edited by Mary G. Dietz.
    p. cm.
    Includes bibliographical references.
    ISBN 0-7006-0420-0 (alk. paper) ISBN 0-7006-0519-3 (pbk.)
    1. Hobbes, Thomas, 1588–1679—Contributions in political science.
I. Dietz, Mary G.
JC153.H66T479 1990
320′.092—dc20   89-37242
                                                          CIP

Printed in the United States of America
10 9 8 7 6 5 4 3 2

The paper used in this publication meets the minimum requirements of the American
National Standard for Permanence of Paper for Printed Library Materials Z39.48-1984.

To the memory of
Benjamin Evans Lippincott
1902–1988

Contents

Acknowledgments

The essays in this volume issue from the Benjamin Evans Lippincott Symposium, "The Political Philosophy of Thomas Hobbes, 1599–1988," held at the University of Minnesota in the spring of 1988. The symposium was made possible by the generous endowment of the Benjamin Evans Lippincott Fund and by the support and assistance of the Department of Political Science.

A number of people deserve thanks for their participation in various aspects, intellectual and organizational, of the symposium and the graduate seminar that accompanied it. I owe special thanks to my colleague Terence Ball, who was diligent and energetic in his role as co-convenor of the symposium and seminar and provided sage advice concerning the production of the manuscript. Substantial appreciation is also due to the fourteen scholars who participated at various times during the Minnesota spring in the spirited discussions of Hobbes and his political thought. For stimulating and provocative papers, I thank the contributors to this volume, and for stirring things up with just the right amount of scholarly criticism and good humor, I thank the symposium commentators: Don Herzog, Hanna Fenichel Pitkin, Patrick Riley, Molly Shanley, Ian Shapiro, George Shulman, and James Boyd White. Thanks also to the graduate students who took the Hobbes seminar and acted as both gadflies and hosts to the visiting scholars. The collective, lively engagement that was an essential part of the symposium's success we owe to them.

The smooth organization and management of the symposium and the efficient coordination required for completion of the manuscript were made possible by Cathy Duvall and Sterline Williams in the Department of Political Science. My thanks to them for making everything seem so easy and uncomplicated and for their unfailing equanimity in the face of an endless parade of duties and demands. My sincerest appreciation also to Gertrude Lippincott for the encouragement and support she continued to extend to this project during a sorrowful time.

The University Press of Kansas has been, from the start, the most efficient and professional publisher an editor could imagine. Thanks are due to the press staff for their enthusiasm and superb assistance at the various stages of production. I am grateful as well to Jeffrey Issac for his good advice and constructive criticism.

Sadly, Benjamin Lippincott did not live to see this volume come to fruition. His love of political philosophy pervades it nonetheless. We dedicate these essays to him.

1

Introduction

Mary G. Dietz

Writing nearly twenty-five years ago about the state of Hobbes studies, the English scholar K. C. Brown observed that "a lively and fruitful discussion has been in progress for considerable time, and no one who is seriously interested in Hobbes's work can altogether avoid being affected by it."[1] Although Brown was referring primarily to Hobbes scholarship in the postwar years, he could easily have extended his point over the past three centuries; for Hobbes is one of a small number of political theorists in the Western tradition who stirred debate in his own lifetime and has continued to do so ever since.

Hobbes's writings emerged in a period of intense political turmoil—a time of civil war and regicide, of puritanical rule and royal restoration. "The so formidable *Leviathan*" (as Aubrey called it) was published in 1651 and constituted, as Hobbes himself characterized it, a defense of any de facto government provided that it governed. Apparently, both Cromwell and Charles II took it as such, for neither seems to have perceived Hobbes as a threat to his regime. Nevertheless, despite Hobbes's personal admission to both the Puritan Commonwealth and the Stuart court, "Hobbism" soon became a target of significant political controversy. Critics were especially alarmed by the so-called Hobbist theory of political obligation, which appeared to root obedience to a given government in self-interested calculation rather than in Christian doctrine. Thus, one commentator wrote, "Most of the bad principles of this age are . . . indeed but the spawn of the *Leviathan*."[2] Hobbes had his defenders as well, however, particularly among those who supported a de facto theory that emphasized a government's ability to protect, not the people's sovereign power, as the basis for political obligation. Whatever else they had accomplished, Hobbes's writings had succeeded in capturing the political imagination of the age. By the end of the century, even his opponents had to concede that Hobbes was a genius, and *Leviathan* one "of the most vendible books in England."[3]

Throughout the eighteenth century and into the nineteenth—when both Hobbesian skepticism and the command theory of law were appropriated by the utilitarians—the hunting of *Leviathan* continued. As the political immediacy of Hobbes's writings receded, their significance as sources of philosophical speculation increased. Displaying a seemingly endless hermeneutical flexibility, his writings were culled for medievalist and modern doctrines, as well as for possible naturalist, neo-Aristotelian, canonical, Erastian, or Stoical foundations. In 1892, Sir James Fitzjames Stephen finally concluded that Hobbes's manner was "half old and half modern," and the debates continued, as disputants variously interpreted Hobbes as a part of the Christian or Stoic natural law tradition on the one hand or firmly embedded in the precepts of natural science on the other.[4]

A brief period of quiescence in the early twentieth century, broken significantly by John Dewey's essay "The Motivations of Hobbes's Political Philosophy," was quickly followed by a resurgence of interest and debate, led by J. Laird, Leo Strauss, and perhaps most significantly, A. E. Taylor, whose essay "The Ethical Doctrine of Thomas Hobbes" set off the lively discussion to which K. C. Brown referred.[5] In response to the increasingly mechanistic and psychological interpretations of the day, the so-called Taylor-Warrender Thesis claimed a deontological status for Hobbes's theory, quite distinct from, and even incompatible with, his egoistic psychology. Hobbes's scientific naturalism and egoism were thus deemed to be at odds with the moral imperatives that could be derived from the Hobbesian laws of nature (which Taylor viewed as divine commands and Warrender associated with Stoic and Roman law thinking).[6] The wide-ranging scholarly debate that followed the introduction of this "thesis" enlisted among its participants Michael Oakeshott, John Plamanatz, Leo Strauss, Sterling P. Lamprecht, Dorothea Krook, J. W. N. Watkins, and Willis B. Glover—all of whom contributed to the thickening of Hobbesian interpretation in various ethical, psychological, and nominalist terms.[7] The literature articulated and focused upon questions that remain alive in current

Hobbesian scholarship: To what extent is Hobbes's naturalist, scientific method compatible with an ethical doctrine of duty and consent? How systematic (and successful) was Hobbes's naturalism as the basis for a theory of political society and moral obligation?

As dominant as this debate was in twentieth-century Hobbesian interpretation, however, the study of Hobbesian theory began to emerge in other, less purely philosophical and ethical forms as well. Under alternative guises, the central issues in interpretation tended to shift from the problem of natural law, obligation, and egoism to more expressly political problems of power and sovereignty, liberty and obedience, religion, ideology, and rationality. At no time was this more evident than in the 1960s, which witnessed a veritable explosion in Hobbes literature on both sides of the Atlantic. Among the influential commentators of the decade we can number Sheldon Wolin, C. B. Macpherson, Samuel I. Mintz, F. C. Hood, J. W. N. Watkins, M. M. Goldsmith, F. S. McNeilly, and David P. Gauthier.[8] K. C. Brown's valuable collection, *Hobbes Studies*, appeared at this moment, as did a series of path-breaking essays by Quentin Skinner.[9] In general, this episode in Hobbesian interpretation continued to press the ethical dimensions of his system of ideas. More important, perhaps, it also gave rise to a series of new directions in Hobbesian scholarship. Historical and sociological interpretations were advanced, as were a variety of logical-formalist discussions of the rational construction of Hobbes's theory. New issues appeared on the intellectual landscape, including the social origins of Hobbes's thought (precipitated by Macpherson's interpretation of Hobbes as a theorist of "possessive individualism"); the historical and intellectual context of Hobbes's writings, spurred by Mintz and Skinner's contextualist critique of the Taylor–Warrender Thesis; and the logical-scientific bases of Hobbes's system, generated by Watkins's naturalistic account on the one hand and Gauthier's rational-actor approach on the other. In all of these guises, Hobbes continued to grip the scholarly imagination; to paraphrase K. C. Brown, Hobbesian theory ignited new revolutions in scholarship and interpretation.

Today, as we celebrate the four hundredth anniversary of the birth of the "little worm" from Malmesbury amidst an abundance of scholarly riches, it might be appropriate to ask: Why yet another volume of Hobbes studies? The answer requires us to acknowledge, as we have already seen, that Hobbes's writings are not mere static artifacts of a particular historical milieu open to a single accounting, but rather rich sources for a variety of interpretations and criticisms that spur discussion and debate in their turn. Whatever else the story of Hobbesian scholarship has been, it is indeed a tale of seemingly limitless hermeneutical possibilities, of cross-generational accounts, critiques, and countercritiques that persistently test and press beyond the established boundaries of the existing literature. To the extent that the essays in this volume emerge from and respond to some of the themes of recent Hobbesian scholarship, they continue in the tradition of expanding the scope of our knowledge of Hobbes and his time.

We hope, however, that these essays do not simply underscore the hermeneutical flexibility of Hobbes studies in some general sense, but develop a particular set of hermeneutical concerns as well. Hence, instead of beginning from purely philosophical premises or rationally reconstructed formalist arguments, these studies start with the following assumption: that Hobbes's writings are motivated by concrete political problems and a practical concern, namely, to secure political order, absolute sovereignty, and civil peace. What emerges is a political theory that is at least partly constitutive of the ways in which we continue to understand and describe our own political practices. Thus, Hobbes's theory raises both contextual and contemporary political questions, and these are the sorts of questions that distinguish the essays in this volume: How might we assess Hobbes's political project in light of the practices, concepts, and political arrangements that constitute our own political culture? How did Hobbes attempt to mediate the practices, concepts, and political institutions of his own time? How, in particular, did he fashion a strategy for controlling rebellious elites and creating obedient citizens? How did he understand the need to reconstitute a dominant political culture, particularly in terms of the relationship between science and rhetoric? In what ways did he perceive the ideology of religious conflict and its relation to the politics of scriptural interpretation? To what extent can Hobbes's political theory be read as an attempt to gain control over nothing less than the entire realm of discourse of a political regime, so that the allegiance of the people, and hence the stability of the state, can be assured?

In short, while taking up these issues in diverse ways, the authors in this volume have in common the interpretive premise that Hobbes was, first and foremost, a political thinker and that his writings were, first and foremost, political acts, rather than preeminently scientific or ethical doctrines or logico-deductive exercises. Since this dimension of Hobbes's work has not been fully explored in the existing literature, we hope our volume will afford the reader a set of competing perspectives that will not only add to the already rich mix of Hobbes studies but thicken it interpretatively as well.

The volume begins with Sheldon Wolin's essay "Hobbes and the Culture of Despotism," which sets the stage for a discussion of Hobbesian politics as structured by a form of theoretical discourse that itself constitutes a particular conception of power. What interests Wolin is the way Hobbes, like Plato, sought to represent a technical knowledge to a general public and transmute that knowledge not only into a "science" of sovereign absolutism but into a deeper culture of despotism as well. Thus, the Hobbesian project has elitist implications that must be confronted, especially in the age of the technocratic state. David Johnston is also concerned with the relationship Hobbes established between a calculating science and a theory of political power. In "Plato, Hobbes, and the Science of Practical Reason," he too pursues the parallel between Plato and Hobbes, arguing that both attempted to construct a science of "practical reason" and a "common measure" that would allow for the adjudication of conflicting political values and demands. Hobbes's conception of appetites, however, permits him to arrive at what he considered a far more precise and unequivocal moral philosophy than Plato's; it replaced the contemplation of eternal goods with the calculation of quantifiable passions. Johnston concludes by reflecting upon the problematical implications this science of practical reason has for contemporary political life.

Like Wolin and Johnston, Gordon Schochet is interested in Hobbes's relation to a particular form of discourse. In "Intending (Political) Obligation: Hobbes and the Voluntary Basis of Society," Schochet reconsiders the various liberal and nonliberal aspects of Hobbesian theory, particularly in light of Hobbes's thinking on intention and obligation. Schochet's analytical examination of the relationship Hobbes struck between intention, consent, and obligation leads him to uncover some decidedly nonliberal elements in Hobbes's political thought. Although we are amiss to see Hobbes as some sort of protoliberal, Schochet argues, Hobbes nevertheless attempted to ground a theory of consent and obligation in something more robust than a doctrine of simple coercion or mere absolutism. By critically reexamining the grounds of Hobbes's views of intentionality, Schochet invites us to discard our shopworn assessments of Hobbes as "liberal" or "antiliberal" and approach Hobbes's thought in other ways.

The next two essays shift the discussion of Hobbes's political theory in a contextual direction, in order to investigate Hobbes's own critical and political purposes concerning masses and elites. Deborah Baumgold's essay "Hobbes's Political Sensibility: The Menace of Political Ambition" approaches the problem of sovereign and subject from a historical perspective. Baumgold argues that Hobbes's political theory is best understood in view of his analysis of civil strife; in particular, Hobbes was primarily preoccupied by the danger of those politically ambitious elites who threatened the order and stability of the commonwealth. Baumgold offers extensive textual warrant for reading in *Leviathan* an attempt to check these "children of pride." Thus, Baumgold argues, Hobbes's political theory emerges not from a detached social analysis but rather from a political sensibility attuned to the political and intellectual conflicts of his day. Mary Dietz pursues a "political contextual" Hobbes as well, but with a different emphasis. In "Hobbes's Subject as Citizen," Dietz presents Hobbes as a theorist of civic virtue who advanced an argument for civic obedience with the political qualities of the common people in mind. Hobbes's conception of the subjects' obedience, Dietz contends, is grounded in a theory of duty as "the science of just and unjust," which itself demonstrates and advances a set of civic qualities and civil commandments designed to establish a healthy citizenry and assure the stability of sovereign power.

Both Baumgold and Dietz raise a possibility that Stephen Holmes pursues in "Political Psychology in Hobbes's *Behemoth*." Holmes suggests that Hobbes's political psychology is far more complex and multifaceted than most previous analytic, subjectivist interpretations have allowed. In particular, we can gain a deeper appreciation of Hobbes as a political psychologist if we consider his assessment of the actual agents and elites involved in the political, social, and religious disputes of his time. Focusing upon *Behemoth*, Holmes contends that Hobbes's "anatomy of disorder" reveals him to be a sophisticated analyst of the passions and interests that percolated beneath the surface of the English Civil War.

The final essays, by Richard Tuck and James Farr, focus directly upon Hobbes's view of the religious disputes that colored mid-seventeenth-century England and his political response to them. In "Hobbes and Locke on Toleration," Tuck offers a detailed historical interpretation of Hobbes's view of state control of religious worship in England. By situating Hobbes within the context of numerous parliamentary acts and ordinances, Tuck suggests that we read *De Cive* and *Leviathan* as texts that argued that there was no source independent of the sovereign on matters of religious judgment and that the absence of any independent source implied toleration. Thus, on matters of policy and politics, Hobbes seems to have had much in common with John Locke. On the basis of his hermeneutical rendering of Hobbes's interpretation of Scripture, James Farr argues that Hobbes was less a tolerationist than he was an astute interpreter of biblical Scripture, whose religious doctrine was promulgated with specifically political ends in mind. In "Atomes of Scripture: Hobbes and the Politics of Biblical Interpretation," Farr uncovers a politics of scriptural interpretation, guided by a set of hermeneutical principles, at work in parts 3 and 4 of *Leviathan*. Reconstructing these principles and the logic behind Hobbes's lengthy discussion of a "Christian Commonwealth," Farr shows how Hobbes attempted to teach the sovereign to mold and present Scripture in a way that would not only establish the state's power over doctrine and opinion but put an end to the divisiveness of "false and seditious doctrines" once and for all. Thus, Farr argues, Hobbes's politics of scriptural interpretation, and his call for a sovereign interpreter of Scripture, are nothing less than an attempt to "reconstitute the language and community of his contemporaries."

Insofar as all of these essays proceed in a spirit of expressly political and theoretical inquiry, I hope that our readers will find in them a valuable addition to the already expansive Hobbes literature. At the least, these essays allow a renewed acquaintance with the genius and multidimensionality of one of the greatest minds in all of political philosophy. But perhaps readers will also discover in this collection a series of rich contributions to the further interpretation of Hobbes's writings as political acts designed to secure power, sovereignty, and civil peace.

NOTES

1. K. C. Brown, "Introduction," *Hobbes Studies*, ed. K. C. Brown (Cambridge, Mass.: Harvard University Press, 1965), p. vii.

2. Quentin Skinner, "The Context of Hobbes's Theory of Political Obligation," in *Hobbes and Rousseau*, ed. Maurice Cranston and Richard S. Peters (Garden City, N.Y.: Doubleday & Company, 1972), p. 114.

3. Ibid., pp. 111, 113.

4. W. H. Greenleaf, "Hobbes: The Problem of Interpretation," in *Hobbes and Rousseau*, pp. 14–15, 24.

5. See John Dewey, "The Motivations of Hobbes's Political Philosophy," in *Thomas Hobbes in His Time* (Minneapolis: University of Minnesota Press, 1974); John Laird, *Hobbes* (London: E. Benn, 1934); Leo Strauss, *The Political Philosophy of Hobbes: Its Basis and Its Genesis*, trans. Elsa M. Sinclair (Chicago: University of

Chicago Press, 1952); and A. E. Taylor, "The Ethical Doctrine of Thomas Hobbes," in *Hobbes Studies*.

6. Howard Warrender, *The Political Philosophy of Hobbes: His Theory of Obligation* (Oxford: Clarendon, 1957).

7. See Michael Oakeshott, Introduction to *Leviathan* (Oxford: Basil Blackwell, 1960); Strauss, *Political Philosophy of Hobbes*; Sterling Lamprecht, "Hobbes and Hobbism," *American Political Science Review* 34 (1940): 31–53; and John Plamanatz, *Man and Society*, 2 vols. (New York: McGraw Hill, 1963). Also Dorothea Krook, *Three Traditions of Moral Thought* (Cambridge: Cambridge University Press, 1959); J. W. N. Watkins, "Philosophy and Politics in Hobbes," in *Hobbes Studies*; and Willis B. Glover, "Human Nature and the State in Hobbes," *Journal of the History of Philosophy* 5 (1966): 293–311.

8. See Sheldon S. Wolin, *Politics and Vision* (Boston: Little, Brown, 1960); C. B. Macpherson, *The Political Theory of Possessive Individualism, Hobbes to Locke* (Oxford: Clarendon Press, 1962); Samuel I. Mintz, *The Hunting of Leviathan: Seventeenth-Century Reactions to the Materialism and Moral Philosophy of Thomas Hobbes* (Cambridge: Cambridge University Press, 1962); F. C. Hood, *The Divine Politics of Thomas Hobbes: An Interpretation of Leviathan* (Oxford: Clarendon Press, 1964); J. W. N. Watkins, *Hobbes's System of Ideas: A Study in the Political Significance of Philosophical Theories* (London: Hutchinson University Library, 1965); M. M. Goldsmith, *Hobbes's Science of Politics* (New York: Columbia University Press, 1966); F. S. McNeilly, "Egoism in Hobbes," *Philosophical Quarterly* 16 (1966): 193–206; David P. Gauthier, *The Logic of Leviathan* (London: Oxford University Press, 1964).

9. K. C. Brown, *Hobbes Studies*; and Quentin Skinner, "Hobbes on Sovereignty: An Unknown Discussion," *Political Studies* 13 (1965): 213–18; "The Ideological Context of Hobbes's Political Thought," *Historical Journal* 9 (1966): 286–317; and "Thomas Hobbes and His Disciples in France and England," *Comparative Studies in Society and History* 8 (1966): 153–67.

2

Hobbes and the Culture of Despotism

Sheldon S. Wolin

Unless either philosophers become kings or those who are now called kings come to be sufficiently inspired with a genuine desire for wisdom; unless power and philosophy meet together . . . .

—Plato *Republic* 473c–d

And my own social theory which favors gradual and piecemeal reform strongly contrasts with my theory of method, which happens to be a theory of scientific and intellectual revolution.

—Karl Popper

Shortly after the end of the war against totalitarianism, Karl Popper launched a famous criticism of Plato. He charged Plato with advocating a totalitarian regime in which philosophers would have absolute power because they alone possessed absolute or true knowledge. Such claims, Popper argued, were based upon a metaphysical conception of absolute truth that was logically false as well as politically pernicious. Thus Plato's system stood condemned as a double absolutism, epistemological and political.

Ironically, the relationship that Popper detected in Plato's thinking between knowledge-claims and forms of rule, between the structure of truth and the structure of power, was unintentionally reproduced when Popper set out his alternative conceptions of truth and politics. Popper, too, relied upon a homology between politics and knowledge that modeled the former upon the latter and would have political practice emulate the "free" methods of science. The result, while not totalitarian as Plato's combination was alleged to be, displays some strikingly authoritarian elements. That such a result should occur in a thinker whose intentions were anti-authoritarian might be explained by suggesting that his scheme disguised the presence of power from the author, not just in the political domain but in the scientific as well. The disguise was provided by reducing politics to a series of technical problems with the result that power, especially in its coercive aspects, virtually disappears. Concurrent with his scientization of politics, Popper's description of scientific method contained authoritarian and intolerant elements, although he believed that his description of science portrayed an "open society."

Popper was concerned primarily to justify a new form of politics—social engineering—by appealing to scientific methods; that is, a politics in which social policies would be treated experimentally was recommended because it was "like" the logic of science. The methods of science represented the rational grounds for demonstrating the truth of a given statement. "The only [sic] course open to the social sciences is . . . to tackle the practical problems of our time with the help of the theoretical methods which are fundamentally the same in *all* sciences."[1] What Popper labeled the "logic of discovery" involved a so-called "crucial experiment" designed to falsify statements submitted to it. Only statements that passed the test of falsification qualified as "acceptable." Popper looked upon the notion of "the falsifying experiment" as a liberating advance over views of science that demanded "ultimate grounds" for statements rather than probable ones. The falsifying experiment, he asserted, "has opened up new vistas into a world of new experiences."[2]

"Piecemeal social engineering" was presented by Popper as the political correlative of falsification procedures. Like the latter, piecemeal engineering was based upon a negative criterion: to attack "the greatest and most urgent evils of society rather than searching for, fighting for, its greatest ultimate good." It involved "the alteration of one social institution at a time . . . without revolutionizing the whole society."[3]

Popper's defense of social engineering was strongly criticized at the time by advocates of central economic planning, a notion then much in favor among democratic socialists and liberal exponents of the interventionist/welfare state. That criticism had the effect of obscuring the strong technological impulse in Popper's political thinking and the similarity between Popper's scientist/social engineer and Plato's philosopher king. Against the "total ideologies" of Plato, Hegel, and Marx, he called for "a social technology . . . whose results can be tested by social engineering."[4] Popper's formulation, in principle, provided no limit to the application of the engineering mentality to society nor to the number of "problems" society might appear to produce. The only limit would be the scale of discrete projects. Unfortunately, incrementalism is no barrier to totality or to what Popper deprecated as "the revolutionizing the whole of society."

At the same time Popper reproduced a comparable form of elitism based on a faith that institutions of knowledge—in his case, the community of scientists—could produce "objective" truth in spite of the frailties of individual scientists or social engineers. The "objectivity" of science, Popper argued, was assured by the "public character" of the experience to which science appealed. From the claim about public experience, Popper slid easily into an unargued implication that Everyman, if he felt dubious about a scientific claim, could simply proceed to test it. Yet as soon as Popper formulated that principle, it became clear that the nature of testing rendered it the preserve of the few: "Everyone who has learned the technique of understanding and testing scientific theories can repeat the experiment and judge for himself."[5] The selfless rule that Plato had hoped to produce by the education of his guardians Popper discovered in the "impartiality" produced in the "institutionally organized objectivity of science."[6] For Plato's rule by mind Popper offered rule by method; for a vision of a virtuous society Popper presented a technological society. Technological society, *technē- + logos* = technical reason, was the perfect combination of a structure of theoretical reasoning: the *logos* represented by scientific reason, "the one method of all rational discussion,"[7] and a structure of rule, the *techne-* represented by "that rational method of piecemeal engineering."[8]

Scarcely two decades after Popper's attack on Plato and radicalism generally, the main target of social criticism in "advanced, developing nations" was "technological society." The terms of the attack were almost identical with those that Popper had used against Plato: critics wrote of "the domination" of nature and the "exploitation" of man, of dehumanization, the arrogance of social engineers, the prevalence of elitism, and, above all, the relentless extension of technology to every corner of existence, from probing the fetus to probing the universe.

Now, nearly a quarter-century after the debates of the sixties, the conception of the technological society has ceased to be in vogue, although its ghost still prowls among environmental groups. However, its reality persists, exalted into "high-tech societies." Social engineers have fallen from favor while genetic engineers have been elevated. At the present moment in the history of most so-called industrial democracies, Plato's formula for rule-by-knowledge appears in a less offensive light and triggers a less negative reaction, not because of the triumph of Platonism but because of the widespread acceptance of Popperism. Knowledge, particularly scientific knowledge useful to high-tech(ne) societies, is assumed to be the *arche*, or ruling principle, of such societies, and in that sense, Plato's formula has been translated into practice. Similarly, the assertion that high-tech societies are necessarily elitist goes virtually uncontested either as a description or as a norm.

What kind of reasoning concludes that a high-tech society requires rule by elites? The commonest answer is that for "advanced societies," science represents the most valued kind of social knowledge. It happens to be the most difficult to comprehend and is most likely, therefore, to be possessed by the few who are technically qualified or scientifically educated. Although this conclusion seems sensible, it dilutes the original question. That question is not solely about "who" should rule but what "principle" rule should be "based" upon. The crux concerns the kind of knowledge that should rule. Those who worry over the economic "threat" of Japan and the other "tigers" of the Far East seldom spend their energies defending elitism. This is because the problems of a high-tech society do not appear to them in a form that requires such a defense. Rather, the "challenge" is usually portrayed as the need to increase scientific research or to hasten the practical application of scientific knowledge or to reform American education at all levels so as to make the United States competitive in the international economy. Such discussions abound with antidemocratic implications and assumptions, but this may owe more to certain political views embedded in conceptions of technical knowledge than to a consciously elitist conception of politics.

What goes unnoticed is the peculiarity of the assumption that "principles of knowledge" should "rule," that the nature of the one is fitted to the nature of the other, that truth and power have not only complementary structures but mimetic ones, that there is a power-structure to truth and a truth-structure to power. The sense in which elitism is a "necessary" feature of advanced societies may have less to do with a theory of politics than with an imperative whose political character is no longer recognized. The imperative is to organize political power in order to best exploit the structural character of truth while concealing from exploiters and especially the exploited the political elements that have helped to constitute the understanding of truth and shaped its structure.

Accordingly, an advanced society might ideally be defined as one whose decision-making structure is so arranged as to present qualified individuals with the opportunity to make the necessary decisions.[9] With only slight exaggeration, one might say that in an ideal high-tech society, the right knowledge would "possess" people while decision-making structures would construct "problems" so as to apply them to the construction which goes under the name of the decision-maker!

II

Virtually every thinker who accepted [early seventeenth-century] mechanistic physics claimed that material bodies followed laws imposed on the world much as good citizens followed laws imposed on society.[10]

When Condorcet referred to the "tyranny of reason," does that apparent oxymoron hint at a correspondence between political structure and forms of theoretical discourse? Is it sufficiently pronounced that we might say that the political structure of a theory intimates/ imitates a corresponding form of political rule? If the relationship holds, we might expect, for example, that a theory which argues that absolute authority is a legitimate political form, because it is a necessary condition for peaceful relationships among the particular persons and groups of a society, will have incorporated a prior commitment to absolutism in the theoretization of its formal structure. Such a theory would not only have proposed absolutism as a political system but represented it in the theorizing of the proposal. One might hypothesize that it would have stipulated certain absolutist conditions in its methodology; for example, that relations between empirical particulars, facts, or definitions, on the one hand, and theoretical generalizations or propositions, on the other, must scrupulously obey certain unappealable notions of rigorous reasoning if the theory is to be authorized.

Perhaps we might secure a better grip on what is being proposed here by repeating the earlier way of posing the question. What is it about, say, scientific, mathematical, or technical knowledge that favors an elitist or antidemocratic regime? The obvious answer is that these forms of knowledge are so complex, abstruse, and difficult that they are beyond the reach of ordinary people. Moreover, the growing political power of elites corresponds to the fact that only a relatively small number of people are capable of grasping the implications of the highly technical character which public policies inevitably assume in "an advanced industrial society."

This seemingly obvious answer is not, however, an answer at all. The question is not whether nonscientific people can master astrophysics or any other body of scientific knowledge. It does not concern the substantive knowledge by which experts communicate with one another. It involves, instead, how highly technical knowledge is (re)presented to a more general public; in what sense such representations are knowledge; and to what genres they belong. Leaving aside such potent considerations as the powers available to those who produce social representations of socially valued knowledge of a highly technical character, is there a political element embedded in the social representation of scientific knowledge, such that to think in certain representational terms is to redescribe certain political postures, depending on the political character of the representations?

In putting the question in this way, no claim is being made that always and everywhere the contents of scientific statements have been "contaminated" by political elements. Rather, as I phrased it above, political elements become "attached," say, as interpretative categories. Such categories need not be, and among twentieth-century scientists rarely are, in use in the scientific community. But it is not primarily scientists who interpret science to general audiences or even to the nonscientific academy. Science, like the gods, needs intermediaries. The common practice is for those who hold credentials bearing the title "of science"—as in philosopher of science, sociologist, historian, or popularizer of science—to mediate, or interpret, science to the rest of us. They endeavor to make science accessible to nonscientists by describing its epistemic importance or "contribution" while embedding that description in a context that gives it social and political meaning as well.[11] The title "of science" lends to the mediator a modest reflection of the aura of power that surrounds "real" science. The philosopher of science or the historian of science is slightly elevated above, say, the philosopher of language or the historian of bourgeois culture, because the mediators are presumed to be in closer proximity to those whose arcane knowledge actually "unlocks" the "powers of nature."

To return to Plato's *Republic*: unlike our high-tech society, Plato made no provision for mediating agencies to interpret the meaning of the Forms to the most numerous class of "bronze" members. The latter were deemed incapable of the higher knowledge. Their understandings were to be the product of the institutional practices which Plato carefully sketched in to control family, sexual relations, labor, and property. In addition, and more striking, the inhabitants of Plato's imaginary society were to be treated to certain so-called noble falsehoods, such as "the myth of the metals" concerning the origins of social distinctions.[12] That the falsehoods were presented by Plato as fabrications is a signal that their discursive structure is discontinuous with that of philosophical knowledge—politically discontinuous, that is, in both their substance and their modes.

Knowledge of the Forms, according to Plato's various accounts, could never be imposed. It yielded only to a combination of dialectical inquiry and the intuitions of a purified mind. In contrast, Plato's "citizens" were to be indoctrinated into the "truth" of the falsehoods. Thus the "true" falsehoods embodied the political element, which Plato's authoritarian mind identified with unthinking submission. Philosophical truths were, ironically, antipolitical because they arose from uncoerced conviction—indeed, so uncoerced that as the mind ascended, Plato had it abandon even its dependence upon hypotheses. Hence the peculiar formulation: the true falsehood is political = imposed while the truly true or philosophic is antipolitical = persuasion.

Thus there is no homology existing between Plato's theory of knowledge and his theory of rule. The structure of truth for Plato does not result from mental activity modeled after political action but from activity modeled after religious rites of purification. It is true that the Platonic dialogue is heavily laden with political motifs. In the encounters, for example, between Socrates and Thrasymachus or between Socrates and Callicles in *Gorgias*, the atmosphere is politically charged and the action is politically symbolic in the extreme. But the dialogues, as most readers recognize, never end in a claim to truth, only to having dispelled errors and glimpsed the shadow of truth. Truth and politics were structurally antithetical for Plato, and so the only way that Platonic truth can rule is through imposition and falsehood; that is, by a non-truth that requires the elimination of politics and other forms of public contestation. The structure of rule is discontinuous with the structure of truth. This is confirmed by arrangements in the *Republic*, requiring that when the guardians take their turn at governing, they cease temporarily to engage in philosophical activity.

But what if the structure of truth were to exhibit features similar to those associated with despotic rule? What if the despotic mind were to emerge as an ideal of theoretical activity and, at the same time, as the subject of a new version of Plato's formula concerning philosophers and kings? These possibilities began to crystallize in the eighteenth century when despotism acquired what it had rarely enjoyed in the ancient world, namely, a theory about its nature. Montesquieu wrote a famous critique of it; the fact that it figures so prominently in his writings suggests that his contemporaries were fascinated by the subject.[13] It is also well known that the idea of "enlightened despotism," while not as ubiquitous as some modern scholars once believed, was nonetheless a theme that surfaced in a number of philosophies and among the early founders of Physiocracy.[14] Despotism can also be detected as a latent element in Bentham's writings, notably those dealing with prison reform (the Panopticon) and the administration of the poor laws.[15]

Prior to the eighteenth century, despotism had appeared mainly in association with tyranny and had signified a particular mode of exercising power that was absolute, willful, and illegitimate, either because the despot had seized power from its rightful owner or because in the course of ruling he would predictably violate the laws, customs, or accepted norms of the society.[16] The legitimation of despotism was made possible by more than two millennia of monotheism and monarchism; and by theological justifications of omnipotence, omniscience, and what might be called omnilegalism, or the corsetting of the world and of man in a totalistic framework of laws divine, natural, and human. In the seventeenth century, the religious bond to that matrix of totality was challenged by philosophers and publicists in the name of science, but the paradigm of power formally represented by science was inspired by the political theology under attack by scientizing theorists.[17]

Ever since antiquity, despotism has exercised a fascination as a potential liberating force, but with modern times, that emancipatory hope has become linked to the theorizing mind and a theorizable world. Accordingly, what is striking about the interest in despotism is that it emerged among thinkers whose modernizing credentials were, save for Montesquieu, impeccable and whose commitment to the advancement of scientific knowledge and to a culture of rationality was strong and steady. This development appears as the intellectualization of despotism. It involves dissolving the person of the despot and reconstituting him as an abstraction—absolute reason, a combination of power and reason that disguises power as rational legislation. This picture found support in common notions about the rationality of physical laws of nature. A law of nature pre(de)scribed regularities and uniformities among natural phenomena, that is, "necessary" relationships that phenomena "obeyed."

These notions are conveniently assembled in a famous document of the Enlightenment, d'Alembert's "Preliminary Discourse" to Diderot's *Encyclopedia.* D'Alembert's statements reveal the extent to which the attempt to explain scientific methods was permeated with bureaucratic and monarchical modes of thought, with themes of superior-inferior, of power, and of domination and submission. Explanation becomes a political metaphor—explanatory power. Describing the "systematic spirit" by which scientists apply mathematical methods to the study of terrestrial bodies, d'Alembert wrote that we come to know about the relationship among such bodies "by the comparisons we make among them, by the art of reducing, as much as that may be possible, a large number of phenomena to a single one that can be regarded as their principle. . . . The more one reduces the number of principles of a science, the more one gives them scope." D'Alembert's account culminates in a vision in which all that is in the world has been reduced to a single center of understanding: "The universe, if we may be permitted to say so, would only be one fact and one great truth for whoever knew how to embrace it from a single point of view."[18]

Eighteenth-century French conceptions of the laws of nature were, one might say, undialogical. Such laws were as arguably "compelling" to the phenomena "obeying" them as they were "irresistible" to the minds being instructed about the "necessary truths" contained in these laws. The laws of nature were the decrees of a rational despot—God—or of a rational despotism—Nature. The science of despotism was the despotism of science, and each had a common opposite: not freedom, because freedom became associated with accepting rational necessity, but prejudice. Thus modernity takes shape as the struggle not simply between scientific rationality and nescience/ignorance but between despotism/science and inherited prejudice.

The political implications of this version of science emerged in a conception of social science which found favor in the 1760s among the members of the so-called Turgot Circle. It was refined by various philosophies and Encyclopedists and kept alive during the French Revolution by former Turgotians such as Condorcet.[19] It was taken up in the first quarter of the nineteenth century by Comte and incorporated into his new science of sociology. The project can be described as the attempt to create a culture of despotism; i.e., a social mentality and practice that enable power to operate unhindered.

III

Geometry is therefore demonstrable, for the lines and figures from which we reason are drawn and described by ourselves; and civil philosophy is demonstrable because we make the commonwealth ourselves.

Wherefore Man is made fit for Society not by Nature, but by Education.
—Hobbes[20]

These preliminaries are germane to our main discussion because of the strong influence that Hobbes and his former employer Francis Bacon exercised over many of the philosophes, particularly those who helped to produce the great *Encyclopédie*. I am concentrating on Hobbes because his theory unites several of the themes alluded to in my previous discussion. Hobbes was one of the first, after Bacon, to interpret the radical political and social implications of modern science and one of the first moderns to undertake the role of political mediator between science and society. Hobbes called simultaneously for the reconstitution of theoretical knowledge and for the reconstitution of society on the new basis of scientific modes of thought. What connects the two is a common thread of despotism.

For Hobbes to achieve both theoretical and political despotism, he had to overcome the bad odor that had trailed despotism since antiquity. His achievement was to help fashion a mind-set in which the despotic eventually would assume the status of an unacknowledged cultural icon. Obviously such an achievement was not solely the work of one man. The mentality celebrated by Hobbes was described in the language of a new form of despotism in which truth and power were released from theological language but not from its presuppositions of monotheistic absolutism.

> If any man . . . by most firm reasons demonstrate that there are no authenticall doctrines concerning right and wrong, good and evill, besides the constituted lawes in each Realme and government; and that the question whether any future action will prove just or unjust, good or ill, is to be demanded of none but those to whom the supreme hath committed the interpretation of his Lawes: surely he will not only shew us the high way to peace, but will also teach us how to avoid the close, darke, and dangerous bypaths of faction and sedition.[21]

Leviathan would become Deuteronomy outfitted as political geometry.

As interpreted by Hobbes, the scientific revolution would both displace as well as replace the absolutist modes nurtured by theological thinking. The most striking features of that revolution were the appropriation of the most available model of omnipotence and omniscience, the creator-god of the Old Testament, and the reversal of his order: instead of God creating man as his subject, man creates a collective being of incomparable power to whom he is perfectly subject (*non est potestas super terram quae comparebur*). Although "the Art whereby God hath made and governes the World is by the *Art* of man . . . imitated,"[22] man's creation is accomplished in full view—a transparent prodigy, as it were. It rests on a simple and open fiction: "as if every man should say to every man . . ."[23] Man could become the self-conscious maker of his own myth, for by a simple exchange of oaths, men would create a "Mortall God" by "conferr(ing) all their power and strength upon one Man," a miracle only slightly less staggering than that in the Book of Genesis—although perhaps less credible, since Hobbes's act of creation involves no exhausting labors such as had compelled a weary god to rest on the seventh day. On the contrary, Hobbesian subjects are receptive to the "architect" of Leviathan because they are "weary" from the fears and anxieties inherent in a society that attempts to reduce or limit its ruling powers or to divide them polytheistically into competing centers of legitimacy, e.g., parliamentary versus royal authority.

IV

Thomas Hobbes is said to have been the first modern "to show an interest in adding the word [despotic] to the stock of terms used in the political discussions of Europe."[24] I further suggest that he was the first modern in whom a despotic mentality was at work. He perpetuated Bacon's political reading of science, and he fully appreciated the political structure implicit in Bacon's conception of scientific knowledge. Bacon's credo "knowledge is power" was transcribed to read "knowledge is for the sake of power" (*scientia propter potentiam*).[25]

Hobbes's despotic mentality is revealed in the several departments of his theory, not just in his political writings: in his thinking about human nature, physical nature, knowledge, scientific inquiry, and thinking itself. He fashioned images of man and mind as subjects fit for despotic rule: the one for the rule or rules of a sovereign lawgiver, the other for the rules of method decreed by a sovereign science. The homogeneity attributed to human nature and the mind was inspired by the success which a comparable assumption concerning matter had had in the construction of scientific laws.

Hobbesian science promised not merely truth but "infallible" knowledge focused on the supreme end of power. The vision of power that science promised went far beyond simple governance to an unlimited capability of producing any desired result at "another time." The necessary condition for the realization of that vision of power was succinctly stated by Hobbes: "For whoso is freed from all bonds is lord over all those that still continue bound."[26] Laws represent the conditions of power decreed by an unconditioned sovereign. They are norms of social behavior that should be designed to enlarge the opportunities for the powers of individuals to be exerted while controlling the harmful social and political consequences of conflict among the aggressive individuals who constitute Hobbesian society. The sovereign tells his subjects what right consists in, what is justice, and what salvation.

Although absolutism is the necessary condition for the maximization of power, it is not sufficient by itself. When legislating, the sovereign must observe the basic requirement of all scientific thinking—logical consistency. The absolute lawmaking authority of the sovereign means that he is the master of meaning in the social world or, more precisely, its monopolist. Hobbes extended the despotic into the very terms of discourse and sought to expel the forms of communication which threatened his monological ideal. The despotic is expressed in his insistence that scientific progress and man's happiness depend upon "exact definitions, first snuffed and purged from ambiguity." What lies behind his obsession for linguistic purity is a concern to constrain the possibilities of interpretation while extending those of undeniable, logically necessary demonstration. The danger, as Hobbes saw it, is represented by "Metaphors and senselesse and ambiguous words" which, instead of falling into the orderly progression promised when reason works with "exact definitions," produces "wandering amongst innumerable absurdities; and their end, contention, and sedition, or contempt."[27] Clearly "Metaphors, Tropes, and other Rhetoricall figures"[28] invite interpretation, prolong controversy, and frequently fail to produce agreement. A metaphor is open-ended: it has no correct meaning.

Hobbes's sovereign is never portrayed as listening, because his function is to reduce the "different tempers, customes, and doctrines of men,"[29] the analogue to the Babel deliberately introduced by the jealous God of the Old Testament in order to halt the dangerous growth of human power and presumption. The monologic of despotism is perfectly conveyed in Hobbes's great metaphor about the law: "Men . . . have made an Artificiall Man, which we call a Commonwealth; so also have they made Artificiall Chains, called Civill Laws, which they themselves, by mutuall covenants, have fastned at one end, to the lips of that Man, or Assembly, to whom they have given the Soveraigne Power; and at the other end to their own Ears."[30]

What is the model for a discourse that produces silence among those addressed? In the passage just cited, as well as in numerous others, there is the visible outline of the Old Testament god who commands, who gives his decalogue to a chosen intermediary, and who demands obedience. That outline has now been overlain by a discourse which promises scientific rather than revealed truth—overlain but not superseded.

Hobbes's guiding assumption is that the structure of scientific truth and the structure of political order are interchangeable, an assumption that, significantly, had its parallel among those who argued for true religion as the structural correlate of political order. His assumption emerges in the remarkable argument introduced to support the claim that the sovereign had the right to determine "what Opinions and Doctrines are averse, and what conducing to Peace." In addressing the obvious objection that this would allow a sovereign to suppress scientific truths, Hobbes acknowledged that "in matter of Doctrine nothing ought to be regarded but the Truth," but he added that "Doctrine repugnant to Peace can no more be true than Peace and Concord can be against the Law of Nature." If a commonwealth was presently enforcing "false Doctrines," it is possible that "contrary Truths may be generally offensive." But even under such circumstances, peace would not be disturbed but rather a latent condition of war stirred. Thus the structure of pseudodoctrines corresponds to the structure of pseudopeace: "Yet the most sudden, and rough busling in of a new Truth, that can be, does never breake the Peace, but only somtimes awake the Warre."[31]

In Hobbes's vision, scientific knowledge parallels the structure of despotic rule: it is knowledge of the power that is guaranteed by a chain of dependency which reason constructs as it links one of its definitions to another while pursuing the connections between cause and effect. The structure of connections is taken as representing the structure of all things in which "cause" signifies power. When scientific reasoning establishes logical connections, it is reproducing a system of power: "*Science* is the knowledge of Consequences, and dependance of one fact upon another. . . . Because when we see how any thing comes about, upon what causes, and by what manner; when the like causes come into our power, wee see how to make it produce the like effects."[32]

The despotic element in Hobbes's vision of science is most fully realized when the objects represent an order of reality that is completely open to human fabrication and manipulation. Geometry is demonstrable in its absolute character because "the generation of the figures depends on our will."[33] The same possibility of truth lies open to politics. Because "neither public good nor public evil was natural among men any more than it was among beasts," politics is like mathematics but unlike physics where "the causes of natural things are not in our power but in the divine will." In politics, too, "we ourselves make the principles . . . whereby it is known what justice and equity and their opposites, injustice and inequity, are."[34]

The "making" of principles has a direct bearing upon politics, for it contains the Hobbesian conception of action: man knows what he can make. Hobbesian political science is the science of political construction in which absolute and arbitrary elements are combined and presuppose one another. It teaches men what they can make, but what they make is arbitrary. If they wish, they can establish a parliamentary sovereign or a monarchical one. Similarly, when once authorized, the sovereign is equally free to establish whatever kind of system of rules he prefers. Thus absolutism in politics parallels absolutism in thought. Each begins from an arbitrary act of definition or identification, and then both proceed to "work out" the dependence of one definition upon another; i.e., fit them into a power relationship with each other. It is a purely mentalized conception of power. Hobbesian political science is indifferent to external facts of geography, economics, and culture that had played such a large role in Aristotelian political science, had been revived by Hobbes's contemporary Jean Bodin, and subsequently would be a crucial factor in Montesquieu's argument against despotism.

V

The most perfect organization of the universe can be called God.

—Nietzsche[35]

Hobbes accomplished the legitimation of despotism through a multiple revolution that challenged several traditional conceptions concerning the scope and meaning of that form of rule. Hobbes denied that despotism was anomalous, a pariah form of political rule; that its mode of arbitrariness was inconsistent with the rule of law; that it furthered only the interests of the despot or that the interests of the despot and society were irreconcilably opposed; and, finally, that the necessarily repressive policies needed to produce political submissiveness would discourage industriousness and thereby impoverish society and weaken the despot as well.[36] When Hobbes completed his revolution, the appearance of despotism was transformed and its substance reproduced as lawfulness and rule-governed behavior, as well as a promise of "commodious living."

The core notion of the Hobbesian revolution was "organization." It was the equivalent of a meta-constitution, the *politeia* of the *despotikos*. It can be thought of as the equivalent of a formal theory of politics in the sense that it specified abstractly what was universally necessary for all "independent political systems."[37] Although the word "organization" was available, Hobbes did not use it. Instead he developed the idea of political society as a rational-scientific construction by transforming older political language. He introduced radically new, even opposing, meanings into two traditional terms—"commonwealth" and "body politic." There could be no sharper contrast than that between the sixteenth-century image of the commonwealth as an organic, natural body and Hobbes's profoundly constructivist conception of "the Pacts and Covenants by which the parts of this Body Politique were at first made, set together, and united."[38] The distinctively organizational character of the Hobbesian commonwealth is manifested most strikingly in two ideas: sovereign authority and covenant. The former embodies the central feature of organization: a sovereign whose arbitrary will expresses itself as rule-rationality. The latter embodies both the trauma that necessitates the institution of sovereign authority and the statement of the conditions that will make it possible.

Constructivism subjects passion to conformity, as mathematical reasoning displaces sense by abstraction. Just as natural phenomena are inherently lawful and only await discovery by the scientific lawgiver, so men exhausted by the anxieties and perils of an insecure existence want to be constructed into order. They need a maker who constructs by instructing.

For men, as they become at last weary of irregular justling, and hewing one another, and desire with all their hearts, to conforme themselves into one firme and lasting edifice; so for want, both of the art of making fit Lawes, to square their actions by, and also of humility, and patience, to suffer the rude and combersome points of their present greatnesse to be taken off, they cannot without the help of a very able Architect be compiled into any other than a crasie building.[39]

Unlike older conceptions of political constitutions, commonwealth/organization signified a premeditated structure, not a perversion of another form, as oligarchy was of aristocracy, or tyranny of monarchy. Nor was it one of the so-called good regimes. It transcended the categories of good and bad, normal and perverted. Thus it did not grow out of anything or derive from it. Instead it "resemble(s) that Fiat, or the Let us make man pronounced by God in the Creation"; that is, it comes from nowhere, *ex nihilo*, and for that reason it is potentially universal, as unconditioned by time or place as scientific truth itself or God. Any type of constitution, normal or perverted, could be rightly organized. Right organization did not imply a pledge to promote justice or any other moral or religious good. Indeed, the quality of relations established by the Hobbesian organization appeared remarkably analogous to the absolute unconditionality of God postulated by theologians. The organization was endowed with a quality which had previously been considered to be the peculiar property of God: it was the defining source of justice, hence it could not be unjust. At the same time, the subjects of the organization were like God's believers, capable of injustice when they violated their covenantal obligations to the sovereign.

Organization represented a departure from all previous forms. It renounced all of the personalizing categories that had characterized the classical types. The sovereign, it should be emphasized, was not identical with the organization but was the supreme "office" of its structure.[40] "I speak not of the men but (in the Abstract) of the Seat of Power."[41] The *politeia*, or constitution, was thus dehumanized. It did not represent a class principle, such as rule by the wealthy, or an ethical principle, such as rule by the best (*aristoi*). Instead, organization represented the convergence of necessity in its two most irresistible forms: the undeniable fact of death and the necessity inherent in logical demonstration of the requirements of peace and prosperity, or what Hobbes called "commodious living." Thus despotism stands for an absolutism of the undeniable. The rudiments of that order were worked out by Hobbes in his conceptions of covenant, sovereign representative, subject, and law.

VI

Fabian: I will prove it legitimate, sir, upon the oaths of judgment and reason.
— Shakespeare, *Twelfth Night*, III. ii. 13

In *Leviathan*, Hobbes attacked the pariah status of despotism by two distinctive claims: that despotic power was entitled to the same rights of authority as any other form of political rule; and that all forms of political authority, whether democratic, aristocratic, or monarchic, had of necessity to incorporate the same despotic principle of a final and uncontrollable rule-making power if they were to survive. "The Rights and Consequences of both *Paternall* and *Despoticall* Dominion are the very same with those of a Soveraign by Institution [i.e., by formal consent]."[42] Tyranny, Hobbes declared, was not a form of government but merely an expression of dislike by those "that are discontented under *Monarchy*."[43] Thus the traditional division between "good" polities and perverted ones is dismissed, and the distinction collapsed. "*Tyranny* and *Oligarchy* . . . are not the names of other Formes of Government, but of the same Formes misliked."[44]

The legitimation of despotism and the destruction of the traditional distinctions between it and all other political life-forms reveals an antipathy toward difference that pervades Hobbes's attitude toward diversity of opinions, of social rank, and of truth-claims. His world is a bare place of abstract space and time, and his man a dehistoricized bit of matter-in-motion. For Aristotle, despotism had been the reflection of natural differences; for Hobbes, it was justified by a common denominator to all men, a "similitude of *Passions*" and natural equality.[45] It was directed at those who strove for preeminence or were obsessed by comparisons of worth, and it threatened the rest who were content with equality.[46]

The reduction of difference signifies that an organization is a creature of conditions rather than grounds. So Hobbes abstracted the sociological, historical, and normative elements from the various political forms and presented them as a choice between "conveniences" and "inconveniences." Those criteria prove to involve essentially matters of efficiency and effectiveness, and they lead to a strikingly new conclusion: since the power is the same in all forms, the choice comes down to which is more likely to produce better "administration of its affairs." Hobbes concluded that absolute monarchy had the fewest inconveniences.[47]

VII

A despotic mentality pervades the structure of Hobbes's arguments. It appears in a coercive quality attaching to Hobbes's demand that all forms of authority must incorporate an absolutist principle, even if the ideology of the regime abhors that principle. He depicted those who would contrive to establish a rational governance as no freer to resist a provision for absolute power than matter-in-motion is able to resist the laws of physics. Whether the government is monarchic, popular, or aristocratic, "the Soveraign Power . . . is as great as possibly men can be imagined to make it." Men may "fancy many evill consequences" of "so unlimited a Power," but the consequences of its lack are the direst possible: "perpetual warre of every man against his neighbour."[48] Hobbes was not trying to persuade his readers but to compel them. The logical structure of his argument is a sequence of stark compulsions forcing on his reader-citizen the choice between controlled violence and violent oblivion: if men are to survive they must establish a sovereign power; if power is less than sovereign, men are condemned to an endless *bellum omnium contra omnes*.[49]

The symbol of the despotic mentality is in its chosen icon, the irresistible force of a geometric proof. "A necessary act is that, the production whereof it is impossible to hinder."[50] Geometry means, first, "Universall rule," which relieves the mind from having to adjust its assertions to local peculiarities. A universal rule "discharges our mentall reckoning, of time and place . . . and makes that which was found true *here* and *now*, to be true in *all times* and *places*."[51] Geometry also means "necessary truths," and the "necessary" signifies power whose unchallengeability simply reduces all talk of legal limits or restraints to irrelevancy. What is necessary already embodies the idea of following a law and of renouncing what is arbitrary or capricious. It is the route whereby *despotikos* is legalized. The origins of the route are crucial, for they not only confirm the despotic character of geometry's necessary truths but also foreshadow the despotic nature of the Hobbesian sovereign.

The necessary truths of geometry originate in the arbitrary—the contradictory opposite of the necessary. They begin with "definitions" (e.g., of a circle) that cannot themselves be proven, that is, legitimated. The fascination with geometrical reasoning is its incredible combination of the undeniability of its proofs, along with the fact that man, the most subjective of all creatures, has nonetheless willed the existence of geometry and freely chosen its starting point. An arbitrary will that reasons consistently/relentlessly can produce perfect "laws" that legitimate the otherwise despotic starting point: "The generation of the figures depends on our will; nothing more is required to know the phenomenon peculiar to any figure whatsoever, than that we consider everything that follows from the construction that we ourselves make in the figure to be described."[52] Cryptically stated, Hobbes's sequence is perfect truth as the product of will; free will as the creator of necessary truths; the necessary as the irresistible. "*Liberty* and *Necessity* are Consistent" because all acts proceed from "causes in a continuall chaine" of "necessity."[53]

Thus logical reasoning functions as the microcosm of despotism, and despotism as the macrocosm of logic. Logical reasoning shares the characteristic that is present absolutely in all men and that will reemerge in the absolute power of the sovereign. Logical reasoning is undeniable; death as the fate of all men and their deepest fear is undeniable; and the power of the sovereign must be as undeniable as the fact of death and the proofs of reason.

VIII

In terms evocative of the slavemaster's authority, Hobbes attributed "the Soveraign Power of life and death" to his creature. In the Hobbesian commonwealth, however, life is secured by the fear of death, by the fear of that which represents the absolute (because unavoidable) coercion. The *despotes* of death, the great leveller to which all men are enslaved, becomes transmuted into the despotism of sovereign authority—the magic solvent before which "The Power and Honour of Subjects vanisheth."[54] Death, in the form of a "Mortall God" or sovereign, authorizes the terms for life: "The Liberty of a Subject, lyeth therefore only in those things, which in regulating their actions the Soveraign hath prætermitted."[55] Despotism exists to institute and maintain a nonpolitical life-space where "men have the Liberty, of doing what their own reasons shall suggest for the most profitable to themselves."[56]

"Fear and Liberty are consistent."[57] Because Hobbes depicted man as timid and fearful by nature, it appears in keeping with that character that Hobbesian man should submit himself to absolute power. Yet the nature with which Hobbes actually endowed man is completely contrary to the picture of timidity, although perhaps its psychological complement. The anatomy of human nature embodies a despotic potential, for its quintessence is power. "Man's nature is the sum of his natural faculties and powers." The faculties of the body are classified as "power nutritive, power motive, and power generative." The "powers of the mind" are "power cognitive" and "power imaginative."[58] Accordingly, the life of such a being can be compared to a race for domination: "But this race we must suppose to have no other goal, nor other garland, but being foremost."[59]

Hobbesian liberty is designed to channel and legitimate the dynamics of domination implanted in every individual. Man is being in continuous motion, for "Life it selfe is but Motion, and can never be without Desire, nor without Feare."[60] Human motion is power, but it is under the same "laws" that control the motions of "Inanimate creatures." This assimilation of man to natural objects—and like them, subject to the necessity of laws—puts the meaning of liberty in a special light.

"*Liberty* and *Necessity* are Consistent."[61] Liberty is not a unique property of man, and it does not signify freedom to choose but "the absence of externall Impediments" that block his power, i.e., his motion according to law.[62] Liberty is the despot's dream of opposition-free rule now held out as the ideal of freedom, of unobstructed individual motion/desire. For just as the despot brooks no opposition or rival, Hobbesian liberty "signifieth (properly) the absence of Opposition; (by Opposition, I mean externall Impediments of motion)." And like the despot who disdains to be constrained by law or by political rivals, the Hobbesian man cannot be "so tyed, or environed, as it cannot move, but within a certain space, which space is determined by the opposition of some externall body."[63]

IX

For life is perpetual motion that, when it cannot progress in a straight line, is converted into circular motion.

—Hobbes[64]

For the use of Lawes . . . is not to bind the People from all Voluntary actions; but to direct and keep them in such a motion, as not to hurt themselves by their own impetuous desires, rashnesse, or indiscretion, as Hedges are set, not to stop Travellers, but to keep them in the way.

—Hobbes[65]

The space left by the silence of the law was not conceived by Hobbes as bounded like a geometric figure but as an unobstructed path capable of accommodating indefinitely the despotic compulsions reflected in the Hobbesian description of human happiness. Men seek more than "a bare Preservation, but also all other Contentments of life."[66] Their happiness is in "proceeding" rather than in contentment. It "consisteth not in having prospered but in prospering."[67]

Hobbesian despotism thus must accommodate the driving motions of men in search of prosperity, as well as the uncertain needs of sovereign power that must defend itself in an international state of nature. "And Law was brought into the world for nothing else, but to limit the naturall liberty of particular men, in such manner, as they might not hurt, but assist one another and joyn together against a common Enemy."[68] Theoretically, a despot could use his absolute power to stifle the energy of society and discourage individual initiatives, but such a course would plainly be self-defeating. Yet man, the relentless pursuer of his own interests and opinions, must be contained. Despotism cannot rule society oppressively in the literal sense of weighing it "down." It must repress but not suppress the vital motions of its members. It must manipulate fear while maintaining anxiety.

Hobbes's resolution of these difficulties is more clearly set out in chapter 10 of *De Corpore*, entitled "Of Power and Act." There he developed a schema in which the fullness of power depends crucially upon the character of the "patient" or object (sc., citizen), not upon the agent alone (sc., sovereign). "Power," Hobbes noted, "and Cause are the same thing," and "power and act" correspond to "cause and effect." To exercise power or "produce" an effect, the agent must have "all those accidents which are necessarily requisite for the production of some effect in the patient." The power of the patient consists of the "accidents" of his which produce a given effect. The power of the patient is "passive." "The power of the agent and patient together" corresponds to "plenary power"; it is the "sum or aggregate of all the accidents" in both parties that produce an effect. Power differs from a cause in that it applies to the future. Power is ineffectual or "impossible" when some of the requisites are lacking in either agent or patient. When the two are closely matched, so that the attributes of the patient mesh with those of the agent, the potential for power is maximized. Then, "every act which is not impossible is possible."[69] The attributes Hobbes assigned to sovereign authority corresponded to the "requisites" of an agent. Given that Hobbes wanted his sovereign authority to be absolute, it follows that a "patient" or subject needs to have or be given the "requisites" for a role that, while passive, is still contributory.

Hobbes turned immediately in part 1 of *Leviathan* to endowing man with a nature whose drives make him a creature fit for despotic rule. The first image of despotism accompanies the basic description of human nature in its natural condition. His right to self-preservation is a statement of despotism in the extreme: "THE RIGHT OF NATURE . . . is the Liberty each man hath, to use his own power, as he will himselfe, for the preservation of his own Nature . . . of doing any thing, which in his own Judgement, and Reason, hee shall conceive to be the aptest means thereunto. . . . in such a condition [of Nature] every man has a Right to every thing; even to one anothers body."[70] In the state of nature, then, the first despot is man himself, and despotism is the original and universal condition.

The despotic nature of man is defined by the fact that he is an endangered and a self-endangering species. His deepest driving force is the fear of death, and the whole of his mechanism of motion is bent toward fleeing death and preserving the self. Man certifies that he is alive by responding to his desires—the Hobbesian definition of death is the cessation of desire—and he acts out his escape from death by the unending pursuit of his desires.[71] He cannot stop without dying: "The object of mans desire is not to enjoy once onely, and for one instant of time; but to assure for ever the way of his future desire. . . . he cannot be content with a moderate power . . . because he cannot assure the power and means to live well . . . without the acquisition of more."[72] "Felicity is a continuall progresse of the desire from one object to another." Man is not so much a seeker of happiness as its victim. Happiness seeks him out and drives him in "a perpetuall and restlesse desire of Power after power that ceaseth onely in Death."[73]

X

And as to the faculties of the mind, (setting aside the arts grounded upon words, and especially that skill of proceeding upon generall, and infallible rules, called Science; which very few have, and but in few things . . .) I find yet a greater equality amongst men, than that of strength.

—Hobbes[74]

Hobbes's attempt to impose laws of behavior upon man prefigured the creation of a sovereign authority who would shape men to obedience. The despotism of theory and the despotism of sovereignty are both produced from the realization that man, the object of their power, is inherently refractory, both in his natural as well as his civil capacity. "The constitution of a mans Body is in continuall mutation; it is impossible that all the same things should always cause in him the same Appetites and Aversions." This damning admission is followed by another that threatens to subvert the basic premise of a sovereign authority created by covenant: "Much lesse can all men consent in the Desire of almost any one and the same Object."[75] An inexpungeable subjectivity that manifests itself in a wide range of human differences, from opinion to types of madness, threatens the basic assumption of the covenant—that all men can agree on the need for an absolute sovereign authority because all fear death and all possess reason.

This difficulty puts Hobbesian science in a certain light. It is a science that resorts to fictions about human nature that, in reality, are lies. Men are not in fact what the requirements of the theory demand that they must be if its theoretical power is to be realized. Before Hobbesian citizens can be the object of absolute sovereignty, they must first be transformed into the abstract subject of a despotic theory. The laws of motion thus turn out to be constructions of the god-theorist who had declared his intention of legislating an "Artificiall Man" who would exceed in power the natural man first created by the theorist-god of the Old Testament.[76] The laws are prescriptive of an ideal form of motion that is "true" of human behavior in the sense that it can serve as a reference point for legislating "real" laws for human conduct. The political problem set for the sovereign is to shape men into law-abiding citizens. "Man is made fit for Society not by Nature, but by Education."[77] Man is taught to be "bound" by the "laws of nature." These laws are "generall rule(s) of Reason" whose observance is necessary if there is to be social peace. Thus they are the analogues to the laws of nature which dictate "order" to physical bodies.[78]

Hobbes's confession—that for all of the analogies between human behavior and physical motion and between cause-and-effect relations in nature and human desires and aversions, there remained a stubbornly subjective core, a "constitution individuall"—defined the tasks of political culture. In order to make man into an animal fit for society, he had to be made into a being who would approximate the "behavior" of natural phenomena. While "terror" was not an insignificant means, it ran the risk of provoking resentment or, worse, paralyzing activity. The solution was indoctrination/education. It begins with Hobbes's legislating "a fifth Law of Nature" by which *"every man strive to accommodate himselfe to the rest."* This law aims at nothing less than to overcome "a diversity of Nature, rising from the diversity of Affections" among men. Men are compared to "stones" assembled for a building, but their "asperity, and irregularity . . . takes more room from others." So some will have to be "cast away" as "unprofitable, and troublesome."[79]

The next step in rendering man's nature lawful is to reform education, beginning with the universities where the nation's teachers are produced. Reform would aim at insuring that "true" political and religious doctrines were taught.[80] More ambitiously, Hobbes proposed a new political cult that would instruct the common people in opinions that would dispose them to submissiveness. "The Common-peoples minds, unlesse they be tainted with dependance on the Potent, or scribbled over with the opinions of their Doctors, are like clean paper, fit to receive whatsoever by Publique Authority shall be imprinted in them."[81] The ideal of a truly "lawfull" subject is caught in Hobbes's despotic image of "rooting out of the consciences of men all those opinions" that potentially might lead to rebellion.[82]

The political and theoretical problem for Hobbes was to find a notion which could render plausible the analogy between the social and the physicalist meanings of the laws of nature. How would man have to be conceived to make him seem as much the "natural" subject of civil laws as natural phenomena were of natural laws? The solution was the notion of natural equality—the analogue to the operation whereby geometers posit abstract triangles divested of the "irregularities" that are present in "actual" triangles. "And therefore for the ninth law of Nature, I put this, *That every man acknowledge other for his Equall by Nature.*"[83]

Nature is thus introduced to legitimate equality, but "nature" really functions as a metaphor for methodological requirements transferred to politics. When Hobbes stated that "the question who is the better man, has no place in the condition of meer Nature,"[84] the statement was equivalent to saying that for purposes of demonstration all objects having certain specified traits will be considered to be the same, regardless of individual variations in other respects. Equality is the consequence of a methodological need rather than a normative claim. Its function is to promote power through equal treatment. "Nature" is identified with abstraction rather than with the "natural" differences apparent to common observation. It is not that men *are* equal; Hobbes acknowledged that some men are stronger and others of "quicker mind." Yet the differences, Hobbes insisted, are "not so considerable" that the strong cannot be killed by the weak or that experience, which is available to all men, has not made them all roughly equal in wisdom. Thus the needs of a political science of nature coincide with the necessary condition for society: politics cannot become a science if it starts from the differences which exist among men, and diverse particulars cannot make a society if those differences are treated as primary. "Men . . . will not enter into conditions of Peace, but upon Equall termes."[85] Absolutism comes into the picture because, according to Hobbes, men want to flee the consequences of natural equality. The rough equality among men leaves each insecure. A man can never become sufficiently powerful in nature to prevent others from harming him. Thus the natural equality which allows for the covenant that makes society possible also makes absolutism necessary.

The extent to which the authority of the Hobbesian sovereign complements the despotic nature of Hobbesian man was not accidental. It rests upon a vision whose unique power lies, not in its defense of absolutism, but in its conception of a culture of despotism that reproduces a conception of mind: it is at one and the same time a conception of mind and an ideal of collective *mentalité*.

NOTES

1. Karl Popper, *The Open Society and Its Enemies*, 2 vols. (London: Routledge, 1945), 2: 210.

2. Karl Popper, *Logic of Discovery* (New York: Basic Books, 1959), p. 80.

3. Popper, *Open Society*, 1:139, 143.

4. Ibid., 2:209, 210.

5. Ibid., 2:205, 206.

6. Ibid., 2:207, 208.

7. Popper, *Logic of Discovery*, p. 16 (italics in original).

8. Popper, *Open Society*, 1:147.

9. This is the type of argument to be found in Niklas Luhmann, *Soziale Systeme* (Frankfurt: Suhrkamp, 1984). See the critique by Jürgen Habermas, *The Philosophical Discourse of Modernity: Twelve Lectures*, trans. Frederick Lawrence (Cambridge, Mass.: MIT Press, 1987).

10. Gary B. Deason, "Reformation Theology and the Mechanistic Conception of Nature," in *God and Nature: Historical Essays on the Encounter between Christianity and Science*, ed. David C. Lindberg and Ronald L. Numbers (Berkeley and Los Angeles: University of California Press, 1986), pp. 168–69.

11. For a recent example see Daniel J. Kevles, *The Physicists: The History of a Scientific Community in Modern America* (Cambridge, Mass.: Harvard University Press, 1971). Kevles says of his book, "It addresses how physicists overcame the difficulties of pure science in the American democratic culture to win world leadership in their discipline and recognition as assets to the modern American state. It is occupied with how they acquired power" (p. ix). For an earlier period see the studies by Margaret C. Jacob, *The Newtonians and the English Revolution, 1689–1720* (Ithaca, N.Y.: Cornell University Press, 1976); and by J. R. Jacob, *Robert Boyle and the English Revolution: A Study in Social and Intellectual Change* (New York: Burt Franklin, 1977).

12. Plato, *Republic* 414b–e. Plato does suggest, though haltingly, that "if possible" the rulers were to be persuaded of the falsehood "but failing that the rest of the city."

13. Montesquieu, *Esprit des Lois* III, 8–10; IV. 12–16; VI. 2.

14. See Leonard Krieger, *An Essay on the Theory of Enlightened Despotism* (Chicago: University of Chicago Press, 1975). See also Melvin Richter, "Despotism," *Dictionary of the History of Ideas*, 5 vols. (New York: Scribner, 1974), 2:1–18. Richter argues (p. 12) unpersuasively that "it is now generally agreed that there is no body of political ideas in the eighteenth century that can accurately be described as 'enlightened despotism,' a term invented by nineteenth century German historians."

15. See Charles F. Bahmueller, *The National Charity Company: Jeremy Bentham's Silent Revolution* (Berkeley and Los Angeles: University of California Press, 1981).

16. Locke denied that despotic rule was a form of government and he associated it with tyranny. He recognized a legitimate moment in despotism in the case of a conqueror involved in a just war. Locke insisted, however, that justifiable conquest created rights only over those who had instigated or actively waged the unjust war. *Two Treatises of Government*, "Second Treatise," secs. 174–76, 196, 199. Compare Hobbes, *Leviathan*, ed. C. B. Macpherson (Harmondsworth, Middlesex: Penguin, 1968). All references to *Leviathan* will be to this edition.

Mario A. Cattaneo has attempted to relate Hobbes's thinking to eighteenth-century currents of enlightened despotism, but he has argued that both should be interpreted as promoting the rule of law. See his article, "Hobbes Théoricien de l'Absolutisme Éclairé," in *Hobbes-Forschungen*, ed. R. Koselleck and R. Schnu (Berlin: Duncker & Humblot, 1969), pp. 199–210. For a recent discussion of the meaning of absolutism in Hobbes's writings see Raymond Polin, *Hobbes, Dieu, et les Hommes* (Paris: Presses Universitaires de France, 1981), p. 105ff. Michel Malherbe's chapter on "La Science de la Nature" in his *Thomas Hobbes ou l'Œuvre de la Raison* (Paris: J. Vrin, 1984), p. 89ff, is also useful. Judging from the absence of entries on the scientific aspects of Hobbes's thought as reported by Bernard Willms, "Der Weg des Leviathan: Die Hobbes-Forschung von 1968–1978," *Der Staat: Zeitschrift für Staatslehre Öffentliches Recht und Verfassungsgeschichte*, Beiheft 3 (1979), there has been a decline of interest in the political implications of Hobbesian science. However, students of the history of science have recently become concerned with Hobbes's critique of the experimental method. See especially Steven Shapin and Simon Schaffer, *Leviathan and the Air-Pump: Hobbes, Boyle, and the Experimental Life* (Princeton, N.J.: Princeton University Press, 1985).

17. I owe a great deal indirectly to the work of Francis Oakley. See his *Omnipotence, Covenant, and Order: An Excursion in the History of Ideas from Abelard to Leibnitz* (Ithaca, N.Y.: Cornell University Press, 1984), and "Christian Theology and the Newtonian Science: The Rise of the Concept of the Laws of Nature," *Church History* 30 (1961):433–55.

18. Jean le Rond d'Alembert, *Preliminary Discourse to the Encyclopedia of Diderot*, trans. Richard N. Schwab and Walter E. Rex (Indianapolis: Bobbs-Merrill, 1963), pp. 22, 29.

19. On Condorcet see Keith M. Baker's fine study, *Condorcet: From Natural Philosophy to Social Mathematics* (Chicago: University of Chicago Press, 1975).

20. "Six Lessons to the Professors of the Mathematics," in *The English Works of Thomas Hobbes*, ed. Sir William Molesworth, 11 vol. (London: John Bohm, 1839–1845), 7:183–84; *De Cive* in *Philosophical Works of Thomas Hobbes*, ed. Howard Warrender (Oxford: Clarendon Press, 1983–), 3:44.

21. *De Cive*, 3:31–32.

22. *Leviathan*, Introduction, p. 81.

23. Ibid., ch. 17, p. 227.

24. R. Koebner, "Despot and Despotism," *Journal of the Warburg and Courtauld Institute* 14 (1951):288.

25. *De Corpore*, in *Body, Mind, and Citizen*, ed. Richard S. Peters (New York: Collier, 1962), ch. I.6., p. 27.

26. *De Cive* II. x. 8.

27. *Leviathan*, ch. 5, pp. 116–17.

28. Ibid., ch. 5, p. 114.

29. Ibid., ch. 15, p. 216.

30. Ibid., ch. 21, pp. 263–64.

31. Ibid, ch. 18, p. 233.

32. Ibid., ch. 5, p. 115.

33. "Six Lessons to the Professors of the Mathematics," in *English Works*, 7:183–84.

34. Thomas Hobbes, *De Homine*, in *Man and Citizen*, ed. Bernard Gert (Garden City, N.Y.: Doubleday, 1972), 10, secs. 4–5, pp. 41–43.

35. The quotation is attributed to Nietzsche by Georges Bataille, *Visions of Excess, 1927–1939*, ed. Allan Stoekl (Minneapolis: University of Minnesota Press, 1985), p. 197, but the reference given does not confirm the quotation literally.

36. See the famous comparison made by the fifteenth-century jurist Sir John Fortescue between the impoverished condition of French society under absolute monarchy and the prosperity of England under a constrained monarchy in *De Laudibus Legum Anglie*, ed. S. B. Chrimes (Cambridge: Cambridge University Press, 1949), ch. 29, pp. 35–36.

37. For Hobbes's discussion of "systems" see *Leviathan*, ch. 22, p. 274.

38. *Leviathan*, Introduction, pp. 81–82. Compare Thomas Starkey, *A Dialogue Between Reginald Pole and Thomas Lupset*, ed. Kathleen M. Burton (London: Chatto and Windus, 1948), pp. 61–62, 95–97.

39. *Leviathan*, ch. 29, p. 363.

40. See ibid., ch. 30, entitled "Of the Office of the Sovereign Representative."

41. Ibid., Epistle Dedicatory, p. 75.

42. Ibid., ch. 20, p. 256.

43. Ibid., ch. 19, p. 240.
44. Ibid.
45. Ibid., Introduction, p. 82; *De Corpore*, ch. I.1., pp. 277–78.
46. *De Corpore*, ch. I.1., pp. 277–78.
47. *De Cive*, 3:138.
48. *Leviathan*, ch. 20, p. 260.
49. Ibid., ch. 21, p. 264.
50. *De Corpore*, ch. 10.5, p. 122.
51. *Leviathan*, ch. 4, p. 104.
52. *De Homine*, ch. 10, sec. 5, p. 41.
53. *Leviathan*, ch. 21, p. 263.
54. Ibid., ch. 18, p. 237 (marginal note).
55. Ibid., ch. 21, p. 264.
56. Ibid.
57. Ibid, ch. 21, p. 262.
58. Thomas Hobbes, *The Elements of Law, Natural and Politic*, ed. Ferdinand Tönnies (Cambridge: Cambridge University Press, 1928), pt. 1, ch. 1, secs. 6–8, pp. 1–11.
59. *Elements of Law*, pt. 1, ch. 9, sec. 21, p. 36.
60. *Leviathan*, ch. 6, p. 130.
61. Ibid., ch. 21, p. 263.
62. Ibid., ch. 14, p. 189; ch. 21, p. 261.
63. Ibid., ch. 21, p. 261.
64. *De Homine*, ch. 11, sec. 15, p. 54.
65. *Leviathan*, ch. 30, p. 388.
66. Ibid., ch. 30, p. 376.
67. *Elements of Law*, pt. 1, ch. 7, sec. 7, p. 23.
68. *Leviathan*, ch. 26, p. 315.
69. *De Corpore*, ch. 10.1-4, pp. 121–22.
70. *Leviathan*, ch. 14, pp. 189, 190.
71. Ibid., ch. 8, p. 139.
72. Ibid., ch. 11, pp. 160–61.
73. Ibid., ch. 11, pp. 160, 161.
74. Ibid., ch. 12, p. 183.
75. Ibid., ch. 6, p. 120.
76. Ibid., Introduction, p. 81.
77. *De Cive*, 3:44.
78. *Leviathan*, ch. 14, pp. 189ff.
79. Ibid., ch. 15, p. 209.
80. Ibid., ch. 30, pp 384–85.
81. Ibid., ch. 30, p. 379.
82. *Elements of Law*, pt. 2, ch. 9, sec. 8.
83. *Leviathan*, ch. 15, p. 211.
84. Ibid.
85. Ibid.

3

Plato, Hobbes, and the Science of Practical Reasoning

David Johnston

It is often assumed that Hobbes's political philosophy has little in common with the work of his ancient predecessors.[1] This assumption is in part a product of Hobbes's own polemics. By berating the "DARKNESS from VAIN PHILOSOPHY, and FABULOUS TRADITIONS"[2] he believed to be lurking within the philosophical practice of his scholastic contemporaries, Hobbes seemed to be placing himself at a great distance from the ancient Greeks as well. Although most modern scholars would demur at Hobbes's claim that his own book *De Cive* deserves to be recognized as the first work of genuine civil philosophy,[3] there is considerable agreement that the presuppositions of his political philosophy differ fundamentally from those of his ancient forebears. Hobbes's world was not their world. How could his outlook have overlapped in any significant way with theirs?

Hobbes's own view of the relationship between his work and that of his ancient precursors appears upon closer examination more entangled than his modern interpreters have generally allowed. His stance toward Plato seems especially complex. Although he insisted that "neither *Plato*, nor any other Philosopher hitherto, hath put into order, and sufficiently, or probably proved all the Theoremes of Morall doctrine,"[4] he also suggested that Plato was "the best Philosopher of the Greeks," the sign of his superiority being that he "forbad entrance into his Schoole, to all that were not already in some measure Geometricians."[5] Moreover, it is striking that Hobbes was deeply interested in Greek history and literature throughout his productive life, which began with his translation and publication of the first complete English version of Thucydides' *History of the Peloponnesian War* and ended (or nearly so) with his composition of a translation of the Homeric poems.

My aim in what follows is to explicate one of the strands of continuity that links Plato's political philosophy with that of Hobbes. Like Plato, Hobbes thought that practical reasoning is capable of being treated as an art of calculation. Both philosophers believed that moral evaluation could be approached fruitfully as a form of measurement. I shall suggest that this approach to evaluation is linked to the ambition—common to both Plato and Hobbes—to construct a comprehensive political philosophy. I shall further suggest that high costs accompany the adoption of this approach to practical reasoning. Although Plato and Hobbes seem to have been insensitive toward or uninterested in these costs, we should not imitate their disregard.

I

Two major literary sources provide a record of one of the central difficulties Plato sought to address in several of his philosophical dialogues. The first is the collected writings of the Greek tragedians. These writers, who were some of the most esteemed moral teachers in ancient Greece, were by the same token among Plato's most formidable rivals. The second is Thucydides' *History of the Peloponnesian War*, which chronicled the ultimately catastrophic events through which Plato lived as a boy and young man in Athens.

In one of the more celebrated passages of his work, Thucydides argued that in the aftermath of the revolution in Corcyra, which occurred several years after the beginning of the war, the

> customary verbal evaluations of deeds were exchanged for new ones as men claimed the right to use words as they would suit their actions. . . . The cause of it all was love of power to gratify greed and personal ambition; from that came the eagerness to quarrel which appeared once strife had begun. The leading men of either side . . . boldly committed villainous outrages and took even more villainous revenge, not stopping where justice or the city's interest demanded, but limiting their actions only by their appetites. . . . Thus did every sort of evil take root in Greece.[6]

Although Thucydides did not argue that linguistic disorder is the cause of moral and political disorder, the connection he drew between these two is close enough to suggest that both forms of disorder are evil and that both might be eliminated by the same means. Our ability to order our actions well recedes hand in hand with our capacity to evaluate our deeds in clear and recognizable terms.

The tragedians, however, taught that clear evaluative terminology cannot always be attained. The sources of goodness, they suggested, are multiple and heterogeneous. Because of this heterogeneity, our evaluations are often complex and sometimes equivocal. Indeed, several of their dramatic works focus upon the inevitable costs of any attempt to eliminate evaluative equivocation. Whether we think of Agamemnon's sacrifice of his daughter Iphigenia or of Antigone's defiance of Creon, her king, the underlying lesson appears to be the same: that in our practical lives we must often make choices that are tragic in the sense that they require us to sacrifice some genuine good; and that we can obliterate the tragic dimension of such choices only by blunting and diminishing our own moral sensibilities.[7]

To Plato this lesson seemed unconvincing. Like Thucydides, he viewed the fact that people differ in their use of evaluative terms as a sign of degeneration in the human condition and not as one of its permanent and normal features. For Plato, Aeschylus' and Sophocles' belief in the inescapability of tragic choices was itself a symptom of moral disintegration, a report of sorts on the diminished condition of the *polis* as an ethical community rather than a reliable account of the nature of things. But how could the tragedians' claims be rebutted? In the dialogues of his early and middle periods, Plato devoted a good deal of his creative energy to formulating a persuasive answer to this question.

Plato took two important steps toward this goal in his early dialogue *Euthyphro*. First, he argued that where the tragedians had seen insuperable moral dilemmas that compel those who face them to choose between courses of action, each of which necessarily entails some evil, we should instead see failures of moral understanding rooted in the intellectual limitations of those involved. In principle, at least, these limitations can be transcended. If they were, then we would be able to see that genuinely tragic choices do not exist. What the tragedians had believed to be ineliminable moral conflicts flowing from irreducible heterogeneity among the sources of goodness, Plato saw as mere moral disagreement resulting from a flawed understanding of the nature of the good. Goodness, for Plato, must ultimately prove to be unitary and homogeneous.

Plato's second step toward the formulation of an answer to the tragedians' notion of moral conflict is suggested by the following exchange in the dialogue between Euthyphro and Socrates:

> *Socrates*: Hatred and wrath, my friend—what kind of disagreement will produce them? Look at the matter thus. If you and I were to differ about numbers, on the question which of two was the greater, would a disagreement about that make us angry at each other, and make enemies of us? Should we not settle things by calculation, and so come to an agreement quickly on any point like that?
> *Euthyphro*: Yes, certainly.
> *Socrates*: And similarly if we differed on a question of greater length or less, we would take a measurement, and quickly put an end to the dispute?
> *Euthyphro*: Just that.
> *Socrates*: And so, I fancy, we should have recourse to scales, and settle any question about a heavier or lighter weight?
> *Euthyphro*: Of course.
> *Socrates*: What sort of thing, then, is it about which we differ, till, unable to arrive at a decision, we might get angry and be enemies to one another? Perhaps you have no answer ready, but listen to me. See if it is not the following—right and wrong, the noble and the base, and good and bad. Are not these the things about which we differ, till, unable to arrive at a decision, we grow hostile, when we do grow hostile, to each other, you and I and everybody else?[8]

What Plato appeared to be suggesting is that disagreements about right and wrong, the noble and the base, and good and bad lead to hatred and wrath in part because of our failure to approach these disagreements through calculation and measurement. The art (*technē*) through which resolution of such disagreements is attempted is highly imprecise, unlike the art through which we resolve disputes about things that can be measured. By juxtaposing these two forms of *technē*, Plato appeared to be hinting that if disputes about moral questions were subject to resolution by means similar to those used to settle disputes involving calculation, moral disputes might be resolved as easily and decisively as disagreements about numbers.

The implementation of this suggestion would of course require the invention of a scheme for quantifying the moral claims and qualities to which it is to be applied. The benefits of such a scheme, in Plato's view, would be very great indeed. Disputes about right and wrong or good and bad would no longer arise—or if they did, they could be settled quickly and definitively. Practical choices could be made by calculating the amounts of goodness and badness that would be generated by each available alternative. Instead of having to "weigh" incommensurable bundles of good and evil, as the dramatic figures Agamemnon and Antigone had been forced to do, we could resort to calculation—to weighing of a more nearly literal kind—to determine our practical decisions. Practical reasoning would be transformed into a science based upon rigorous measurement and calculation.

However, the possibility of effecting this transformation was contingent upon the discovery of a unit of measure—a metric by reference to which all values could be rendered commensurable with one another. The obstacles to any such discovery appear great. Goods as diverse as love, political loyalty, and personal integrity would all have to be reduced to a common measure and regarded for the purpose of practical calculation as subject to mutual trading in precise quantities. The view that we should be able to quantify the value of any of these goods in units of the others seems to contradict our ordinary intuitions about the diversity of goods and perhaps even to degrade the value of all goods potentially subject to such comparisons. The implementation of Plato's suggestion thus presented anyone willing to pursue it with a formidable task.

This task occupied a considerable portion of Plato's philosophical energy for some time after he completed the *Euthyphro*. Signs of his effort to grapple with it appear in several subsequent dialogues of his early period.[9] But by the time he composed the dialogues of his middle period, including *The Republic*, Plato seemed to have arrived at a resolution of the problem of a metric, at least to his own satisfaction. In these dialogues Plato argued that activities alone—and not experiences—are intrinsically valuable. The various states of mind or body that we generally consider pleasurable possess no inherent goodness or value. Moreover, not all activities are equally valuable. Activities of all kinds can be arranged on a hierarchical scale in accordance with their varying degrees of intrinsic worth. The most valuable of all activities is contemplation of eternal things, of things "as they really are,"[10] as Plato was fond of saying. The value of all other activities can be measured by comparison with this highest and most worthy of pursuits; the resulting values can then provide the basis necessary to transform practical reasoning into a precise, calculative science.

The results of this line of reasoning are exemplified by Plato's discussion of the tyrant in book IX of *The Republic*. Having established that the life of a tyrant is inferior to that of a king, Socrates goes on to ask whether his interlocutors know *"how much* more unpleasant the tyrant's life is than the king's?" This exchange follows:

Well, there seem to be three kinds of pleasure, one genuine and two false. Shunning law and reason, he even disdains the limits set for the false pleasures. He goes beyond them, gives himself over to certain slavish and mercenary pleasures. It is no easy task to measure his debasement, except perhaps in the following way.

How?

The tyrant, you remember, stands third from the oligarch. The democratic man stands between.

Yes?

So his illusionary pleasures are thrice removed from those of the oligarch—that is, if what we said before is true.

It is true.

Now if we agree that king and aristocrat are one and the same, we can place the oligarch at third remove from the king.

Third is right.

Then the tyrant must be separated from pleasure by a number that is three times three.

So it seems.

In that case the tyrant's illusion of pleasure, measured in terms of length, is a plane number.

Quite.

Finally, the square and the cube define the true distance separating the tyrant from pleasure.

All that is obvious to one skilled in mathematics.

Then turn it around and say how far the king is removed from the tyrant in terms of true pleasure. When we are finished with multiplication, it will be evident that the king experiences 729 times more pleasure than the tyrant. The tyrant's pain may be measured by the same number.

Your calculations concerning the distance between pleasure and pain for the just and unjust man overwhelm and baffle us.

But if days and nights and months and years have relevance to men's lives, the number is relevant and true.[11]

In Plato's view, calculation is precisely what is required for sound practical reasoning.

Plato's argument for a calculative *technē* of practical reasoning had theoretical as well as practical implications. By arguing that we should look toward "things as they really are" as the measure of all values, he was in effect proposing a method for simplifying both our practical choices and the task of constructing a political philosophy. The final product of his effort to transform practical reasoning into a calculative science was a philosophy that provided firm guidance to what its author regarded as the best way of life both for individuals and for the polity as a whole. By persuading himself that he had discovered a single unit of measure through which the values of all goods could be specified, Plato was enabled to put the problem with which he had struggled throughout much of his early period behind him and to go on with the composition of the masterpieces of his middle and later periods. Plato could construct the first comprehensive political philosophy in part because he was convinced that he had discovered the key to a *technē* of practical reasoning that would render that art of decision clear, precise, and unequivocal in its results.

II

Hobbes appeared to have shared Plato's conviction about the need for practical reasoning to assume a scientific, quantitative form. In a passage from *The Elements of Law*, he suggested that

> those men who have taken in hand to consider nothing else but the comparison of magnitudes, numbers, times, and motions, and their proportions one to another, have thereby been the authors of all those excellences, wherein we differ from such savage people as are now the inhabitants of divers places in America; . . . to this day was it never heard of, that there was any controversy concerning any conclusion in this subject.[12]

This pointed comment that the constructive activities made possible by the mathematical sciences engender no controversy stands in contrast to Hobbes's depiction of the state of affairs that exist when agreement upon units of measure is lacking:

> In the state of nature, where every man is his own judge, and
> differeth from other concerning the names and appellations of
> things, and from those differences arise quarrels, and breach of
> peace; it was necessary there should be a common measure of
> all things that might fall in controversy; as for example: of what
> is to be called right, what good, what virtue, what much, what
> little, what *meum* and *tuum*, what a pound, what a quart, &c.
> For in these things private judgments may differ, and beget con-
> troversy.[13]

Taken together, these two passages are strikingly reminiscent of the
argument in Plato's *Euthyphro* cited above. Indeed, Hobbes was even
more explicit than Plato in suggesting that clearly defined units of
measure are as appropriate and necessary for the resolution of disputes about what is right, good, and virtuous as they are for settling
quarrels about property and ordinary material goods. Like Plato,
Hobbes believed that practical reasoning at its best is reasoning by
means of measurement and calculation.

Hobbes could not, however, accept the unit of measure Plato had
proposed for this science. Contemplation of things "as they really
are" was to him an unacceptable measure of value for both epistemological and political reasons. Hobbes was deeply skeptical about the
accessibility of eternal things to the human mind. His oft-repeated
insistence that human beings are incapable of knowing anything
whatsoever about the substantive attributes of God[14] is probably the
best-known sign of this skepticism, but it is far from being the only
one. One of his most general statements on the subject occurs in *Leviathan*, where Hobbes declared that "the Principles of naturall science . . . are so farre from teaching us any thing of Gods nature, as
they cannot teach us our own nature, nor the nature of the smallest
creature living."[15] If things "as they really are" genuinely exist, we
cannot fathom or contemplate their true natures at all: although we
can have *faith* in the existence of such things, we cannot obtain
knowledge of them.[16] And even if such things were accessible to the
human mind, they would not be susceptible to measurement and
calculation, or to what Hobbes generally calls "ratiocination" ("Adding and Substracting . . . of the Consequences of generall names
agreed upon, for the *marking* and *Signifying* of our thoughts").[17]
These operations can be performed *only* upon "every body of which
any generation can be conceived and of which a comparison can be
made after any consideration of it; or in which composition and resolution has a place,"[18] and this description does not apply to Pla-

tonic things "as they really are," which by definition are not subject to change. In Hobbes's view, philosophical contemplation of such things is not even possible. It can therefore hardly be considered the activity by reference to which the values of all other goods should be determined.

Furthermore, the political consequences of Plato's proposal must have struck Hobbes as exceedingly dangerous. The thesis that contemplation of eternal things is the most valuable activity available to human beings has obvious affinities with (and would likely provide encouragement to) some of the doctrines Hobbes identified as among the most seditious known. Foremost among these, as detailed in *Leviathan*, are the notions of private judgment (*"That every private man is Judge of Good and Evill actions"*), conscience (*"that whatsoever a man does against his Conscience, is Sinne"*), and supernatural inspiration (*"That Faith and Sanctity, are not to be attained by Study and Reason, but by supernaturall Inspiration, or Infusion"*).[19] Although none of these doctrines is genuinely Platonic, all share with Plato's notion of intellectual contemplation the idea that we come to understand the highest and most important goods through a kind of activity that is intensely private—and thus, in Hobbes's view, relatively immune to social controls. Indeed, Hobbes's argument that this understanding "is by the flame of the Passions, never enlightned, but dazled,"[20] seems designed to echo and reverse the meaning of Plato's famous description of the experience of the ordinary person who has just emerged from the cave for the first time to enter into "the world of light, whose brightness then dazzled the soul's eye."[21] For Hobbes, enlightenment by necessity tends to produce irenical effects, never inflammatory or disturbing ones. What Plato regarded as an experience of illumination, Hobbes seemed to consider a dangerous perturbation by the passions.

Hence Hobbes could not agree with Plato's implicit claim that he had discovered the metric by means of which practical reasoning could be made over into a science. Did Hobbes nevertheless believe that such a science could be brought into being by other means? One line of argument that can be teased out of his writings is that a unit of measure suitable for the purpose of practical calculation can be derived in some way from the appetites. As is well known, Hobbes argued that people call things good or evil because of the effects those things produce upon them. In *The Elements of Law*, for example, he claimed that "every man, for his own part, calleth that which pleaseth, and is delightful to himself, GOOD; and that EVIL which displeaseth him: insomuch that while every man differeth from other in constitution, they differ also one from another concerning the common distinction of good and evil."[22]

That passage, the substance of which is reproduced in Hobbes's later political writings as well, suggests that the evaluative disorder Thucydides had regarded as a sign of the deterioration of human social life was seen by Hobbes as a normal attribute of the human condition. But Hobbes did not consider this disorder inevitable. He argued that it is important to distinguish different ways in which people use evaluative terminology:

> Every man by natural passion, calleth that good which pleaseth him for the present, or so far forth as he can foresee; and in like manner that which displeaseth him evil. And therefore he that foreseeth the whole way to his preservation (which is the end that every one by nature aimeth at) must also call it good, and the contrary evil. And this is that good and evil, which not every man in passion calleth so, but all men by reason.[23]

By subjecting our appetitive responses to the discipline of "right reason"—ratiocination "from principles that are found indubitable by experience, all deceptions of sense and equivocation of words avoided"[24]—we should be able to approach practical reasoning in a calculative way. In the end, this calculative approach should enable us to deduce the "Immutable and Eternall" laws of nature, the "Science" of which "is the true and onely Moral Philosophy."[25]

The idea that satisfaction of the appetites is the appropriate basis of calculation in our practical affairs seems consistent with Hobbes's rejection of Plato's theory of the soul. Although Hobbes occasionally alluded to the parts of the soul in hierarchical, Platonic terms,[26] his more developed discussions of motivation and reasoning make it clear that his conception of the parts of human nature is very different from Plato's. For Plato (at least in *The Republic*), each of the three major components of the soul—intellect, emotions, and appetites—has its own distinctive motivational energy. Part of what is involved in his famous account of the souls' conversion, or "turning around," in book VII is the development of a powerful attraction toward the goods distinctive to the intellect—an attraction ordinary, unphilosophical people sense very little or not at all. For Hobbes, by contrast, the "passions of man . . . are the beginning of *all* his voluntary motions."[27] One implication of this claim is that no conversion or turning around of the soul like that described by Plato is possible.

Our appetites supply us with the only sort of motivation we can ever have.

Traditionally, of course, the appetites and emotions were thought to be so unstable that many philosophers considered them unsuitable objects of speculative inquiry and *a fortiori* poor bases for practical calculation. Within the human soul they were often regarded as emblematic of the world of transitory things, of things that appear otherwise than "as they really are." In *The Republic*, Plato went so far as to deny that the appetites and emotions are integral parts of a whole human being: to him they were more akin to attributes of the shell or cage that houses human beings than to parts of the true self.[28] Hobbes accepted Plato's view that the appetites are insatiable by nature. At the same time, however, he suggested that their celebrated capriciousness is only apparent. In the introduction to *Leviathan*, for example, he argues that the saying *"Nosce teipsum, Read thy self"* is intended "to teach us, that for the similitude of the thoughts, and Passions of one man, to the thoughts, and Passions of another, whosoever looketh into himself, . . . shall thereby read and know, what are the thoughts, and Passions of all other men, upon the like occasions. I say the similitude of *Passions*, which are the same in all men, . . . not the similitude of *the objects* of the Passions."[29]

For Hobbes, therefore, the appetites are susceptible to scientific inquiry. Indeed, Hobbes argued that the appetites can actually be changed as a result of this sort of inquiry. Perhaps his most dramatic statement of this view occurs in *De Cive*:

> For were the nature of humane Actions as distinctly knowne, as the nature of *Quantity* in Geometricall Figures, the strength of *Avarice* and *Ambition*, which is sustained by the erroneous opinions of the Vulgar, as touching the nature of *Right* and *Wrong*, would presently faint and languish; And Mankinde should enjoy such an Immortall Peace, that (unless it were for habitation, on supposition that the Earth should grow too narrow for her inhabitants) there would hardly be left any pretence for war.[30]

The almost utopian tone of this passage suggests that Hobbes believed he had taken possession of a genuinely new science of human affairs that promised to deliver the irenical, conflict-resolving results that Plato's *technē* of practical reasoning had failed to produce. This suggestion is confirmed by his subsequent claim that "Civil Philosophy [is] yet much younger [than natural philosophy,] as being no older . . . than my own book *De Cive*."³¹ Was Hobbes claiming that he had discovered the true foundation for a science of practical reasoning, the need for which he had seemed so clearly to identify in *The Elements of Law*?

The best answer to this question is, yes and no. The obstacle to a straightforward "yes" is the fact that for Hobbes the concept of right reason is itself problematical. After pointing out the undesirable consequences that flow from the lack of a common measure of right, good, and virtue in *The Elements of Law*, Hobbes observed that

> this common measure, some say, is right reason: with whom I should consent, if there were any such thing to be found or known *in rerum naturā*. But commonly they that call for right reason to decide any controversy, do mean their own. But this is certain, seeing right reason is not existent, the reason of some man, or men, must supply the place thereof; and that man, or men, is he or they, that have the sovereign power.³²

Whereas Plato had suggested that disagreements about right and wrong, noble and base, and good and bad could be resolved easily and authoritatively if they could be rendered susceptible to measurement and calculation, Hobbes suggested that the unit of measure itself would always be subject to dispute. The difficulty is not merely that we lack a unit of measure that can be applied to *values* of all kinds; it is that we lack a unit of measure acceptable to all *parties* involved in evaluative disagreements. A measure that is common in this second sense cannot simply be discovered by moral philosophers. It must, Hobbes believed, be promulgated and enforced by a sovereign.

For Hobbes, then, right reason—the instrument through which we order our appetites and subject our ends to calculation—is an artifact. The effect of this conclusion is to suggest that the idea of devising a calculative *technē* of practical reasoning cannot succeed in the form in which Plato had conceived this idea. No unit of measure capable of transcending evaluative disagreements can be discovered. But it would be a mistake to infer that Hobbes was led by this line of reasoning to abandon Plato's project altogether. It is crucial to bear in mind that for Hobbes the reason of the person or persons who possess sovereign power *supplies the place of* right reason. Hobbes's wording suggests that he intended the sovereign's reason to perform some of the functions that would be performed by right reason if it were discoverable *in rerum natura*. One of these functions is to define that common measure without which evaluative disorder cannot be overcome. Hobbes's objective—the devising of a calculative science of practical reasoning capable of definitively resolving evaluative disagreements—remained the same as Plato's. In his view, however, that objective could be attained only by reformulating Plato's project to take into account both Hobbes's un-Platonic view of the nature of goods as objects of appetite and the indispensable role of the sovereign in defining a common measure of these goods. Rather than abandoning Plato's project, Hobbes proposed to transform it.

If this interpretation is correct, then it would appear that in Hobbes's view, sovereigns, like political theorists, perform philosophical as well as political functions. Hobbes restated the problem of evaluative disorder in *De Cive* by arguing that "it happens, that though all men doe agree in the commendation of the foresaid vertues, yet they disagree still concerning their Nature, to wit, in what each of them doth consist . . . whence it comes to passe that the same Action is prais'd by these, and call'd Vertue, and dispraised by those, and termed vice. Neither is there as yet any remedy found by Philosophers for this matter."[33] Hobbes was of course trying to call attention to the novelty of his own philosophical work. But he seemed also to be hinting that the remedy for evaluative disorder cannot be merely philosophical. The difficulty with Plato's *technē* of practical reasoning is not only that it is "uselesse."[34] It is that any attempt to construct such a science in abstraction from the *actual* reason or measure it must deploy in the act of practical calculation is chimerical. Those who have sought to found a calculative science of practical reasoning by discovering a universal metric in the nature of things have been pursuing a "FICTION of the mind"[35] as fantastic as any golden mountain or imaginary beast. The metric, if one exists, has to be the result of an act of creation at once philosophical and political in nature. Sovereigns consitute reason as well as commonwealths.[36]

This transformation of Plato's project enabled Hobbes to formulate a political theory of his own on a scale that rivaled that of Plato's work. Like Plato and many other ancient and modern thinkers, Hobbes identified his own theoretical activities through the metaphors of founding and architecture. For him political theory is the extraordinary activity of giving a form or constitution to collective life, of designing the structure within which ordinary, more routinized political activities take place. But the "Principles of Reason"[37] upon which any sound design must be based—the presuppositions of theorizing—are for him products of art. Hobbes believed that his own comprehensive theorizing activity was dependent upon sovereign power not only to provide conditions favorable to its pursuit but to supply or at least legitimate the standards by which that activity could be judged. Sovereign power was axiomatic for Hobbes because he believed that without it there could be "no Knowledge of the face of the Earth; no account of Time; no Arts; no Letters; no Society"[38]—and no political philosophy, either.

III

The appeal of the project in which both Plato and Hobbes were engaged rests upon its promise to provide a means for the authoritative resolution of disputes involving evaluation. The concerns that motivated these two philosophers to search for such a means differed. Whereas Plato seemed to be interested primarily in minimizing disturbances that might interfere with the pursuit of philosophical truth, Hobbes was devoted principally to the avoidance of physical conflict and its destructive consequences. Yet these differing aims converged upon a single project: the transformation of practical reasoning into a calculative science that would enable its practitioners to put an end to disputes about the nature of right and wrong—disputes that, by Hobbes's testimony, account for the bulk of all human violence, including war.

If Plato's aim in pursuing this project is unappealing, Hobbes's objective seems beyond reproach. But the invention of a quantitative *technē* of practical reasoning would have some significant disadvantages. Suppose that the obstacles to such an invention were suddenly overcome. What would be the effects of its adoption?

I suggest that there would be at least two foreseeable effects that should cause us to draw back from this project. First, expertise in practical reasoning would become highly refined and more highly valued than it is today. Of course, such expertise already exists: there are philosophers and other specialists in practical reasoning, and it is surely advisable for ordinary people to listen to and incorporate these specialists' arguments into their own reasoning when these arguments help make sense of difficult situations of practical choice. But if practical reasoning were allowed to become a calculative science, it would most likely generate its own cadre of technical specialists similar to those which dominate other specialized fields of study. The effect of this development would probably be to diminish rather than to enlarge the capacities of ordinary people to make practical decisions.[39] In place of a democratic society that prizes its citizens' skills of deliberation and practical judgment—skills of which we currently possess no great surplus—we would see an increasingly deferential society take shape. Evaluative disagreements would diminish but at the cost of a flight by ordinary people from responsibility for practical choices.

A second likely effect of the transformation of practical reasoning into a quantitative science would be to lessen our evaluative sensibilities. Intuitions tell us that the value of goods such as love and personal integrity cannot be measured in units of money, nor even in units of one another, as they would have to be if the project on which Plato and Hobbes concurred were taken seriously.[40] Certainly there are occasions on which we must choose between these different goods. Usually, however, we do not think of these choices in quantitative terms. The Platonic and Hobbesian solutions to the problem of commensurability are illustrative of the pitfalls inherent in doing so. For just as Plato denigrated the emotions and appetites in order to surmount this problem, Hobbes was compelled to portray intellectual activities as mere manifestations of particular appetites—a characterization that seems alien to their nature. Human beings are not maximizing machines by nature, nor does it seem desirable that they should be made over into such machines.[41]

Are these consequences so undesirable as to constitute a decisive objection to the transformation of practical reasoning into a quantitative science? The answer is not easy to discern. If the irenical effects of the science they envisaged were really as great as Hobbes imagined, then we might be inclined to say no. Violence has plagued human societies since long before the beginning of recorded history. Any device we can invent that would help alleviate this plague should be welcomed.

There is good reason, however, to be suspicious of the capacity of this *technē* to achieve the result promised—and indeed to wonder whether this promise really explains our two philosophers' adoption of this goal. Both Plato and Hobbes were attracted by the idea of a precise science of practical reasoning in part because both were driven by a wish for theoretical as well as political order. In a justly famous passage from *Leviathan*, Hobbes argued that

as the art of well building, is derived from Principles of Reason, observed by industrious men, that had long studied the nature of materials, and the divers effects of figure, and proportion, long after mankind began (though poorly) to build: So, long

time after men have begun to constitute Common-wealths, im-
perfect, and apt to relapse into disorder, there may, Principles of
Reason be found out, by industrious meditation, to make their
constitution (excepting by externall violence) everlasting. And
such are those which I have in this discourse set forth.[42]

The architectonic pretensions for political philosophy to which
this passage gives voice were shared by Plato and Hobbes and by
many other political philosophers since ancient times. The invention
of a quantitative science of practical reasoning greatly simplified
their theoretical task. The successes of Plato and Hobbes as comprehensive political philosophers may even have been made possible by
their willingness to adopt the simplifying device represented by such
a science. But comprehensiveness should not be confused with political or theoretical wisdom.

Of even greater antiquity than the images of architect and
founder through which Plato and Hobbes interpreted their own theoretical activities is another image—less ambitious, perhaps, and certainly less controlling—of the political theorist as a physician of the
body politic. Unlike architects, who must direct that materials be
fashioned to suit a design of their imagining alone, physicians must
listen carefully and respond to their patients in order to perform
their functions well. They possess considerable authority based
upon medical expertise, but unless they are willing to enter into a dialogue and become attuned to their patients' quirks and sensibilities,
their success as medical practitioners will be less than their potential
would allow. Physicians are not creators of a comprehensive science,
nor do they draw their advice from a single, integrated body of
knowledge. They are pragmatists who draw information from whatever sources they may have at their disposal, including knowledge
of their patients' characters as well as their formal medical training.
In short, physicians respond as well as prescribe; they listen as well
as speak. Their aim is not to create but to heal.

The idea that practical reasoning should be transformed into a
quantitative science belongs to the image of the theorist as an architect and founder, not to that of the theorist as physician. It is motivated as much by theoretical ambition as by practical promise. Its
presupposition is that the "matter" of a political "structure" must be
made "to suffer the rude and combersome points of their present
greatnesse to be taken off" in accordance with the design of "a very
able Architect" in order "to conforme themselves into one firme and
lasting edifice."[43] It is antithetical to the ideal of theoretical activity

as a form of care. It may be that we should simply discard the idea of precise moral measurement along with the architectonic pretensions for political philosophy with which it is linked, in order to return to an older and more human image of the theoretician's role.

NOTES

1. I should like to thank Terence Ball, Mary Dietz, George Shulman, and the other participants in the Benjamin Evans Lippincott Symposium on the Political Philosophy of Hobbes at the University of Minnesota (spring 1988) for many helpful comments and suggestions on an earlier draft of this paper and to thank the American Council of Learned Societies, the Columbia University Council for Research in the Social Sciences, and the National Endowment for the Humanities for financial support during the period of its composition.

2. *Leviathan*, ch. 46, p. 682; *English Works*, 3:664. In this paper, references to Hobbes's *Leviathan* will be to chapter and page number of C. B. Macpherson's edition (Harmondsworth, Middlesex: Penguin, 1968), followed by reference to the text in *The English Works of Thomas Hobbes*, ed. Sir William Molesworth, 11 vols. (London: John Bohn, 1839–1845), by volume and page.

3. *De Corpore* (English translation under the title *Elements of Philosophy concerning Body*), in *English Works*, 1:ix. Hobbes repeated this claim in his *Considerations upon the Reputation, Loyalty, Manners, and Religion of Thomas Hobbes*, in *English Works*, 4:409–40.

4. *Leviathan*, ch. 31, p. 407; *English Works*, 3:357.

5. *Leviathan*, ch. 46, p. 686; *English Works*, 3:667.

6. I have followed the translation given by A. W. Gomme in his *Historical Commentary on Thucydides*, vol. 2 (Oxford: Clarendon Press, 1969), pp. 383–85, except for the first sentence, where I have accepted the arguments of J. Wilson in "'The Customary Meanings of Words Were Changed'—or Were They? A Note on Thucydides 3.82.4," *Classical Quarterly*, n.s. 32 (1982):18–20.

7. For an extensive elaboration of this perspective on Greek tragedy see Martha C. Nussbaum, *The Fragility of Goodness: Luck and Ethics in Greek Tragedy and Philosophy* (Cambridge: Cambridge University Press, 1986).

8. Plato *Euthyphro* 7b–d, trans. Lane Cooper in *Plato: The Collected Dialogues*, ed. Edith Hamilton and Huntington Cairns (Princeton, N.J.: Princeton University Press, 1973).

9. For a very interesting interpretation of Plato's *Protagoras* along these lines, see Nussbaum, *The Fragility of Goodness*, ch. 4.

10. Plato *Republic* 582c, trans. Richard W. Sterling and William C. Scott (New York: W. W. Norton and Co., 1985).

11. Plato *Republic* 587b–588a.

12. Thomas Hobbes, *The Elements of Law, Natural and Politic*, 2d ed., ed. Ferdinand Tönnies (London: Frank Cass and Co., 1969), pt. 1, ch. 13, sec. 3, pp. 65–66.

13. *Elements*, pt. 2, ch. 10, sec. 8, p. 188.

14. See *Elements*, pt. 1, ch. 11, secs. 2 and 3, pp. 53–54; and *Leviathan*, ch. 3, p. 99; *English Works*, 3:17.

15. *Leviathan*, ch. 31, p. 404; *English Works*, 3:354.

16. This distinction is drawn by Hobbes with special clarity and force in his *Thomas White's De Mundo Examined*, trans. Harold Whitmore Jones (London: Bradford University Press, 1976), although it is also drawn in a number of Hobbes's other works, including *Leviathan*. For a discussion see David Johnston, "Hobbes's Mortalism," *History of Political Thought* (forthcoming).

17. *Leviathan*, ch. 5, p. 111; *English Works*, 3:30.

18. Thomas Hobbes, *Computatio Sive Logica*, trans. Aloysius Martinich, ed. Isabel C. Hungerland and George R. Vick (New York: Abaris Books, 1981), ch. 1, sec. 8.

19. *Leviathan*, ch. 29, pp. 365–66; *English Works*, 3:310–11.

20. *Leviathan*, ch. 19, p. 242; *English Works*, 3:174.

21. Plato *Republic* 518a.

22. *Elements*, pt. 1, ch. 7, sec. 3, p. 29. For parallel passages see *Leviathan*, ch. 6, p. 120, and ch. 15, p. 216; *English Works*, 3:41, 146.

23. *Elements*, pt. 1, ch. 17, sec. 14, pp. 93–94. For a similar argument see *Leviathan*, ch. 6, p. 129; *English Works*, 3:50–51.

24. *Elements*, pt. 1, ch. 5, sec. 12, p. 22.

25. *Leviathan*, ch. 15, pp. 215–16; *English Works*, 3:146.

26. E.g., in *De Cive, The English Version*, ed. Howard Warrender (Oxford: Clarendon Press, 1983), pt. 2, ch. 7. sec. 18, p. 116.

27. *Elements*, pt. 1, ch. 5, sec. 14, p. 23, emphasis added. See also *Leviathan*, ch. 6, pp. 118–19; *English Works*, 3:39.

28. Plato *Republic* 443, 589.

29. *Leviathan*, Introduction, pp. 82–83; *English Works*, 3:xi.

30. *De Cive*, Epistle Dedicatory, pp. 25–26.

31. *De Corpore*, 1:ix.

32. *Elements*, pt. 2, ch. 10, sec. 8, p. 188.

33. *De Cive*, pt. 1, ch. 3, sec. 32, p. 75.

34. *Leviathan*, ch. 31, p. 407; *English Works*, 3:357.

35. *Elements*, pt. 1, ch. 3, sec. 4, p. 10.

36. For arguments about the constitutive linguistic functions of a sovereign that approach the view suggested here, see Sheldon S. Wolin, *Politics and Vision* (Boston: Little, Brown, 1960), ch. 8; and Terence Ball, "Hobbes's Linguistic Turn," *Polity* 17 (1985): 739–60.

37. *Leviathan*, ch. 30, p. 378; *English Works*, 3:324.

38. *Leviathan*, ch. 13, p. 186; *English Works*, 3:113.

39. It is possible, of course, that ordinary people's capacities might be improved through the acquisition of knowledge from experts. But it is likely that there would also be a tendency for them to delegate their decision-making functions to these experts, resulting in a diminution of ordinary people's capacities.

40. For discussions relevant to this observation see Thomas Nagel, "The Fragmentation of Value," in *Mortal Questions* (Cambridge: Cambridge University Press, 1979), pp. 128–41; and Bernard Williams, "Conflicts of Values," in *Moral Luck* (Cambridge: Cambridge University Press, 1981), pp. 71–82.

41. Of course, for certain purposes human beings may fruitfully be thought of as if they were such machines. For an example, see Jon Elster, *Ulysses and the Sirens*, 2d ed. (Cambridge: Cambridge University Press, 1984).

42. *Leviathan*, ch. 30, p. 378; *English Works*, 3:324–25.

43. *Leviathan*, ch. 29, p. 363; *English Works*, 3:308.

4

Intending (Political) Obligation: Hobbes and the Voluntary Basis of Society

Gordon J. Schochet

I

The unembellished "designe" of *Leviathan*, as Hobbes asserted at the end of his book, was "to set before mens eyes the mutuall Relation between Protection and Obedience."[1] Hobbes was not alone in his acceptance of this notion that the duty of obedience was a consequence of being provided with security. Several scholars have discussed the popularity of this de facto theory as a solution to the problem of political obligation in England after the execution of Charles I on 30 January 1649.[2]

The king was dead, and his government had been uprooted. One of the initial problems facing the Commonwealth that had quickly replaced the monarchy was to establish itself as the legitimate authority entitled to allegiance. A loyalty—or "Engagement"—oath was instituted in February for members of the governing Council of State, and a year later, it was extended to "all men whatsoever within the Commonwealth of England, of the age of eighteen years and upward." Each such person was ordered to "*declare and promise, that I will be true and faithful to the Commonwealth of England as it is now established, without a king or House of Lords.*"[3] The oath raised considerable problems for people who questioned the legality of the new government, either because they had previously declared their loyalty to the dead king and his successors (who were still alive and well) or because they "scrupled" at revolution and regicide.[4]

The de facto insistence upon the extraction of the duty to obey from the fact of protection was designed to answer precisely such complaints and to eliminate personal moral judgments from politics. The ultimate moral judgment, of course, was that the government itself is illegitimate. Hobbes launched a strong attack on the "false doctrine" that *"every private man is Judge of Good and Evill actions"* because it "disposed [men] to debate with themselves, and dispute the commands of the Common-wealth; and afterwards to obey, or disobey them, and in their private judgements they shall think fit. Whereby the Common-wealth is distracted and *Weakened.*"[5] The remedy for the conditions that had led to the disastrous Civil War was simple obedience to the government in power, and *Leviathan* was designed to show the inevitability of that conclusion.

In one sense, then, Hobbes extended and modified the political doctrines he had previously worked out in *De Cive* (1642 and 1647) and *De Corpore Politico* (written before 1640 and first published in 1650) and applied them to the conditions of 1650, especially the Engagement Oath debates. This much has become a near-commonplace in the Hobbes literature, and we have grown accustomed to regarding the contextual *point* of *Leviathan* as a contribution to the same debates that exercised the likes of Francis Rous, Marchamont Nedham, Anthony Ascham, and even John Milton and Sir Robert Filmer. Its aim was to encourage men to take the Engagement, and in this respect, it is possible to regard all the discussions of "compact," "contract," "covenant," and "consent" in *Leviathan* as theoretical and conceptual analogues to the Engagement Oath.

But there is a further and deeper dimension both to the Engagement Oath debates and to *Leviathan* that has been left out of this recent, contextualizing literature. From the perspective of a prescriptive theory of authority, what is to be gained by insisting that subjects take an oath of allegiance? If it is the case that people are already bound to obey governors who protect them as a result—and perhaps even as the virtual "cost"—of that protection, what is *added* to their duty by having them give their words?

The consent or oath cannot create or justify the duty to obey, for that duty preceded the consent. In these terms, consent is no more than an overt recognition, acceptance, or acknowledgement of a preexisting duty. Its function, therefore, is largely social and psychological: it serves as a reminder and intensifier of the duty. Having already agreed that something is her duty, a person is perhaps more likely to fulfill it than she might otherwise be; it may induce others to behave similarly; and a commitment of this sort can help to keep one from wavering at a later date. In short, while the commitment provides something additional to "think about" in determining how to act, it does not establish a condition in which one is obliged *because* she has consented or agreed.

None of this is insignificant or trivial, however far removed it may be from moral reasoning. Political legitimacy and the widespread beliefs in political obligation that sustain a regime probably turn more on psychological than on irreducibly moral factors. And it is reasonable to suggest that de facto supporters of the Commonwealth and its Engagement Oath appreciated this fact. But it is also the case that, with the significant exception of Hobbes, these writers were not so much concerned to construct coherent philosophic systems as they were to shore up the Commonwealth. Hobbes, on the other hand, appears to have pursued both objectives and to have attempted to put philosophy to work in the service of politics.

The chief conceptual problem for *Leviathan* was to devise (or discover) a means of obliging people—specifically men—to obey the absolute political authority that could protect them from their own worst inclinations and behaviors. Hobbes's solution, as it was for the defenders of the Engagement Oath, was to tie that obligation to the personal undertaking of the subject. The other theorists, at best, argued that it was appropriate and desirable for men to subscribe to the Engagement and that doing so would not violate previous undertakings or moral principles. The Commonwealth was legitimate because it protected them and was therefore entitled to their obedience without further qualification.

The central axiom of *Leviathan*, on the other hand, is that political obligation is a product of personal will, that it is consent or agreement that actually ties one to the sovereign ruler. It is the burden of the book to demonstrate to people that they have already consented and are obliged to the regime and to provide them with reasons grounded in personal commitment, self-interest, and rationality for accepting and acting on their obligations.

In the process of making these arguments, of course, Hobbes constructed an intriguing and elaborate theory of social *and* political obligation that not long ago was treated as the core of his political philosophy. Howard Warrender's *The Political Philosophy of Hobbes*—a strikingly deontological, ahistorical, and virtually "Kantian" reading of Hobbes published in 1957[6]—ushered in nearly two decades of scholarly debate about the nature and place of obligation in Hobbes's thought.[7] Quentin Skinner's having shown the relationship of Hobbes's theory to the Engagement Oath debates—to say nothing of C. B. Macpherson's derivation of Hobbes's doctrines from the putative "possessive individualism" of seventeenth-century England[8]—turned attention from conceptual to historical analysis. In the process, discussions of the theory of obligation have been left dissatisfyingly incomplete.

This paper reopens some of those older questions. Taking seriously Hobbes's insistence that all obligation is a consequence of some individual act—"there being no Obligation on any man, which ariseth not from some Act of his own"[9]—it focuses particularly on the role of intentionality in his account and justification of obligation. No one made the case for the intentional sources and justifications of political duties more fully or forcefully than Hobbes, and the power and clarity of his argument make Hobbes's presentation the best exemplar we have of the intentionalist claim. Thus, an analysis of Hobbes's arguments should reveal some of the inherent shortcomings of strict intentionalism and help point the way toward a more satisfactory account of political obligation.

This final goal is especially important, for it is widely presumed both that modern liberalism is largely voluntaristic and intentionalist and that Hobbesian doctrines are quintessentially liberal. Part of the increasingly popular insistence upon the "bankruptcy," inadequacy, inconsistency, or erroneous quality of liberal ideology rests upon the presumed identity of liberal and Hobbesian values. It is my belief that this view of Hobbes as a liberal theorist is mistaken. One of the implicit but subsidiary aims of this paper, therefore, is to demonstrate something of the distance between the Hobbesian and liberal accounts of political obligation.

The intentionalist core of his theory, I argue, provided Hobbes with the conceptual apparatus necessary to subject people to the structures and constraints of society without violating their natural freedom. This is most clearly seen in the discussions of the origins of sovereign power and civil society, of which Hobbes provided two distinct versions, "institution" and "acquisition." Each of these conceptions has its own strengths and weaknesses, and each of them plays a different role in the larger theory of *Leviathan*.

"Institution," I shall argue, makes possible the conceptions of authorization and representation that are essential to the organic relationship between sovereign and subjects whereby the mighty Leviathan becomes an artificial person. "Acquisition," on the other hand, provides a context in which the individual's sole, preserved right against the sovereign, the right of self-defense, can be understood and from which the dependence of obligation upon protection can be derived. The explanation of acquisition, however, was conceptually incomplete; it required the addition of Hobbes's doctrine of "gratitude," but that, in turn, violated the insistence that obligations must be grounded in a person's intentional and voluntary acts. In the end, Hobbes shored up his argument by transforming gratitude into consent and by making the willingness to accept one's legitimate obligations a sign of rationality, which was itself a cornerstone of his conception of human nature.

II

For Hobbes, it was a foregone conclusion that any situation in which there was obligation or duty—indeed, any relationship between human beings—had to be the result of some prior "paction," "covenant," or act of consent. The only way a person could be subject to the power and authority of another was through the former's actual agreement or consent. Because there was no status in nature, all differentiations were conventional.

The "natural" and original human situation, as is well known, was one of utter equality and independence. This was no idyllic state of nature, but a desperate, insecure, and unstable isolation from which all the consequences, conventions, and conveniences of human sociability were absent. Self-interest and fear—the rawest and most basic of human emotions—reigned supreme, and people lived only by their wits and strengths. For beneath the equality and liberty of "meer nature" were the drive for self-preservation and the accompanying entitlement ("right" is the Hobbesian locution) to do anything that was conceived necessary to sustain one's life. This "right" included defensively attacking and even killing other humans, all of whom were regarded as enemies because they wanted the same things as the self, were driven by the same fears, and had the same entitlements. Such were the conditions that precipitated the bleak "war of all against all."[10] How, then, could it ever have been the case that people escaped this situation and found themselves in (long-term) relationships with others?

The same power and sheer, brute strength that characterized life in the state of nature provided the only route to a stable and secure existence. But the *imposition* of "authority" and the establishment of social ties by means of strength and might would destroy natural "freedom" and equality. Society, with its hierarchical structures—of which authority is preeminent—and the various behaviors it *requires* of people, appears to be in violation of the original provisions and guarantees of nature. What had happened to, and what was the point of, natural freedom and equality if they could *legitimately* be overcome simply by strength?

The point of freedom for Hobbes, seen in conjunction with his conception of natural rights, was that it made each person the sovereign lord over his—and pointedly *her*—own movements and activities. People had to be the authors of whatever statuses they occupied, which required the engagement, in some sense, of their wills. If the route from the state of nature to society was, paradoxically perhaps, by way of that very power whose absence made the natural condition so precarious, it was paved with the *intentional* surrender of equality and liberty. Anything short of strict intentionality deprived people of their rights in violation of the dictates of nature. But Hobbes found an effective way around what could have been a serious dilemma for his theory: he simply read consent back into the generation of all relationships, including that between parents and children.

III

Hobbes distinguished two sources of sovereign power: "acquisition" and "institution," the one based on the "Naturall force" of the sovereign-to-be, the other derived from people's "agreement amongst themselves, to submit to some Man, or Assembly of men, voluntarily."[11] In both cases, it was the "consent" of the individual that translated physical power into civil entitlement, thereby legitimating the existence of the sovereign. The general arguments are familiar enough, and we need not linger over their details.

Institution is the better known of the two processes and the one that seems more satisfactorily to comport with what is taken to be the primary structure of *Leviathan*. The awful state of nature, with its equality of natural rights and natural-law dictates that people *"endeavour Peace"* and *"be willing, when others are so too, . . . to lay down this right to all things,"*[12] would play little role in Hobbes's argument were there no account of sovereignty by institution. It is the *general* and collective or mutual fear of one's co-residents of the state of nature that leads to the renunciation in the so-called social contract, to which the emergent sovereign is not a party.

The rights of acquisition, on the other hand, have their roots in individual self-preservation, the fear of a *specific* person, and a direct relationship between subject and sovereign. Remarking that "the

Rights and Consequences" of acquired sovereignty "are the very same with those of a Soveraign by Institution,"[13] Hobbes dropped the distinction after chapter 20 of *Leviathan*.[14]

It would be very difficult to put the two conceptions together, however, for there are important distinctions between the accounts of sovereign origins that Hobbes simply ignored. The rights of acquisition spring from the "gratitude" of subjects in response to the benevolence of the conquering sovereigns who spared their lives. Gratitude was the fourth law of nature and seems to have imposed a substantive rule of social behavior on the inhabitants of the state of nature apart from and prior to their agreement. In one of the most interesting but neglected passages in *Leviathan*, Hobbes wrote:

> As Justice dependeth on Antecedent Covenant; so does GRATI-TUDE depend on Antecedent Grace; that is to say, Antecedent Free-gift . . . [and] may be conceived in this Forme, *That a man which receiveth Benefit from another of meer Grace, Endeavour that he which giveth it, have no reasonable cause to repent him of his good will.* For no man giveth, but with intention of Good to himselfe; because Gift is Voluntary; and of all Voluntary Acts, the Object is to every man his own Good; of which if men see they shall be frustrated, there will be no beginning of benevolence, or trust; nor consequently of mutuall help; nor of reconciliation of one man to another; and therefore they are to remain still in the condition of *War*; which is contrary to the first and Fundamentall Law of Nature, which commandeth men to *Seek Peace*.[15]

When applied to conquest or the imposition of power by "Naturall Force," gratitude requires that people commit themselves to their new sovereigns *because* their lives have not been taken.

I shall argue below that sovereigns by acquisition, in effect, enter into reciprocal agreements with their subjects—to spare their lives in return for their obedience—and that the resultant obligation is directly conditional. These aspects of acquisition are related to the debt of gratitude and further distinguish it from institution. While it is true that subjects who collectively institute sovereign authority over themselves do so in the expectation that their lives will be rendered more secure, there is nothing in their agreement to impose that requirement upon the ruler. They and all subsequent members of civil society retain their rights to self-preservation because that is the one natural right that is not surrendered in the social compact.

Hobbes's reasons for this claim are logical rather than empirical or contractual: people cannot be supposed to have surrendered control over the very thing—security of life—for which they sought the safety and protection of civil society. Accordingly, their duties do not reach so far as to require that they cooperate in sovereign commands that jeopardize their lives, even if their prior actions would have justified the sovereign's attempt to take their lives.

This situation presents one of the most troublesome, but one of the clearest, dilemmas of *Leviathan*. The general principle—derived from Hobbes's notions of "personation" and "authorization"[16]—is that every subject is the author of every act of the sovereign and so cannot resist what he or she has already consented to. This principle is limited by each individual's retention of the right of self-preservation.[17] Nonetheless, the sovereign possesses the right of capital punishment, which is also a state of nature right carried over into civil society.[18] Any attempt to exercise it, however, places the sovereign in a state of nature relationship with the particular subject whose life is threatened.

True, no other subjects are entitled to join in the resistance to sovereign authority[19]—unless, of course, they perceive the threat to one subject's life as an attack on their own as well, in which case they too presumably have the right to resist[20]—so the entire fabric of the society is not destroyed. Also, subjects are not permitted to threaten one another's lives. Only the sovereign has that entitlement, but it is an entitlement that places no constraints on anyone else. It is a legitimate and proper right that is not matched by a corresponding duty on the part of whomever it is claimed against. Instead, the sovereign's right to take the lives of his or her subjects is actually challenged by an equally legitimate and proper right to resist the sovereign's power. This is precisely the theoretical impasse that characterized the state of nature and required the establishment of sovereignty for its resolution; but in this instance, it is the presence of sovereignty that creates the conflict. The negation of the sovereign's authority in cases such as this is a consequence of the private reservations unavoidably made by each party to the contract that created governance. It is a rare—if not unique and somewhat peculiar—circumstance in which Hobbes permitted the intrusion of private judgment into civil affairs.

Although Hobbesian sovereigns do not (ought not to?) wantonly or indifferently threaten the lives of their subjects, even though they have the right to do so, their grounds or reasons for refraining are strictly prudential.[21] Their actions are not based on a principled conception of the nature of sovereignty nor upon a necessary concern for the welfare of their subjects. Rulers do not (or should not) invade their subjects without sufficient cause because they know that subjects who feel threatened are not so likely to obey as those who are contented. In short, the stable continuation of authority is a direct consequence of the subjects' continued obedience.

But this is hardly a limit on sovereign power, and certainly not a contractual one. Hobbes insisted that there could be no limits imposed on sovereignty without destroying it and the commonwealth as well.[22] Even though it is the reason people in the state of nature agree to the institution of a commonwealth and, from their perspectives, constitutes the ground of their obedience to the sovereign's rule, guaranteeing the personal security of the life and interests of each subject (by the provision of public peace and freedom from external threats) is not the sovereign's *duty*. Sovereigns—at least those who are instituted—have no duties other than those imposed by God.

Acquired sovereignty presents rather a different picture from all this, for the political relationship is a consequence of a bargain struck between the sovereign—typically represented by Hobbes as a conqueror of some sort—and each would-be subject: "Every subject in a Common-wealth, hath covenanted to obey the Civill Law, (either one with another, as when they assemble to make a common Representative, or *with the Representative it selfe one by one, when subdued by the Sword they promise obedience, that they may receive life;*)."[23]

The context is suggestive of a "gunman situation" in which one is faced with the choice of surrendering either "your money or your life." In this case, the choice is "your liberty or your life." So far as Hobbes was concerned, the alternatives were not at all difficult for the rational person, who would naturally prefer life. In return for sparing their lives, the conqueror is entitled to the obedience of the vanquished foes. The obligation to obey the sovereign is rooted in the subject's consent and is therefore no less complete than that which results from the state of nature compact: "It is not therefore the Victory, that giveth the right of Dominion over the Vanquished, but his own Covenant."[24] Furthermore, the covenant is no less valid because coerced, for "Covenants entred into by fear, in the condition of meer Nature, are obligatory."[25]

There is at least one major difference between institution and acquisition that Hobbes never addressed: the sovereign is a party to the agreement. That agreement is actually a contract imposing conditions on both sides.[26] When the sovereign either ceases to protect the subject's life or appears to threaten it, the duty to obey is at an end.[27] This reading has the advantage of being able to account for the sovereign's protection of the subjects' lives on grounds that are theoretically more plausible than the prudence that results from the social contract. But by giving the subject a theoretical or moral claim against the sovereign, it calls into question Hobbes's insistence that the sovereign was answerable to no one on earth.[28]

The other form of acquired sovereignty that Hobbes discussed was "Dominion Paternall," the power of parents over their children in the state of nature. Like the rights of conquest, paternal authority was said to be derived from consent rather than the circumstance that brought parent and child together: "The right of Dominion by Generation, is that, which the Parent hath over his Children; and is called PATERNALL. And is not so derived from the Generation, as if therefore the Parent had Dominion over his Child because he begat him; but from the Childs Consent, either expresse, or by other sufficient arguments declared."[29] The actual consent of the child had to be projected into the future, because along with "naturall fooles" and "mad-men," they "had never the power to make any covenant, or to understand the consequences thereof; and consequently never took upon them to authorise the actions of any Soveraign."[30]

This entire discussion is rather strange and strained. It is part of Hobbes's attempt to deny the existence of status relationships in the condition of "meer Nature." It makes sense, ultimately, on the ground that in the prepolitical world of the state of nature, parents were sovereigns: "A great Family if it be not part of some Commonwealth, is of it self, as to the Rights of Soveraignty, a little Monarchy; whether that Family consist of a man and his children; or of a man and his servants; or of a man, and his children, and servants together: wherein the Father or Master is the Soveraign."[31]

The argument reveals a kind of conceptual embarrassment. Mothers did give birth in the state of nature, but Hobbes insisted upon rooting the consequences of this undeniably natural phenomenon in convention. Appealing to the law of gratitude without calling it by name, he said that children owed their parents obedience because they had let them live: "Preservation of life being the end, for which one man becomes subject to another, every man is *supposed*[32] to promise obedience, to him, in whose power it is to save, or destroy him."[33]

IV

One further point is worth mentioning in this context. Hobbes divided the process of instituting civil society into two forms, which can conveniently be termed "surrender" and "transfer." In the one case, prospective subjects simply set aside or renounced their natural rights to all things without further qualification;[34] whereas in the other, those rights were explicitly and specifically transferred or conveyed to someone else.[35] This distinction is not usually recognized in the literature, but even where it is, the prevailing interpretation is that no significant differences follow from one or the other method of institution.

Generally speaking, this is a correct but incomplete interpretation. By standing outside the state of nature agreement, the sovereign surrenders nothing and retains the natural right to all things, which cannot be increased by any transfer from those who do take part. More to the point, those state of nature rights are sufficient to establish sovereign power and entitlement, which do not require the addition of the rights previously belonging to the members of the civil society:

> He that renounceth, or passeth away his Right, giveth not any other man a Right which he had not before; because there is nothing to which every man had not Right by Nature: but onely standeth out of his way, that he may enjoy his own originall Right, without hindrance from him; not without hindrance from another. So that the effect which redoundeth to one man, by another mans defect of Right, is but so much diminution of impediments to the use of his own Right originall.[36]

This is but a part of the picture, however, and the starkest one at that, for it contains only the absolutist kernel of sovereignty and nothing of the richness of Hobbes's conceptions of representation, "personation," and authorization. Without that part of the theory and without some means of linking it to the voluntary and intentional movement from the state of nature to civil society, the larger argument of *Leviathan* must collapse. Only if they have actually *transferred* some part of their own power and authority to the sovereign who is to exercise it in their behalf can the members of a commonwealth be said to be the *authors* of as well as to have *willed*—and therefore in both senses to have *intended*—the sovereign's laws. All the acts of the sovereign are equally the acts of every member of the commonwealth:

> A Multitude of men, are made *One* Person, when they are by one man, or one Person, Represented; so that it be done with the consent of every one of that Multitude in particular. For it is the

Unity of the Representer, not the *Unity* of the Represented, that maketh the Person *One*. And it is the Representer that beareth the Person, and but one Person: And *Unity*, cannot otherwise be understood in a Multitude.

And because the Multitude naturally is not *One*, but *Many*; they cannot be understood for one; but many Authors, of every thing their Representative saith,[37] or doth in their name; Every man giving their common Representer, Authority from himselfe in particular; and owning all the Actions the Representer doth, in case they give him Authority without stint.[38]

Political obligation is thus direct and, as it were, organic—almost Rousseauian, for people are required merely to obey themselves when they are commanded by their sovereign (with the obvious difference, of course, that they are hardly "as free as they were before").

In the absence of this connection, there is no tie between subject and sovereign. The *Reason* for obeying remains the fact that the sovereign's might replaces the instability and generalized and "continuall feare"[39] of the state of nature—instead of fearing everyone, subjects need only fear the sovereign—and provides the security that is prerequisite to the commodious industries and arts of organized society. The *justification* of the duty to obey is simply the obligation of the oath of renunciation itself and its commitment "not to hinder those, to whom such Right is granted, or abandoned, from the benefit of it."[40]

V

Theories of political obligation represent attempts to reconcile the conflicts between *duty* and *interest*, for it is at the intersection of those radically different concepts that the most significant and troublesome questions arise. The history of these theories appears to resemble a game in which only two winning moves are possible: either interest must be reduced to duty, or duty must be derived from interest. Only by collapsing one of the categories into the other can the conflicts between them be overcome.

It is the burden of *Leviathan* to validate the second of those moves and to argue, in rather complex but never convoluted way, that whatever is revealed as one's duty is so because it fulfills her or his interests. As the sole and independent guardians of their own interests, people must personally be the authors of all their duties; they must *will* them upon themselves.

It is here, incidentally, that Hobbes's solution to the problem of political obligation in the Engagement Oath controversy is at its most brilliant. He held that the confusions and upheavals of the Civil War resulted from the intrusion of private conscience and judgment into the public, political realm. It was certainly true in the state of nature "and also under Civill Government, in such cases as are not determined by the law," that *"every private man is Judge of Good and Evill actions."* But this was not the case where the sovereign's will had been declared, for "the Law is the publique Conscience" by which everyone living in a commonwealth "hath already undertaken to be guided."[41] Hobbes distinguished between obligation and commitment, which were matters of will, and belief, which was a matter of conscience and judgment.[42] Thus, one could safely take the Engagement no matter what his moral, religious, or political scruples. Interest and duty happily coincided—as they always did according to Hobbes if they were properly understood—and the sanctity of conscience was preserved.

At the same time, Hobbes's insistence upon basing obligation on the self-willed act of the individual subject has the makings of an astoundingly anarchistic doctrine, for it followed from this premise that any one who had not committed himself or herself to the commonwealth was not bound by its laws. Such a person, of course, was in the condition of "meer nature" and was an outlaw and enemy to the commonwealth, one of those "masterlesse men" about whom Hobbes was so concerned.[43] But that was not the end of the story, for Hobbes had a number of traps set for his readers, starting with his indifference to coercion.

VI

An obligation one is *forced* to acknowledge because the costs of refusal are greater than those of acceptance is no less valid, no less binding than one that is fully and happily accepted. An obligation of recompense that stems from some "benefit" bestowed where there was no opportunity to reject is equally binding—not because "one good turn deserves another," as the adage goes, but because by reaping the benefits, a person was presumed to have agreed to their costs. Even the content of a prospective obligation was of little moment for Hobbes, so long as it did not violate the laws of the commonwealth or threaten the subject's sole, remaining natural right, the right to life.

Another of the snares employed by Hobbes is his conception of rationality. He argued that a proper and rational understanding of one's interests would lead to the recognition that the political order imposed by an absolute sovereign was always to be preferred to a situation in which each person individually sought to maximize his or her advantages. Rejection of sovereign rule would be a prima facie sign of nonrationality and, therefore, of a failure to comprehend the nature of one's own interests. The duty to obey the sovereign— political obligation—was thus a consequence of rationality. By using the subject's intentional act to create the *mechanism* that tied him or her to the sovereign, rationality permitted a person to appreciate and efficiently to pursue the objects of interest.

In the end, the argument rested upon a circular account of the relationship of rationality to consent. It appears to support Hobbes's case for the intentional origins of political organization and certainly strengthens his implicit case for the derivation of duty from interest. On closer examination, however, it turns out that the cost is part of the plausibility of his position. A consent that definitionally one cannot help but give lest she or he be deemed nonrational and therefore incapable of consenting in the first place is hardly consent in any standard sense of the term and adds nothing to the theoretical claim.

The very point of consent and intention, as Hobbes well appreciated, is that one *could have* done otherwise but, for whatever reason, *chose* not to do so and committed herself or himself. In these terms, it is possible to understand without necessarily embracing Hobbes's indifference to the coercive force of the conqueror's offer to spare a person's life as the intentional source of the subject's obligation to accept his rule. Life is filled with difficult and painful choices, but they are choices nonetheless. The fact that we can conceive of circumstances in which people would choose death over servitude or gross immorality[44] underscores the role of intention. On the other hand, a situation in which one had no choice—in which failure to make the requisite selection would be taken as a sign of incapacity—by its nature cannot be one that is controlled by volition. So-called acts of consent given under such circumstances would be no more intentional than the breaths drawn by someone who is asleep.

Hobbes was certainly correct in his implicit presumption that self-assumed obligations are in general more legitimate than those that are imposed on someone against her or his will. To say this is to agree with him that the starting point of a theory of obligation is human liberty,[45] for an individual can only be *bound* to do that which before becoming so obliged he or she was free not to do. This is especially true of promise making and, correspondingly, of consenting, for in these cases it is the engagement of the will that legitimately circumscribes personal freedom.

What problems there are with Hobbes's theory are consequences of both his presumption of the conventional nature of all forms of status among human beings and his corresponding insistence upon their voluntary origins. The "conventional state" is one of the identifying features of modern politics, and at its most basic level, it numbers Hobbes among its primary architects. But it does not follow from the view of the state as a malleable contrivance that can be tailored to suit human needs that all its structures were *intentionally* erected. Hobbes's reductionist claims reveal the futility of attempting to root all duties and obligations in personal consent. Some of his arguments are conceptually flawed or require strange or absurd distortions, but others are simply outrageous. Interestingly enough, he had at hand a means of salvaging the most substantial of his claims—his fourth law of nature, the law of gratitude—but he chose to derive even that dictate from consent.

The difficulty with a doctrine of strict intentionality, as Hobbes apparently understood, is that the failure or absence of intention defeats any claim for the existence of obligation or duty. For Hobbes, intentionality was necessary to preserve original and natural human freedom and equality. Some modern theories, notably those of Robert Nozick and other individualist libertarians, make the same presuppositions as Hobbes but end with strikingly different conclusions. Whereas the objectives for Hobbes were the preservation of social and political duties and the *practical* denigration of human freedom, libertarians seek to preserve freedom at the expense of the political order. Accordingly, Hobbes deduced intention from obligation, and libertarianism denies obligation in the absence of individual intentions to be bound. Hobbes's polity is maximal; that of libertarianism is minimal. Although not necessarily politically more acceptable than the theory of *Leviathan*, libertarianism on its face is more coherent and less exaggerated. Both doctrines show the difficulties inherent in any attempt to extract the whole of political duty from consent and intention.

VII

A "liberal" theory of political obligation would have to be very different from that of Hobbes. The essence of liberalism is its opposition to the absolutist conception of the "conventional state," of which Hobbes was an early and exceptionally articulate champion. That opposition usually takes the form of some version or another of *constitutionalism*, the doctrine that there are substantive limits to political authority as well as specific procedures through which it should act; the violation of either of these restrictions renders state action illegal. Constitutionalist restrictions spring from and have as their chief goal the preservation and enhancement of the rights and liberties of the members of the civil society. The contrasts with Hobbes are virtually self-evident, and it is something of a mystery that critics of liberalism should be so blind to these differences.

Far from being a "liberal" himself, Hobbes represented what emergent liberal ideology would have to overcome in order to sustain its defense of constitutionalist politics. The goal was to defend a conventional account of the state that did not collapse into absolutism or ineffectually wither away, leaving its members undefended in either case. It is a goal that still motivates the liberal spirit.[46]

NOTES

1. Thomas Hobbes, *Leviathan*, ed. C. B. Macpherson (Baltimore: Penguin, 1968), Review and Conclusion, p. 728. All references to *Leviathan* will be to this edition.

2. See the following (listed in order of publication): John M. Wallace, "The Engagement Controversy, 1649-1652: An Annotated List of Pamphlets," *Bulletin of the New York Public Library* 68 (1964): 384-405, which remains the bibliographic starting point for the subject; idem, *Destiny His Choice: The Loyalism of Andrew Marvell* (Cambridge: Cambridge University Press, 1968), ch. 1; Quentin Skinner, "The Context of Hobbes's Theory of Political Obligation," in *Hobbes and Rousseau: A Collection of Critical Essays*, ed. Maurice Cranston and Richard Peters (Garden City, N.Y.: Doubleday & Co., 1972), pp. 108-42; idem, "Conquest and Consent: Thomas Hobbes and the Engagement Controversy," in *The Interregnum: The Quest for Settlement, 1646-1660*, ed. G. E. Aylmer (London: Macmillan, 1972), ch. 3; Margaret A. Judson, *From Tradition to Political Reality: A Study of the Ideas Set Forth in Support of the Commonwealth Government in England, 1649-1653* (Hamden, Conn.: Shoe String Press, 1980), esp. ch. 5; Glenn Burgess, "Usurpation, Obligation and Obedience in the Thought of the Engagement Controversy," *Historical Journal* 29 (1986): 515-36; and Deborah Baumgold, *Hobbes's Political Theory* (Cambridge: Cambridge University Press, 1988), pp. 124-33.

3. An Act for Subscribing the Engagement, 2 January 1650, from *The Stuart*

Constitution: Documents and Commentary, ed. J. P. Kenyon (Cambridge: Cambridge University Press, 1966), p. 341 (italics in Kenyon's text). The oath was not widely subscribed and apparently not strongly enforced (see Kenyon, p. 330, and Burgess, p. 515), but it was intensely debated.

4. The argument worked for some people. Even Sir Robert Filmer, the staunch defender of divine right royalism, was willing to accept the de facto doctrine, writing in 1652 that "protection and subjection are reciprocal, so that where the first fails, the latter ceaseth" (Sir Robert Filmer, *Directions for Obedience to Government in Dangerous or Doubtful Times* [1652], reprinted in his *Patriarcha and Other Political Works*, ed. Peter Laslett [Oxford: Basil Blackwell, 1949], p. 234). On this basis, he justified taking the Engagement Oath and yet claimed that he remained loyal to the exiled Charles II whose interests he was actually protecting by helping to preserve the peace and stability of the nation. (These refinements on the argument of the *Directions* are in the manuscript essays by Filmer, "Two Treatises against Rebellion," Bodleian Library, MS. Tanner 233, fols. 135–47 and 172–82. Another version of this manuscript was anonymously published in 1680 as *A Discourse concerning Supreme Power and Common Right*, which is traditionally but incorrectly ascribed to Sir John Monson. For discussion of Filmer's authorship and other matters, see my "Sir Robert Filmer: Some New Bibliographic Discoveries," *The Library* 26 [1971]: 135–60.)

5. *Leviathan*, ch. 29, p. 365; see also ch. 46, p. 697.

6. Howard Warrender, *The Political Philosophy of Hobbes: His Theory of Obligation* (Oxford: Clarendon Press, 1957).

7. Warrender certainly did not start this preoccupation, but the brilliance and single-mindedness of his book were a catalyst for subsequent scholarship, some of which is available in Cranston and Peters, ed., *Hobbes and Rousseau*, and in K. C. Brown, ed., *Hobbes Studies* (Cambridge, Mass.: Harvard University Press, 1965). It was Warrender's interpretation that provided the textual starting point for Skinner, and that debate continues; see Brian T. Trainor, "Warrender and Skinner on Hobbes," *Political Studies* 36 (1988): 680–91, and Quentin Skinner, "Warrender and Skinner on Hobbes: A Reply," ibid., 692–95. Reappraisals of Warrender can be found in recent issues of the *Hobbes Newsletter*, but there has been no systematic survey of the literature or reconsideration of the entire question.

8. I refer, of course, to *The Political Theory of Possessive Individualism: Hobbes to Locke* (Oxford: Oxford University Press, 1962), chs. 1 and 2, and to his introduction to the Penguin edition of *Leviathan*.

9. *Leviathan*, ch. 21, p. 268.

10. See, of course, ibid., ch. 13, esp. p. 186.

11. Ibid., ch. 17, p. 228.

12. Ibid., ch. 14, p. 190.

13. Ibid., ch. 20, p. 256. See also ch. 20, p. 252: "But the Rights, and Consequences of Sovereignty are the same in both."

14. In his earlier *The Elements of Law, Natural and Politic*, he wrote of "monarchy by acquisition" and monarchy "made by political institution, . . . whatsoever rights be in the one, the same also be in the other. And therefore I shall no longer speak of them, as distinct, but of monarchy in general" (2d ed., ed. Ferdinand Tönnies with an introduction by M. M. Goldsmith [London: Frank Cass and Co., 1969], pt. 2, ch. 4, sec. 10, p. 135).

15. *Leviathan*, ch. 15, p. 209. See also ch. 11, p. 163, and ch. 30, p. 382; cf. ch. 6, p. 123.

16. See ibid., ch. 16, esp. pp. 217–18, 221; and ch. 21, p. 265 ("Every Subject is Author of every act the Sovereign doth"); cf. ch. 27, p. 346.

17. Ibid., ch. 21, pp. 268–69.

18. Why the sovereign retains this right of nature will be considered shortly.

19. *Leviathan*, ch. 21, p. 270: "To resist the Sword of the Common-wealth, in defence of another man, guilty, or innocent, no man hath Liberty."

20. This is not merely a moot or arcane point, for there are many situations in which it is already too late to act in self-defense by the time one perceives *direct* threats to her or his life. One must be not only cautious and careful but prudent as well.

21. That is, they are based on inferences drawn from experience—which is the standard Hobbesian meaning of "prudence"—and are not merely the results of rationally calculated self-interest—which is one of the modern meanings of "prudence" that is often incorrectly read back into Hobbes. In this case, it is easy to understand the source of this interpretation, for it is clearly in the interest of sovereigns to protect and preserve their subjects.

22. *Leviathan*, ch. 29, esp. pp. 367–68 and 372–73.

23. Ibid., ch. 26, p. 314; emphasis added. See also ch. 21, p. 268: Sovereignty "by Acquisition [is] by Covenants of the Vanquished to the Victor, or Child to the Parent."

24. Ibid., ch. 20, pp. 255–56.

25. Ibid., ch. 19, p. 198; see also ch. 21, p. 262.

26. Cf. ibid., ch. 18, p. 231: "The opinion that any Monarch receiveth his Power by Covenant, that is to say on Condition, proceedeth from want of understanding.

27. Immediately after the passage just quoted, Hobbes wrote, "Nor is the Victor obliged by an enemies rendering himselfe, (without promise of life,) to spare him for this his yeelding to discretion; which obliges not the Victor longer, than in his own discretion hee shall think fit" (*Leviathan*, ch. 20, p. 256). The parenthesis especially supports my contention that upon acceptance of the offer of life, a reciprocal relationship is established between sovereign and vanquished subject.

28. See, e.g., *Leviathan*, ch. 19, p. 246, and ch. 21, p. 265.

29. Ibid., ch. 20, p. 253. For a fuller account of "Dominion Paternall," see chapter 12 of my *The Authoritarian Family and Political Attitudes in 17th-Century England: Patriarchalism in Political Thought*, 2d ed. (New Brunswick, N.J.: Transaction Books, 1987), part of which is summarized here.

30. *Leviathan*, ch. 26, p. 317.

31. Ibid., ch. 20, p. 257.

32. "Supposed" is used here by Hobbes in the sense of presumed, not in the modern sense of ought.

33. *Leviathan*, ch. 20, p. 254; emphasis added.

34. E.g., ibid., ch. 14, p. 190.

35. E.g., ibid, ch. 17, p. 227.

36. Ibid., ch. 14, p. 191.

37. I have silently corrected an apparent and amusing typographer's error in Macpherson's text, which reads "faith," presumably due to the substitution of an *f* for the elongated seventeenth-century *s*.

38. *Leviathan*, ch. 16, pp. 220–21. See also ch. 21, p. 265: "Every Subject is Author of every act the Soveraign doth."

39. Ibid., ch. 13, p. 186.

40. Ibid., ch. 14, p. 191. Obviously, this argument applies to the transfer of natural rights as well. My contention is that when rights are specifically transferred to someone else, an additional and more overtly *intentional* tie on the subject is created.

41. Ibid., ch. 29, pp. 365–66. The same argument had been made in *De Cive*, ch. 12, and *The Elements of Law*, pt. 2, ch. 8, sec. 4, but with considerably less force than in *Leviathan*.

42. Considering the command or law of a sovereign who claimed to be enforcing God's will, Hobbes wrote that the subject is "bound I say to obey it, but not bound to believe it" (*Leviathan*, ch. 26, p. 332; see also ch. 29, p. 366).

43. *Leviathan*, chs. 17 and 21, pp. 238 and 266.

44. On Hobbes's account, of course, such people would not be rational, which raises again the issues I have just discussed. Although we may agree with such characterizations in some general sense, there are significant exceptions, and presumably, we would not definitively consign those who opted for the "less desirable" alternative to some status beyond the reach of this theory.

45. H. L. A. Hart's classic article, "Are There Any Natural Rights?" *Philosophical Review* 64 (1955): 175–91, still seems persuasive on this issue and unsurpassed in the subsequent literature.

46. The original impetus for this paper was provided many years ago by the late Benjamin Evans Lippincott, then my adviser and subsequently a valued friend. Even before I enrolled as a graduate student at the University of Minnesota, Ben imposed Warrender's *Political Philosophy of Hobbes* on me, and I have been dazzled by the book's conceptual brilliance but troubled by its interpretative perversity ever since. This paper is something of a response to the general problem posed by Warrender in terms that I hope Ben would have appreciated.

The first draft was completed during my tenure as a Fellow of the Center for the History of Freedom at Washington University, St. Louis, Missouri, during the winter and spring of 1988; both the Fellowship and Research Divisions of the National Endowment for the Humanities have supported the research out of which this essay has grown. It is a pleasure to record my indebtedness to these institutions. I also wish to thank Molly Shanley, Sharon Lloyd, Robinson Grover, Sharon Achinstein, David Wootton, Mary Dietz, and especially Louise Haberman, all of whom made valuable suggestions that helped to bridge the gap between this version and the initial draft as presented to the Benjamin Evans Lippincott Symposium on the Political Philosophy of Hobbes, at the University of Minnesota (spring 1988).

5

Hobbes's Political Sensibility: The Menace of Political Ambition

Deborah Baumgold

Some time ago, Leo Strauss advanced the view that taming men's desire for power is the focal problem of Hobbes's theory.[1] These days, more attention is being paid to his account of rational action than to his observations about the passions. It is now more fashionable to reconstruct Hobbism around the problem of generating cooperation among rational egoists than to accent his concern with controlling men's appetite for power. The Straussian thesis merits revival, in my view, although it is not my intention to defend his reading of Hobbism. Strauss interpreted the desire for power as a psychological theme and discerned in Hobbesian psychology the outlines of a modern, bourgeois moral sensibility. Most commentaries on Hobbes's account of the passions have similarly treated the desire for power as a psychological attribute and have been preoccupied with the sociological bias or the moral import of his observations. My concerns lie in a different direction. The revisionist version of the Straussian argument to be presented here concentrates on the role that the desire for power plays in Hobbes's analysis of politics.

Examining his understanding of ambition for power as a force in politics, I arrive at an unorthodox view of Hobbes's conception of political agency. An analysis of the role of the passions in politics is necessarily, since these are not disembodied forces, an analysis of the desires of some persons. The identity of the power-hungry—the "children of pride"—in Hobbes's imagination is a topic that touches directly on received ideas about the subject of his political theory. Twentieth-century readers commonly suppose that he was concerned principally with the motivation, rights, and duties of ordinary people. According to Strauss, for instance, Hobbes "deduces the form of the right State" from "motives on whose force one can depend in the case of all men under all circumstances."[2] But this orthodoxy is belied, I will argue, by Hobbes's observations on the desire for power as a force in politics. To the contrary, his political analysis discriminates between political elites and ordinary subjects, and it was the ambition of the former for power that occupied his attention.

After examining the identity of the power-hungry in Hobbes's political imagination and, next, his conception of the role ordinary subjects play in politics, I consider last his analysis of the causes of civil war. Here the main issue is the explanatory significance of the desire for power relative to other hypothesized causes of civil disorder, namely class or ideological conflict. The issue bears on another dimension of political agency and raises a further question about the identity of the "children of pride." Are ambitious leaders merely the agents of more fundamental historical forces, as many twentieth-century readers of Hobbes presumably imagine? By his lights, I suggest, this is a romantic view: contention for power is all there is to politics.

THE IDENTITY OF THE "CHILDREN OF PRIDE"

Upon earth there is not his like, who is made without fear. He beholdeth all high things: he is a king over all the children of pride.
—Job 41:33–34

Leviathan, the sea monster in the story of Job that Hobbes took as the symbol for government, is described in the biblical story as the "King of the Proud."[3] Translation of the metaphor into a political analysis hinges on defining the salient persons and passion: who are the "children of pride" whom Leviathan must master? Based on Hobbes's statement that his image of a barbarous state of nature is an "Inference . . . from the Passions,"[4] most twentieth-century interpreters have agreed they are Everyman: the dangerous passion is the "desire of Power after power" that Hobbes "put for a generall inclination of all mankind."[5] Within this broad consensus, there is disagreement whether Hobbesian psychology describes human nature *sub specie aeternitatis* or merely human nature in some social contexts. In C. B. Macpherson's well-known view, the postulate of a universal struggle for power is accurate only to bourgeois ("possessive") market societies, such as Hobbesian England was in most respects.[6] This dispute over the purchase of his vision does not, however, affect the main thesis that Hobbes was obsessed with the appetite for power of Everyman—ordinary subjects as well as grandees.

Yet some readers have suggested that his obsession has a narrower and different target. Criticizing Macpherson's thesis that Hobbes possessed a bourgeois sociological imagination, Keith Thomas advanced the view that his animadversions are directed at the aristocracy and at the passion characteristic of that class—pride. Hobbes, he observed, "explicitly excluded the poor from this contention for honour" and therefore "was by implication confining his analysis to that section of the population, 'who have most leisure to be idle.'"[7] Arguing in a similar vein, Neal Wood relates Hobbes's description of human nature to the "crisis of the aristocracy" at that time: "Who are more likely models for those 'children of pride' than the fiercely competitive and combative English landed gentlemen in their frenetic pursuit of honours, offices and riches in the first half of the seventeenth century?"[8]

In Hobbes's *political* imagination, however, the class of dangerous people is even narrower and more determinate. He held, certainly, that desire for power is a ubiquitous human passion, which makes conflict and competition inherent features of human social relationships.[9] But, as Thomas and Wood correctly note (and Strauss grants), he did not find politically worrisome the ordinary person's desire for power.[10] "Those men are of most trouble to the Republique," according to *De Cive*, "who have most leisure to be idle; for they use not to contend for publique places before they have gotten the victory over hunger, and cold."[11] In connection with politics, it was a less general disposition that Hobbes feared: the salient disposition is "ambition," connoting an "immoderate love of political power" or "*Desire* of Office, or precedence."[12] "Amongst men," he observed in *Leviathan*, "there are very many, that thinke themselves wiser, and abler to govern the Publique, better than the rest; and these strive to reforme and innovate, one this way, another that way; and thereby bring it into Distraction and Civill warre."[13] The statement is indicative of a political sensibility trained not on a vice of the aristocracy as a class (nor on Everyman's or Every-bourgeois-man's desire for power) but rather—and much more concretely—on the threat to political order coming from politically ambitious elites. The

"children of pride" whom Leviathan must master are, quite straightforwardly, those who would be sovereign. In the story of Job, the enemy of Leviathan is the land monster Behemoth, which is the name
Hobbes gave to the institution that in his view was responsible for
the Civil War. His history of the war carries the title *Behemoth or The
Long Parliament*,[14] referring to the Parliament that revolted against
Charles I and remained in session throughout the Interregnum.

Hobbes's commentary on the passions—in particular, the ubiquitous desire for power and its significance in politics—is more dis-
criminating than is sometimes noticed. It is in chapter 11 of *Leviathan*
that he posited a general inclination to seek "Power after power." In
the same chapter, Hobbes distinguished among various character
types.[15] While our passions are uniform, we attach these to different
objects and have therefore different "dispositions" or "inclinations
toward certain things."[16] Ambition is technically a disposition,
which Hobbes characterized as a species of self-conceit consisting in
"a strong opinion of [one's] own wisdom in matter of government."[17] Only men who are "at ease" in life, who have "gotten the
victory over hunger and cold," are likely to develop such a conceit:
"For then it is that he loves to shew his Wisdome, and controule the
Actions of them that governe the Common-wealth."[18] Observing the
political scene prior to the Civil War, Hobbes thought that lack of political opportunity played a part in exacerbating the menace of elite
ambition. "Amongst all those that pretend to, or are ambitious of
such honour [of public employment]," he wrote in *The Elements of
Law*, "a few only can be served, unless it be in a democracy; the rest
therefore must be discontent."[19]

Hobbes's sensitivity to the reality of political inequality is evident
in the advice to rulers on how to govern that complements his doctrine of absolute (unconditional and unified) sovereign right. Formally, all are equally subject to the Hobbesian sovereign. Nonetheless, he counseled rulers to see that justice is administered
with a politic eye to differences among persons and crimes. "The se-
verest Punishments are to be inflicted for those Crimes, that are of
most Danger to the Publique; such as are those which proceed from
malice to the Government established."[20] Furthermore, punishment
should be particularly directed at the "Leaders, and teachers" in a rebellion, as opposed to the "poore seduced People." Punishing leaders sets a good example, while "to be severe to the People, is to
punish that ignorance, which may in great part be imputed to the
Soveraign, whose fault it was, they were no better instructed."[21]

In addition to advising severe treatment of rebel leaders, Hobbes warned repeatedly about the dangers of favoritism and leniency toward grandees. Flattering "a stiffe-neckt subject . . . for fear of his power" may defer a civil war in the short term,[22] but the tack only increases the long-term danger: "It is a contention with Ambition, like that of *Hercules* with the Monster *Hydra*, which having many heads, for every one that was vanquished, there grew up three. For in like manner, when the stubbornnesse of one Popular man, is overcome with Reward, there arise many more (by the Example) that do the same Mischiefe."[23] In summary, "It conduces to the preservation of peace, to depresse the ambitious."[24]

THE ROLE OF ORDINARY SUBJECTS

Common Souldiers resembling Cocks . . . fight for the benefit and ambition of others.

—Francis Osborn, *Advice to a Son*

Hobbes hoped that *Leviathan* would be taught in university because "by that means the most men, knowing their Duties, will be the less subject to serve the Ambition of a few discontented persons, in their purposes against the State."[25] The work is widely considered to be a treatise on political obligation, that is, an inquiry into the ground and extent of citizens' duties. But this is an interpretive construction which distorts Hobbes's understanding of politics by overestimating the importance of ordinary subjects as political actors. Far from seeing "poore, obscure, and simple men, comprehended under the name of the *Vulgar*" as major figures on the political landscape,[26] he pictured them as followers and victims. Explaining why it would be profitable to make *Leviathan* part of a higher education, for instance, he described universities as "the Fountains of Civill, and Morall Doctrine, from whence the Preachers, and the Gentry, drawing such water as they find, use to sprinkle the same . . . upon the People."[27] The people "receive their motion" from the sovereign or from his ambitious rivals.[28] Hobbes addressed subjects in the preface to the second edition of *De Cive* (1647), appealing to them "no longer [to] suffer ambitious men through the streames of your blood to wade to their owne power."[29]

These were commonplace observations in the early Stuart period about the place of the people and their part in the political universe. *The Trew Law of Free Monarchies* (1598), the political treatise of James I, describes rebels as "bare men" who set themselves up to "fly with other men's feathers."[30] Nor was it only conservatives who saw politics in this way. Writing a half-century later and with opposing political sentiments, Anthony Ascham would compare the people to an "Anvill on which all sorts of Hammers discharge themselves; they seldome or never begin a Warre, but are all concenr'd in it after it is begun."[31] Ascham's *Confusions and Revolutions of Goverments* (1649), a tract counseling "engagement" (i.e., submission) to Cromwell's regime, displays a sensitivity to the victimization of ordinary people reminiscent of Hobbes's appeal in the preface to the 1647 *De Cive*. It is the worst aspect of civil war, Ascham observes, "that many times ambitious or angry men forme subtilties and pretences, and afterwards the poore people (who understand them not) are taken out of their houses . . . to fight and maintaine them at the perils of one an-others lives; and such Wars not being of their Interest, they are sure to reape nothing but desolation by them."[32]

The idea of the political universe shared by James I, Hobbes, and Ascham corresponds to the traditional conceptualization of the right of resistance against tyrannous governments. Orthodox Protestant and monarchomach ("king-killer") resistance theory narrowly legitimized rebellion led by "inferior magistrates," viz., religious authorities and parliaments.[33] "To private persons it is said: 'Put thy sword into its scabbard'; to magistrates, however: 'You do not bear the sword in vain.'"[34] It is a subject of dispute among historians when the ideas of fundamental popular sovereignty and a popular right of resistance emerged. Quentin Skinner traces the ideas back to the sixteenth century; others ascribe authorship to the Levellers in the Civil War period or date their emergence even later, to the post-Restoration era.[35] In any case, traditional resistance doctrine continued to represent mainstream opinion during the Civil War period. Parliamentarians, for example, customarily identified their institution with the nation and denied a popular right of rebellion against it. Charles Herle declared it "a position which no man I know maintains": "'that in case the King and the Parliaments should *neither* discharge their trust, the people might rise and make resistance against both.' . . . The Parliament *is* the people's own consent, which once passed, they cannot revoke."[36]

James I and Hobbes, to be sure, were both concerned to deny any right of resistance against established government; while Ascham, for his part, dismissed from consideration in his treatise questions about the just causes for civil war.[37] But what traditional resistance doctrine cast as right these men took to be a fact about politics: the people are led into rebellion by elite rivals to the established government. As will be seen in the next section, Hobbes gave considerable attention to the process whereby ordinary people are "seduced"—i.e., mobilized—into supporting the designs of ambitious leaders.

A number of questions can be raised regarding the duties of subjects. Twentieth-century commentators have fastened on issues of two sorts: subjects' motivation to obey and cooperate with government (broadly understood as encompassing considerations of psychological motivation, rational calculation, as well as moral duty); and the extent and nature of subjects' duties. I think it safe to generalize that most readers have been more attracted by the puzzle of explaining obligation on Hobbist premises than by the satisfactoriness of his arguments themselves. For Hobbes's contemporaries, however, a third issue took precedence: "To whom is allegiance due?"[38] Throughout the Civil War period, both in the prewar era of constitutional debate between king and Parliament in which Hobbes first framed his theory of politics and in the postwar period of the Engagement controversy in which the theory was made accessible to a broad audience, the question of allegiance was the primary problem confronting ordinary Englishmen.

To a much greater extent than is commonly recognized, Hobbes's political theory is directed at this question.[39] Consider, for example, *Leviathan's* authorization covenant. One of the conundrums for readers of Hobbes is the rationale behind the introduction in the work of this novel, and many think unsatisfactory, account of the political covenant. The previous version of the theory, *De Cive*, describes a compact between incipient subjects not to resist the will of the person (or persons) who has been designated sovereign.[40] Retaining the idea that the sovereign is not a party to the covenant, Hobbes added in *Leviathan* the stipulation that each subject is "to owne, and acknowledge himselfe to be Author" of the sovereign's actions.[41] The new formulation seems to be anticipated in *De Cive*, where it is asserted that "government is upheld by a double obligation from the Citizens, first that which is due to their fellow citizens, next *that which they owe to their Prince*," and therefore, "no subjects how many soever they be, can with any Right despoyle him who bears the chiefe Rule, of his authority."[42] Although *De Cive's* version of the covenant proscribes resistance to the sovereign,[43] it does not sustain the stronger claim that subjects owe exclusive allegiance to the government in place. In *Leviathan*, the authorization formulation is brought in specifically to support this latter proposition:

They that are subjects to a Monarch, cannot without his leave cast off Monarchy, and return to the confusion of a disunited Multitude; *nor transferre their Person from him that beareth it, to another Man, or other Assembly of men*: for they are bound, every man to every man, to Own, and be reputed Author of all, that he that already is their Soveraigne, shall do, and judge fit to be done.[44]

I do not mean to imply that Hobbes was *un*concerned with the questions about the nature of subjects' duties that have preoccupied twentieth-century readers. He seemed actually to become more concerned over time with the subject. Besides introducing the authorization covenant in *Leviathan*, Hobbes made several other additions to this last version of his theory that focus specifically on the scope and limits of subjects' political obligations. Only in this version is a chapter (21) devoted to the "liberty of subjects." Yet Hobbes also stipulated, more strongly than before, that subjects are obliged to give the sovereign their active support. The review and conclusion of the work introduces a further law of nature: "That every man is bound by Nature, as much as in him lieth, to protect in Warre, the Authority, by which he is himself protected in time of Peace."[45] These additions betoken a recognition, perhaps born of reflection on the civil war, that more needed to be explained to subjects than "who to follow." Nevertheless, the main argument of *Leviathan*'s review and conclusion continues to concern the issue of allegiance. "The Civill warres have not yet sufficiently taught men, in what point of time it is, that a Subject becomes obliged to the Conquerour"; Hobbes's instruction consists in the familiar Engagement principle, that there is a "mutuall Relation between Protection and Obedience."[46]

THE CAUSATION OF CIVIL WAR

I intended only the story of their injustice, impudence, and hypocrisy; therefore, for the proceeding of the war, I refer you to the history thereof written at large in English. I shall only make use of such a thread as is necessary for the filling up of such knavery, and folly also, as I shall observe in their several actions.

—*Behemoth*, Dialogue 3

The menace of ambitious elites is a principal theme of *Behemoth*, which was written after the Restoration. The work identifies ambitious Presbyterian ministers and ambitious gentlemen—i.e., Puritan leaders and Parliamentarians—as the chief leaders in the Civil War, who seduced the common people into rebellion.[47] The puzzling issue, as Richard Ashcraft has observed, concerns the relationship between ambition and other possible causes and contributing factors—especially, ideas and class interest.[48] Besides targeting elite ambition, Hobbes also gave an ideological explanation of the war, tracing it to seditious and erroneous doctrines. "What civill war was there ever in the Christian world," he asked rhetorically in *De Cive*, "which did not either grow from, or was nourisht by this Root" of seditious (religious) doctrines?[49] Although a concept of class is absent from the theory, some readers have seen an analysis in terms of material causes in his remarks concerning the role in the rebellion of merchants and the city of London.[50]

Properly located in the context of these other causal variables, how significant is elite ambition in Hobbes's analysis of politics? To start with, this collection of causal hypotheses raises the familiar questions of the importance of leaders in history and of elite competition for power in politics. Interpreting the Hobbesian analysis in a Whiggish manner, i.e., with an emphasis on ideas as the principal causal force, or with a Marxist stress on material causes, ambitious elites are conceived as merely the agents for more fundamental historical forces. That is, the Puritan leaders and Parliamentarians who made the Civil War were but the carriers of ideas or the representatives of socio-economic interests. In my view, the analysis advanced in *Behemoth*, together with the accounts of the causation of rebellion in the several versions of Hobbes's political theory, corresponds more closely to a third explanatory model. Revisionist historians are currently putting forward the anti-teleological, "high politics" view that the Civil War was a struggle for power among political elites—as opposed to an ideological or a class conflict.[51]

Hobbes had worked out a causal analysis of rebellion long before writing *Behemoth*. *The Elements of Law* (part 2, chapter 8) and *De Cive* (chapter 12), both written prior to the Civil War, give an account of the necessary and sufficient causes of rebellion:[52] (1) discontent; (2) pretense of right; and (3) hope of success.[53] Material causes fall under the first category, along with frustrated ambition. Hobbes counted burdensome taxation and fear of punishment for a previous uprising as the two prime sources of popular discontent, while frustrated ambition for political office figures in bringing about elite discontent.[54] Second, rebellion requires ideological legitimation.

Seditious ideas of the period included the following constitutional and religious doctrines: the sovereign is bound by civil law; sovereignty may be divided; subjects have an absolute property right; resistance and tyrannicide can be lawful; and the opinion that private conscience should override civil duty.[55] Third, rebels must have a "hope of success," which dictates that they have "Numbers, Instruments, mutuall trust [i.e., organization], and Commanders."[56] The process of organizing a faction is given most attention in *De Cive*, which Hobbes was working on in the period just prior to the outbreak of the Civil War. Ambitious men, he observed, gather the "ill affected" to debate reform of the present government while also holding secret meetings to organize the proceedings, until the faction is sufficiently large to move against the government.[57] To bring about rebellion, finally, "there wanteth nothing . . . but a man of credit to set up the standard, and to blow the trumpet."[58]

Absent from this analytic model is any notion that rebellion and civil war have underlying structural causes or teleological direction, as well as the associated conception of political actors as agents of such historical forces. Hobbes's analysis of rebellion differs from later Marxist and Whig models at two key points. The Hobbesian idea of a faction is incompatible with the concept of class; while his discussion of the legitimizing function of ideology contrasts with the Whig picture of a conflict over ideology.

To Hobbes's mind, elites do not (and cannot) represent the interests of groups in society such as classes because these are fictional entities. Rather, the direction of agency runs in the opposite direction: elites organize and mobilize the groups they lead.[59] It is a basic tenet of Hobbesian philosophy to deny the existence of natural social agency and to insist instead that corporate bodies are constituted by leadership and organization. He distinguished between a "multitude" of "many single Citizens," which cannot act as a body, and a "people": "If the same Multitude doe Contract one with another, that the will of one man, or the agreeing wills of the major part of them, shall be received for the will of all, then it becomes one Person; for it is endu'd with a will, and therefore can doe voluntary actions."[60] The force of the distinction is to expose as fictitious such supposed corporate bodies as nations with a popular will or, by implication, social classes. By contrast, a "faction," as defined in *De Cive*, qualifies as a "people" by virtue of being an organized body. "I call a faction, a multitude of subjects gathered together, either by mutuall *contracts* among themselves, or by the power of some one, without his or their [authority] who bear the supreme Rule."[61]

Hobbes chiefly applied the distinction between a multitude and a people in support of the proposition that sovereignty is necessarily unconditional:[62] no such entity as a nation or a popular will, to which rulers could be accountable, exists. But the argument is also used to rebut the pretension of rebels to be agents of the popular will: "When men say: the people rebelleth, it is to be understood of those particular persons only, and not of the whole nation. And when the people claimeth any thing otherwise than by the voice of the sovereign power, it is not the claim of the people, but only of those particular men, that claim in their own persons."[63] Such nominalist skepticism regarding social agency precludes conceiving of elites as representing (in any substantive sense) interests and groups in society. Rather, it underwrites an analysis trained on the mobilization and organization of discontent by ambitious leaders.

Second, sedition requires legitimation. With respect to the role of ideas as causes of rebellion and civil war, it is important to distinguish the idea of a conflict over ideology from that of conflict legitimized by ideology. Hobbes held the latter view of rebellion, but not the former. While on the one hand giving great weight to the role of pernicious doctrines in bringing about rebellion, and indeed dedicating his political treatises largely to rebutting the arguments used to justify the Civil War, it was also Hobbes's intent to expose ideas as no more than pretenses masking ambition. He observed, for instance, in *Behemoth*: "For those that by ambition were once set upon the enterprise of changing the government, they cared not much what was reason and justice in the cause, but what strength they might procure by seducing the multitude with remonstrances from the Parliament House, or by sermons in the churches."[64] The view is the reverse of the Whig notion that politicians are the carriers of ideas: rather, it is ideas that carry politicians to power.

If, in Hobbes's view, ideology serves ambition, not vice versa, it is also the case that some ideas are more pernicious than others. *De Cive* defines seditious doctrines in two categories: doctrines legitimizing rebellion and doctrines requiring "obedience to be given to others beside them to whom the supreme authority is committed."[65] The latter doctrines, whether religious or political, reduce to variations on the principle of divided sovereignty.[66] "*That the Supreme Authority may be divided*, is a most fatall Opinion to all Commonweales."[67] Hobbes thought the opinion had been fatal, in particular, to the Stuart monarchy: "If there had not first been an opinion received of the greatest part of *England*, that these Powers [of sovereignty] were divided . . . the people had never been divided, and fallen into this Civill Warre."[68] He explained:

> Where there is already erected a Soveraign Power, there can be no other Representative of the same people, but onely to certain particular ends, by the Soveraign limited. For that were to erect two Soveraigns; and every man to have his person represented by two Actors, that by opposing one another, must needs divide that Power, which (if men will live in Peace) is indivisible; and thereby reduce the Multitude into the condition of Warre, contrary to the end for which all Soveraignty is instituted.[69]

Divided sovereignty—or what comes to the same thing, especially in a country where the constitution is unwritten, the popular opinion that sovereignty is divided—institutionalizes elite conflict. Moreover, and most importantly, all such constitutional doctrines provide ambitious elites with a claim on the allegiance of ordinary people.

Hobbes's emphasis on constitutional doctrines, broadly conceived, provides the final clue to the identity of the "children of pride." Some would-be rulers have better "pretences of right" than others, namely those holding positions of authority in rival institutions. "To have a known Right to Soveraign Power," he observed in *Leviathan* regarding the sovereign, "is so popular a quality, as he that has it needs [do little] . . . to turn the hearts of his Subjects to him."[70] The observation applies to the enemies of the sovereign, as well. Institutional authority, allied with one species or another of the doctrine of divided sovereignty, provides ambitious elites with a legitimate title to govern. Thus it is finally institutionalized ambition that Hobbes feared. *Behemoth's* attribution of the Civil War to ambitious Parliamentarians and ministers does not merely represent, as might be thought, an arbitrary political judgment, nor is it, except in specifics, a judgment pertaining narrowly to that war. It encapsulates a larger empirical analysis of the malignancy of ambition in politics.

One does not have to be a Whig or a Marxist to conceive political ambition in a more positive light. These philosophies of history take their appeal from the commonplace, if vague, sense that posterity has benefited from the great revolutions of the modern era, including the English Civil War. Above and beyond reductively arguing that contention for power is all there is to political conflict, Hobbes bleakly dismissed this consideration. Most leaders of rebellion, *Levi-*

athan observes, perish in the conflict: "so that the benefit of their Crimes, redoundeth to Posterity"—"which argues," he concludes, "they were not so wise, as they thought they were."[71] It is one thing to accentuate the sacrifice of ordinary lives in elite power struggles or to take a skeptical view of the motives of politicians and the constructions of historians; but it is another thing altogether to argue that rebellion is an unwise undertaking because its benefits accrue to others. This last is conservatism of a profoundly egoistic and unattractive ilk.

NOTES

1. Leo Strauss, *Natural Right and History* (Chicago: University of Chicago Press, 1953), ch. 5. Cf. idem, *The Political Philosophy of Hobbes: Its Basis and Its Genesis*, trans. Elsa M. Sinclair (Chicago: University of Chicago Press, Phoenix Books, 1963), esp. pp. 168–69. The earlier work distinguishes "vanity" from desire for power and emphasizes the former.

2. Strauss, *The Political Philosophy of Hobbes*, p. 151.

3. This passage taken from the Book of Job is quoted by Hobbes in *Leviathan* (ed. C. B. Macpherson [Harmondsworth, Middlesex: Penguin, 1968]), ch. 28, p. 362.

4. Ibid., ch. 13, p. 186.

5. Ibid., ch. 11, p. 161.

6. C. B. Macpherson, *The Political Theory of Possessive Individualism: Hobbes to Locke* (1962; paperback repr., Oxford: Oxford University Press, 1964), ch. 2, esp. pp. 67–68. Cf. the psychological interpretation advanced by Norman Jacobson in *Pride and Solace: The Functions and Limits of Political Theory* (Berkeley and Los Angeles: University of California Press, 1978), ch. 3. The debate over universalistic versus parochial interpretations of Hobbesian psychology is discussed by Isaiah Berlin, "Hobbes, Locke and Professor Macpherson," *Political Quarterly* 35 (1964):444–68.

7. Keith Thomas, "The Social Origins of Hobbes's Political Thought," in *Hobbes Studies*, ed. K. C. Brown (Cambridge, Mass.: Harvard University Press, 1965), p. 191.

8. Neal Wood, "Thomas Hobbes and the Crisis of the English Aristocracy," *History of Political Thought* 1 (1980):437. The article draws on Lawrence Stone, *The Crisis of the Aristocracy 1558–1641* (Oxford: Clarendon Press, 1965).

9. E.g., *Leviathan*, ch. 13, p. 185: "In the nature of man, we find three principall causes of quarrell. First, Competition; Secondly, Diffidence; Thirdly, Glory."

10. In *Natural Right and History* (p. 200n), Strauss recognizes that Hobbes thought "the ambition that endangers civil society is characteristic of a minority . . . 'the rich and potent subjects of a kingdom.'"

11. Thomas Hobbes, *De Cive, the English Version, entitled in the first edition Philosophicall Rudiments concerning Government and Society*, ed. Howard Warrender (Oxford: Clarendon Press, 1983), ch. 5, sec. 5, p. 88.

12. Thomas Hobbes, *De Homine*, trans. Charles T. Wood, T. S. K. Scott-Craig, and Bernard Gert, in *Man and Citizen*, ed. Bernard Gert (Garden City, N.Y.: Doubleday, Anchor Books, 1972), ch. 12, sec. 8, p. 60. The second quotation is from *Leviathan*, ch. 6, p. 123.

13. *Leviathan*, ch. 17, p. 226.

14. The possibility has been raised that this was not Hobbes's title for the work. Although the standard Tönnies edition is so named, this edition is based on a manuscript written by an amanuensis. According to Royce MacGillivray, earlier editions of the work did not include the reference to Behemoth in their titles ("Thomas Hobbes's History of the English Civil War: A Study of *Behemoth*," *Journal of the History of Ideas* 31 [1970]:184–85). Ferdinand Tönnies states, on the other hand, that it was the phrase "or the Long Parliament" which was omitted from the title in previous editions (preface to *Behemoth or The Long Parliament*, by Thomas Hobbes, 2d ed. [London: Frank Cass & Co., 1969], p. xi).

15. In *Leviathan*, the chapter is titled "Of the difference of MANNERS." Cf. *De Homine*, ch. 13 ("On Dispositions and Manners").

16. *Leviathan*, Introduction, pp. 82–83; *De Homine*, ch. 13, secs. 1 and 8, pp. 63, 68. The latter work lists six causes for the variation in people's dispositions: the constitution of the body; habit; experience; the goods of fortune; the opinion we have of ourselves; and the teaching and example of authorities (ch. 13, secs. 1–7, pp. 63–68). Cf. *Leviathan*, ch. 8, pp. 138–39 (differences attributed to physical constitution and to education), and ch. 11, p. 161 (diversity of passions and of knowledge).

17. *Leviathan*, ch. 11, p. 164. In ch. 13 (pp. 183–84), "conceipt of ones owne wisdome" is said to be a general human phenomenon.

18. Ibid., ch. 17, p. 226.

19. Thomas Hobbes, *The Elements of Law, Natural and Politic*, ed. Ferdinand Tönnies (Cambridge: Cambridge University Press, 1928), pt. 2, ch. 8, sec. 3, p. 135. See *De Cive*, ch. 12, sec. 10, p. 153; and *Behemoth*, pp. 27, 155–56. Wood discusses the observation in "Thomas Hobbes and the Crisis of the English Aristocracy," pp. 443–47.

20. *Leviathan*, ch. 30, p. 389; see also ch. 27, pp. 347–52, esp. 350–51.

21. Ibid., ch. 30, p. 390.

22. *De Cive*, ch. 13, sec. 12, p. 163; *Leviathan*, ch. 30, pp. 390–91.

23. *Leviathan*, ch. 30, p. 390.

24. *De Cive*, ch. 13, sec. 12, p. 162 (margin note). The passage advises: "Because ambition and greedinesse of honours cannot be rooted out of the mindes of men, its not the duty of Rulers to endeavour it; but by constant application of rewards, and punishments, they may so order it, that men may know that the way to honour is, not by contempt of the present government, nor by factions, and the popular ayre, but by the contraries." See also *The Elements of Law*, pt. 2, ch. 9, sec. 7, p. 145.

25. *Leviathan*, Review and Conclusion, p. 728. The motto for this section is taken from *The Works of Francis Osborn Esq; Divine, Historical, Moral, Political*, 9th ed. (London, 1689), pp. 57–58.

26. *Leviathan*, ch. 27, p. 341.

27. Ibid., Review and Conclusion, p. 728. See *Behemoth*, pp. 39–40, 59, 159.

28. *Leviathan*, ch. 29, p. 374: "The Popularity of a potent Subject . . . is a dangerous Disease; because the people (which should receive their motion from the Authority of the Soveraign,) by the flattery, and by the reputation of an ambitious man, are drawn away from their obedience to the Lawes."

29. *De Cive*, Authors Preface to the Reader, p. 36 (emphasis omitted).

30. James VI and I, *The Trew Law of Free Monarchies* (1598), in *Divine Right and Democracy: An Anthology of Political Writing in Stuart England*, ed. David Wootton (Harmondsworth, Middlesex: Penguin, 1986), p. 101. In the same volume, see also the excerpt from Philip Hunton's *Treatise of Monarchy* (1643), p. 196, in which the Civil War is traced to the actions of "evil turbulent men."

31. Anthony Ascham, *Of the Confusions and Revolutions of Goverments* (1649), intro. G. W. S. V. Rumble (Delmar, N.Y.: Scholars' Facsimiles & Reprints, 1975), p. 2. See also Ascham's Preface to the Reader (n.p.): the people "were not the first movers of those calamitous confusions, but were afterwards by a strict necessity involv'd in them."

32. Ibid., p. 144. The affinity between Ascham's and Hobbes's writings is discussed by Quentin Skinner, "The Ideological Context of Hobbes's Political Thought," *Historical Journal* 9 (1966):286–317; and idem, "Conquest and Consent: Thomas Hobbes and the Engagement Controversy," in *The Interregnum: The Quest for Settlement 1646–1660*, ed. G. E. Aylmer (London: Macmillan, 1972), pp. 79–98. Cf. Deborah Baumgold, *Hobbes's Political Theory* (Cambridge: Cambridge University Press, 1988), ch. 7.

33. See, e.g., Quentin Skinner, *The Foundations of Modern Political Thought*, vol. 2, *The Age of Reformation* (Cambridge: Cambridge University Press, 1978), chs. 7–9.

34. [Philippe du Plessis-Mornay], *Vindiciae contra Tyrannos* (1579), in *Constitutionalism and Resistance in the Sixteenth Century: Three Treatises by Hotman, Beza, and Mornay*, trans. and ed. Julian H. Franklin (New York: Pegasus, 1969), p. 154.

35. Skinner, *Foundations of Modern Political Thought*, 2:339–45. Cf. Julian H. Franklin, *John Locke and the Theory of Sovereignty: Mixed Monarchy and the Right of Resistance in the Political Thought of the English Revolution* (1978; paperback repr., Cambridge: Cambridge University Press, 1981), preface and ch. 3, who highlights George Lawson's *Politica Sacra et Civilis* (1660); and Wootton, introduction to *Divine Right and Democracy*, pp. 40–55, who associates the ideas with the Levellers.

36. Charles Herle, *A Fuller Answer to a Treatise Written by Doctor Ferne* (1642), in *Political Ideas of the English Civil Wars 1641–1649*, ed. Andrew Sharp (London: Longman, 1983), p. 73.

37. Ascham, *Confusions and Revolutions of Goverments*, pp. 1–2.

38. David Hume, "Of the Original Contract," in *Hume's Moral and Political Philosophy*, ed. Henry D. Aiken (New York: Hafner, 1948), p. 368: "But *to whom is allegiance due, and who is our lawful sovereign?* This question is often the most difficult of any, and liable to infinite discussions."

39. For a fuller exposition of my interpretation, see Baumgold, *Hobbes's Political Theory*, esp. the discussion in chs. 2 and 3 of the bearing of Hobbes's covenant arguments on the claims of the Parliamentarians.

40. *De Cive*, ch. 5, sec. 7, p. 88. Cf. *The Elements of Law*, pt. 1, ch. 19, sec. 10, p. 81.

41. *Leviathan*, ch. 17, p. 227.

42. *De Cive*, ch. 6, sec. 20, p. 105 (emphasis added).

43. Hobbes granted the exception that a subject "is supposed still to retain a Right of defending himselfe against violence" (ibid., ch. 5, sec. 7, pp. 88–89).

44. *Leviathan*, ch. 18, p. 229 (emphasis added).

45. Ibid., Review and Conclusion, pp. 718–19 (emphasis omitted). See also ch. 29, pp. 375–76: a subject is obliged "to protect his Protection as long as he is able." In addition, Hobbes stipulated that a subject "obligeth himselfe, to assist him that hath the Soveraignty, in the Punishing of another" (ch. 28, p. 353). Cf. *De Cive*, ch. 2, sec. 18, p. 59, which asserts merely that subjects promise not "to defend others" from the sovereign.

46. *Leviathan*, Review and Conclusion, pp. 719, 728. See, e.g., Ascham, *Confusions and Revolutions of Goverments*, p. 92: "Protection infers publique obedience."

47. *Behemoth*, pp. 2, 23, and passim. According to MacGillivray, Hobbes probably meant by "Presbyterian" "a wide range of politically and theologically conservative English Puritans" ("Hobbes's History of the English Civil War," p. 188).

48. Richard Ashcraft, "Ideology and Class in Hobbes' Political Theory," *Political Theory* 6 (1978):27–62.

49. *De Cive*, ch. 6, sec. 11, p. 96 (emphasis omitted).

50. Ashcraft makes this case in "Ideology and Class in Hobbes' Political Theory," esp. pp. 41–50.

51. J. C. D. Clark, *Revolution and Rebellion: State and Society in England in the Seventeenth and Eighteenth Centuries* (Cambridge: Cambridge University Press, 1986), surveys the work of this revisionist school and contrasts it with "Old Hat" (Whig) and "Old Guard" (Marxist) interpretations of the Civil War.

52. The parallel chapter in *Leviathan* (29) was revised using an organic model of society. Here, Hobbes listed "infirmities" or "diseases" to which commonwealths are prone.

53. *The Elements of Law*, pt. 2, ch. 8, sec. 1, p. 133. The account in *De Cive* is more abstract, referring to "internall disposition," "externall Agent," and "the action it selfe" (ch. 12, sec. 1, p. 146, emphasis omitted). Hobbes explained: "In a Common-weale where the subjects begin to raise tumults, three things present themselves to our regard; First the *Doctrines* and the *Passions* contrary to Peace, wherewith the mindes of men are fitted and disposed; next their quality and condition who sollicite, assemble, and direct them already thus disposed, to take up armes, and quit their allegiance; Lastly, the manner how this is done, or the *faction* it selfe."

54. *The Elements of Law*, pt. 2, ch. 8, secs. 2–3, pp. 133–35; *De Cive*, ch. 12, secs. 9–10, pp. 152–53; *Behemoth*, p. 27.

55. *The Elements of Law*, pt. 2, ch. 8, secs. 4–10, pp. 135–38. See *De Cive*, ch. 9, secs. 1–7, pp. 146–51; and *Leviathan*, ch. 29, pp. 365–70. In the latter two versions of the theory, the list is expanded to include the doctrine of "private judgment of good and evil" and "pretence of inspiration."

56. *De Cive*, ch. 12, sec. 11, p. 153; see *The Elements of Law*, pt. 2, ch. 8, sec. 11, pp. 138–39.

57. *De Cive*, ch. 12, sec. 13, p. 155. See the passage quoted in n. 53 above.

58. *The Elements of Law*, pt. 2, ch. 8, sec. 1, p. 133; see *De Cive*, ch. 12, sec. 11, p. 154.

59. Cf. Ashcraft, "Ideology and Class in Hobbes' Political Theory," pp. 42–43.

60. *De Cive*, ch. 6, sec. 1, p. 92 (emphasis omitted). See *The Elements of Law*, pt. 2, ch. 2, sec. 11, pp. 97–98; and *Leviathan*, ch. 16, p. 220.

61. *De Cive*, ch. 13, sec. 13, p. 163. Cf. *Leviathan*, ch. 22, p. 286.

62. E.g., *Leviathan*, ch. 18, p. 230: "There can happen no breach of Covenant on the part of the Soveraigne. . . . That he which is made Soveraigne maketh no Covenant with his Subjects beforehand, is manifest; because either he must make it with the whole multitude, as one party to the Covenant; or he must make a severall Covenant with every man. With the whole, as one party, it is impossible; because as yet they are not one Person: and if he make so many severall Covenants as there be men, those Covenants after he hath the Soveraignty are voyd."

63. *The Elements of Law*, pt. 2, ch. 8, sec. 9, p. 138. See also pt. 2, ch. 1, sec. 2, p. 84; and *De Cive*, ch. 6, sec. 1, p. 91, and ch. 12, sec. 8, pp. 151–52.

64. *Behemoth*, pp. 115–16. See also p. 121: "You may see by this, what weak people they were, that were carried into the rebellion by such reasoning as the Parliament used, and how impudent they were that did put such fallacies upon them."

65. *De Cive*, ch. 6, sec. 11, pp. 95–96 (emphasis omitted).

66. Ibid., ch. 12, sec. 5, pp. 149–50; *Leviathan*, ch. 29, pp. 370–72.

67. *De Cive*, ch. 12, sec. 5, p. 149.

68. *Leviathan*, ch. 18, pp. 236–37.

69. Ibid., ch. 19, p. 240. See also ch. 18, p. 236 (emphasis omitted): "A Kingdome divided in it selfe cannot stand." The point is stated with regard to ecclesiastical authority in chapter 39, p. 499: "That the Governor must be one; or else there must needs follow Faction, and Civil war in the Common-wealth, between the *Church* and *State*; between *Spiritualists*, and *Temporalists*; between the *Sword of Justice*, and the *Shield of Faith*; and (which is more) in every Christian mans own brest, between the *Christian*, and the *Man*."

70. Ibid., ch. 30, p. 394. With Charles I's troubles rather evidently in mind, Hobbes added that it is important that a sovereign appear able to govern his family and that his enemies disband their armies.

71. Ibid., ch. 27, p. 342. See *De Cive*, Authors Preface to the Reader, p. 36, where Hobbes admonished ordinary subjects: "Esteeme it better to enjoy your selves in the present state though perhaps not the best, then by waging Warre, indeavour to procure a reformation for other men in another age, your selves in the meane while either kill'd, or consumed with age" (emphasis omitted).

6

Hobbes's Subject as Citizen

Mary G. Dietz

The awesome frontispiece of the 1651 edition of *Leviathan* captures much of Thomas Hobbes's view of sovereign and subjects. Leviathan is a "Mortall God," an all-seeing sovereign who is literally constituted by the faceless, immobile subjects of its body. The visual power of this image influenced countless subsequent readers. It surely accounts for Shaftesbury's later sardonic observation that the "Hobbist" operates "under monstrous visages of dragons, Leviathans, and I know not what devouring creatures."[1] Hobbes himself noted that the sovereign is absolute or else there is no sovereignty at all and bluntly asserted that "the Power and Honor of Subjects vanisheth in the presence of the Soveraign."[2] Just to ensure that there was no doubt about the subjects' status, Hobbes added, "though they shine, some more, some lesse, when they are out of his sight; yet in his presence, they shine no more than the Starres in the presence of the Sun."[3] Under the gaze of Leviathan, then, the Hobbesian subject is a pale and diminished creature.[4]

This image of the Hobbesian subject has sustained countless readings of Hobbes's masterwork. These readings make *Leviathan* out to be a text concerned primarily with the sovereign, not subjects, and when about subjects, then about subjection, fear, and force. But if one of Hobbes's principal messages is "That Subjects owe to Soveraigns, simple Obedience, in all things," we should not take from that a simplistic conception of the subject.[5] The Hobbesian subject can be more accurately depicted if we acknowledge what Hobbes certainly understood: that fear or force alone could not sustain long-term allegiance to a political regime. Other, more richly constituted qualities are required if citizens are to remain at peace and supportive of the sovereign state. These qualities, I shall argue here, are precisely what Hobbes had in mind when he characterized his civil philosophy as a "science of Vertue and Vice" and deemed it fit for public instruction. Thus, *Leviathan* can be read not simply as a theory of sovereignty but as an exploration of the dispositions necessary to citizenship, and Hobbes himself can be read as a theorist of civic virtue.

Lest anyone think that this civic perspective on Hobbes achieves what no alchemist could—turning an arch-authoritarian into a classical republican—let us begin with some features of Hobbes's conception of the subject that are undeniably true. From there we can assess the limitations of this account and begin the case for *Leviathan* as a tract on civic virtue.

I

Whatever other generous politics interpreters might accord to Hobbes—that he is a protoliberal, or a defender of toleration, or a spokesperson for the bourgeoisie—no one can make of him a classical republican or a champion of the people. Despite some notable affinities with Cicero and Machiavelli, Hobbes was no proponent of the *res publica*, or a theorist of politics as "the people's affair." In his introduction to his translation of *The Peloponnesian War*, he clearly warmed to his account of Thucydides' dislike of democracy, no doubt finding it compatible with his own:

> It is manifest that Thucydides least of all liked the democracy. And upon divers occasions he noteth the emulation and contention of the demagogues for reputation and glory of wit; with their crossing of each other's counsels, to the damage of the public; the inconsistency of resolutions, caused by the diversity of ends and power of rhetoric in the orators; and the desperate actions undertaken . . . to hold what they had attained, of authority and sway amongst the common people.[6]

In the defenders of "things democratical" in seventeenth-century England, Hobbes found the counterparts to the demagogues Thucydides condemned in fifth-century Athens. And he held them in special contempt, not only because they encourage a specious view of liberty but also because they threaten to do damage to the public.

Demagogues may damage the public and manipulate the common folk because the people are, at the same time, manipulable and easily seduced. One need only reflect upon the state of affairs between 1640 and 1660, as Hobbes did in the opening pages of *Behemoth*, to realize how readily the people had been swayed, lured by seducers of divers sorts into believing that "the disobedient were the best patriots" and the best governors were those averse to the granting of subsidies or public payments.[7] Quite simply, then, Hobbes thought the commoners a thoroughly gulled lot. Not only was the English public "ignorant of its duty," it had also traduced all rule of equity. The papists and sectaries had thus worked their wills, finding within the body politic a mass ripe for popular sedition.

Hobbes's conviction that the common people were not suited for self-government is not merely an immediate political observation, however. His sociological imagination does not lead him to suggest that, once the rhetors and demagogues have been eliminated and the terror of civil war brought to an end, the populace might reconstitute itself as a democratic polity or a true *res publica*. Whatever the hopes of political recovery, they do not, for Hobbes, extend to the possibility of a republic of participatory citizens. This he made clear in *Leviathan*, where he deployed his egoistic account of human psychology to underscore the limitations of "the Multitude" in any form:

> And be there never so great a Multitude; yet if their actions be directed according to their particular judgements, and particular appetites, they can expect thereby no defence, nor protection, neither against a Common enemy, nor against the injuries of one another. For being distracted in opinions concerning the best use and application of their strength, they do not help, but hinder one another; and reduce their strength by mutuall opposition to nothing.[8]

In short, the fractious clash of interests that Machiavelli believed constituted politics—which could also be tempered within a properly balanced republican constitution—Hobbes took as an endlessly disruptive given of human nature. Accordingly, in Hobbes's science, the problem is not how to temper the clash of interests and opinions within the multitude but rather how to eliminate it. And the answer lies not in republican institutions that moderate yet allow for civic action but in a sovereign absolutism that fosters absolute obedience. Yet one may well ask, what *sustains* the absolute obedience of the people and so the absolute rule of the sovereign? Two responses are consistent with conventional readings of Hobbes.

A first response holds that sovereign power will be sustained because Hobbesian subjects find it in their interest to do so; for the "Common Power" directs the actions of the subjects to the "Common Benefit."[9] In this "utilitarian" response, Hobbes is taken to argue that the subjects, as calculators of their own advantage, assess the dangers and uncertainties of life in the multitude and, out of a rational aversion to anarchy, submit to the sovereign protector with a view toward long-term gain. In return, the sovereign "defend[s] them from the invasion of Forraigners, and the injuries of one another, and thereby . . . [secures] them in such sort, as that by their owne industrie, and by the fruites of the Earth, they may nourish themselves and live contentedly."[10] On this telling, then, popular obedience to the sovereign guarantees industry, stability, and contentment. Once the subjects realize this and understand the direct advantage of sovereign absolutism, the longevity of Leviathan will be ensured. Thus their mutual recognition of individual, long-term gain is what sustains the subjects' absolute obedience to the state.

The second response is not unrelated to the first: the sovereign, that "Mortall God," will exact obedience through the power of the sword. As Hobbes put it, "For by this Authoritie, given him by every particular man in the Common-Wealth, he hath the use of so much Power and Strength conferred on him, that by terror thereof, he is inabled to forme the wills of them all, to Peace at home, and mutuall ayd against their enemies abroad."[11] In this "despotic" response, Hobbes established that Leviathan's authority is granted by the subjects who are the authors of sovereign power and, after the act of authorization, are bound by it. But he also established that the government which the subjects authorize has the capacity and the will to impose the fiercest penalties and the most lethal punishments upon malefactors and discontents. It can, in other words, sustain its authorization through sheer terror.

Both the utilitarian and the despotic responses concerning the grounding of political obedience are frequently emphasized in Hobbesian studies. On second look, however, neither the calculation of advantage nor the power of the sword seems to offer a sufficient accounting for what might sustain the absolute obedience of subjects in the Hobbesian commonwealth. In the first place, the utilitarian response fails to account for Hobbes's clear-eyed recognition that even under the gaze of a sovereign protector, some men will be motivated by "avarice, ambition, lust, or other strong desire" to take advantage of the moment and even to risk the danger and uncertainty of war. In other words, even in the face of rationally calculated long-term advantage, some men will still act in passionate haste and immediate self-interest. In their world, security is less compelling than glory, contentment less rewarding than gain. *Behemoth* is a tale rife with accounts of such men, and it does not lend much evidence to the notion that, for Hobbes, sheer rational calculation of long-term interest is a sufficient basis for civil obedience. There is always the problem of ambitious elites, not to mention "masterlesse men."[12]

The despotic response, so much a part of the dominant interpretation of Hobbes, also seems incomplete. It raises the possibility that the obedience of the people is, in the end, sustained primarily through an absolute power that can discipline and punish. But the regime of force this argument presupposes is a conception of the Hobbesian commonwealth that is simply not supported in *Leviathan*. Despite his absolutism, Hobbes was not merely a theorist of the subjugating security-state. In the famous passage on the state of nature that charts the "incommodities" of war—the loss of industry, culture, commodious building, arts, letters, society, and "culture of the Earth"—Hobbes invoked, in converse, a vision of the commonwealth as a civilized society wherein citizens enjoy those things necessary for the living of a prosperous and peaceful life. Seen in this light, Hobbes's subject is less an abject creature confined within a system of public rules than a prosperous and contributing member of a society replete with commercial, cultural, and intellectual achievements.[13] The Hobbesian commonwealth, to paraphrase Plato, is a luxurious city, not a city of pigs (or state police). Fear may help explain submission, but it does not adequately capture the lively and prosperous polity Hobbes imagined nor, it seems, the attitudes of the people within it. Thus, the despotic account, like the utilitarian one, is not comprehensive enough to serve as a complete explanation for what sustains the subject's obedience to the sovereign.

A third response is possible, however. Hobbes intimated it twice. In a crucial but neglected observation in *Behemoth* he wrote, "The power of the mighty hath no foundation, but in the opinion and belief of the people"; and in an admonition in *Leviathan* he observed, "The Office of the Soveraign . . . consisteth in the end, for which he was trusted with the Soveraign Power, namely the procuration of *the safety of the people;* . . . And this is intended should be done . . . by a generall Providence, contained in publique Instruction, both of Doctrine and Example, and in the making, and executing of good Lawes."[14] The sovereign's power will be sustained, that is, only if the subjects harbor right opinions and beliefs, rooted in public instruction of the sort that reinforces a sense of allegiance to the commonwealth. The implication of this argument is that the longevity of the sovereign is primarily dependent upon neither external force nor an individualized utilitarian calculation, but upon the internalization of something deeper within the subjects. What I believe Hobbes had in mind is the inculcation of a kind of civic virtue, compatible with the pursuit of civil peace.

This "civic virtue" response, whereby Hobbes offered a view of the subject-as-citizen, has received virtually no attention to date. But it deserves scrutiny, for by these lights, the Hobbesian subject emerges as a more fully dimensional public being than heretofore understood. In addition, if we pursue this possibility more closely, we may even discover that it is not so much Hobbes's theory of sovereign absolutism that guides his thinking about the subject, but rather his conception of civic virtue that ensures the power and strength of Leviathan itself.

II

To understand Hobbes as a theorist of civic virtue, it is perhaps best to begin with *Behemoth*, his history of the Long Parliament and the English Civil War. *Behemoth* elucidates in a historical setting certain aspects of the science of politics developed more systematically in *Leviathan*. Indeed, cast in light of *Behemoth*, Hobbes's science begins to look less like a theory of modern politics based solely on the calculation of interest and the geometry of force and more like a complex civil philosophy concerned with questions of citizen morality.

Behemoth is full of invective against the forces in English politics that Hobbes considered dangerous and divisive, particularly ambitious ministers and ambitious gentlemen: "the ministers, envying the authority of bishops, whom they thought less learned; and the gentlemen envying the privy-council, whom they thought less wise than themselves."[15] Hobbes located the seedbed of sedition in the universities, "as the Presbyterians brought with them into their churches their divinity from the universities so did many of the gentlemen bring their politics from thence into the Parliament."[16] The universities, Hobbes continued with a different metaphor, "have been to this nation as the wooden horse was to the Trojans"; they have nurtured the preachers of seditious doctrines and then "poured them out into city and country" to undermine the commonwealth and destroy the sovereignty of the Crown. Hobbes's insights on these matters and, indeed, his account of the causes of the Civil War, lend credence to the claim that his vision of politics is largely determined by a conception of ambitious elites vying for power and ideological supremacy.[17]

But there is much more to *Behemoth* than simply an account of "high politics" and, accordingly, more at stake in Hobbes's analysis than an emphasis on the "struggle for power." In particular, notice that the question that sets off the lengthy exchange between teacher A and student B—the discussants in *Behemoth*—concerns neither elites nor ambitious interests. Instead, it addresses the people and raises the problem of public virtue (or, more precisely, the lack of it): "How came the people to be so corrupted?"[18] This question, which burns beneath so much of the discussion, illuminates the problem of civic virtue as a central aspect of Hobbes's analysis of this period. Reflecting upon the political crisis, questioner B observes: "The seditious doctrine of the Presbyterians has been struck so hard in the people's heads and memories, (I cannot say their hearts: for they understand nothing in it but that they may lawfully rebel), that I fear the commonwealth will never be cured."[19] In true Thucydidean fashion, Hobbes was intent on deciphering the problem of a degenerate *demos*. The issue, then, is not simply about warring demagogic elites but about the *corruption of a citizenry*.

As noted earlier, Hobbes was not a thinker tempted to romanticize the common people or to find within them an innocence that renders them easy prey for ambitious men. Prey they are, but not because they are innocent or unsullied. In *Behemoth*, teacher A offers a more intriguing political analysis—the people champion knaves and betray their king, he says, because they are ignorant and incapable of distinguishing between men of wisdom and fools who play "by the advantage of false dice and packing of cards."[20] Student B attempts to elaborate: "For the common people have been, and always will be, ignorant of their duty to the public, as never mediating any thing but their particular interest; in other things following their immediate leaders . . . as common soldiers for the most part follow their immediate captains, if they like them. If you think the late miseries have made them wiser, that will quickly be forgot, and then we shall be no wiser than we were."[21]

Read in light of the preceding discussion, B's pessimistic assessment of the common people is not surprising. But his conception of a "public" that *is* more than an arena for the mediation of particular interests, and to which the people have a duty even if they are ignorant of it, is compelling indeed. Given conventional readings of Hobbes, however, we would expect A (who is often taken as Hobbes's alter ego) to endorse the pessimistic reading of the common people and to contest both the notion that a "public" is more than a conduit for private interests and the conception of "duty" that presents itself as the commitment to such a public. But A does no such thing. To the contrary, he not only appropriates B's conception of duty but also corrects B by stressing that this duty *can* be taught to the common people: "Why may not men be taught their duty, that is, the science of just and unjust, as divers other sciences have been taught, from true principles and evident demonstration; and much more easily than any of those preachers and democratical gentlemen could teach rebellion and treason?"[22]

At least two elements in this exchange deserve mention. First, it is significant that neither A nor B equates "public" with "sovereign" or seems to presume a commensurability between the language of "duty to the public" and the language of submission to the commands of king or Parliament. In fact, when A elaborates later upon what he explicitly calls the "virtue of the subject," he notes that it is "comprehended wholly in obedience to the laws of the commonwealth . . . for without such obedience the commonwealth (which is every subject's safety and protection) cannot subsist."[23] Even though the people's duty to the public certainly presupposes submission to the sovereign (who determines the civil laws), it also appears to encompass more than mere submission. The people's duty extends beyond allegiance to the commands of Crown or Parliament and is directed toward the inclusive "body politique"—toward the commonwealth that, through its laws, ensures civil peace. In developing this broader notion of the public, A also makes clear that the sovereign is not synonymous with the commonwealth. He notes, instead, that the virtues of the sovereign are such as tend *to serve* the commonwealth. Thus, the actions and habits of the sovereign "are to be esteemed good or evil by their causes and usefulness in reference to the commonwealth."[24] It seems, then, that whatever their differences, both the subject and the sovereign have a common interest in preserving that which allows them to flourish—the subjects do this through obedience to the commonwealth, the sovereign through actions and habits that contribute to its security and strength and, hence, to the "safety of the people" themselves.[25]

Without making too much of the wedge Hobbes seemed to be

driving between sovereign and commonwealth, we might at least allow that, by distinguishing the two, he opened the possibility of a broader conception of the public and thus a more developed conception of duty than mere submission. The people's duty to this public must be taken to include allegiance to the sovereign, of course, but it can also be read as something beyond this: as perhaps a duty to promote and preserve civil peace (which the laws of the commonwealth ensure). And it is this duty to promote civil peace that requires much more of a subject, by way of habits, virtues, and beliefs, than does mere submission through fear.

This leads to a second important element in the discussion between A and B that is implicit in the notion of duty as a more demanding attribute than simple submission. The subject who practices his or her duty to the public must have a rich blend of political qualities that goes well beyond what Edmund Burke once called "heavy, lumpish acquiescence." Or, as A informs B, "You may perhaps think a man has need of nothing else to know the duty he owes his governor, and what right he has to order him, but a good natural wit, but it is otherwise."[26] Public duty, in A's view, depends upon something more substantial than just being in command of your wits or displaying common sense or correct perception in the presence of your governor. In his earlier response to B, A makes this very plain indeed, by equating the subject's knowledge of duty with "the science of just and unjust." Like any other science, A argues, this one proceeds from true principles which can be demonstrated or logically deduced and thereby taught to anyone, including the common people. Thus, A's conviction that the people are not doomed to ignorance concerning their duty to the public is rooted in the claim that this duty is a form of scientific knowledge that can be put into practice once the proper demonstration of "just and unjust" principles has taken place.

The "science of just and unjust," then, is a civic doctrine of a very specific kind. Whatever else it names, "just" names a virtue, and "unjust" a vice, and "justice" requires certain attendant virtues and injunctions against those who exhibit vice. Thus the science that informs the subject's exercise of duty—the science that makes of the subject a citizen—must be aimed toward the inculcation of particular precepts, admonitions, and injunctions into the common people. According to this reasoning, one of the primary tasks of Hobbesian political philosophy is to develop a science of public virtues, with an eye toward obedience, and not just a logic of sovereign power. Likewise, the science of politics must be attentive to the cultural and sociological conditions that encourage the development of these public virtues—foremost among them being "duty to the public."

Why Hobbes placed such great emphasis upon the schools, the universities, and the pulpit should now be clear. They are not simply the seedbeds of "potent men" and ambitious elites but, once transformed, the culture beds of civic education. The universities train the men of the pulpit, and the pulpit itself, from which the sovereign's ministers preach, is where we find "the rules of just and unjust sufficiently demonstrated, and from principles evident to the meanest capacity."[27] Before the pulpit, the multitude "should ever learn their duty."[28]

There is, of course, an instrumental purpose to Hobbes's advocacy of the teaching of civic duty; a truly moral citizenry that knows its duty can smother the most dangerous threat of all—the ruinous doctrines and seditious murmurings of ambitious men. As Hobbes put it:

> The Greeks had for awhile their petty kings and then by sedition came to be petty commonwealths; and then growing to be greater commonwealths, by sedition again became monarchies; and *by all for want of rules of justice for the common people to take notice of*; which if the people had known in the beginning of every of these seditions, the ambitious persons could never have had the hope to disturb their government after it had been once settled. For ambition can do little without hands, and few hands it would have, if the common people were as diligently instructed in the true principles of their duty, as they are terrified and amazed by preachers.[29]

In *Behemoth*, Hobbes made no case for a citizenry educated in justice as a good in and of itself. As the passage above indicates, his are not so much the sentiments of a virtuous civic republican as the conclusions of a political instrumentalist who loathed ambitious men and viewed the right education of the multitude in their duty as the means to keep ambitious men in check.[30] But Hobbes's civil philosophy is no less concerned with virtue for that. If anything, his contempt for the fractious elites made his case for the people's duty to the public all the more central to his political science. *Behemoth*'s contribution, in addition to its astute analysis of the causes of civil strife, is to bring this case for civic education in public duty to the forefront of English political life.

Yet, despite its oft-repeated arguments for teaching the common people "the grounds of their duty," *Behemoth* does not itself provide that teaching or make the "science of just and unjust" known. In fact, this had already been done. "Notwithstanding the obscurity of their author," A tells B, principles of this civic science "have shined, not only in this, but also in foreign countries, to men of good education."[31] The author of these principles is, of course, none other than Hobbes himself, and the science shines especially in *Leviathan*. It is to *Leviathan*, then, that we must turn (or turn back), for there Hobbes crafted a moral and civil philosophy with "the *qualities* that dispose men to peace, and to obedience" in mind.[32]

III

In *Leviathan*, Hobbes wrote that "all men agree on this, that Peace is Good, and therefore also the way, or means of Peace, which (as I have shewed before) are *Justice, Gratitude, Modesty, Equity, Mercy,* and the rest of the Lawes of Nature, are good; that is to say, *Morall Vertues*; and their contrarie *Vices*, Evil. Now the science of Vertue and Vice is Morall Philosophie; and therefore the true Doctrine of the Lawes of Nature, is the true Morall Philosophie."[33] For most readers of Hobbes, it has become a commonplace to take the laws of nature as dictates, general injunctions, or prudential maxims, found out by reason, open to agreement, and without which social life and the pursuit of private goals would be impossible. Hobbes himself gave us ample reason for reading the natural laws this way, since he referred to them explicitly and often as "precepts," "generall rules," "Principles of Reason," or "Theorems" that uncover articles of peace relevant to "the conservation of men in multitudes."[34] But given my preceding argument—that Hobbes was concerned with educating subjects in civic virtue and the science of just and unjust, so that they would effectively exercise their duty to the public—we might now consider the natural laws in a slightly different way, although still in terms that Hobbes himself used.

In the passage above and elsewhere in *Leviathan*, Hobbes cast the laws of nature as "morall vertues" and their true doctrine as a "science of Vertue and Vice," or the true moral philosophy. The "means of Peace" he enumerated are drawn from the third, fourth, tenth, eleventh, and sixth laws respectively and deal with the conduct and character of humans as beings who live in "multitudes." Although Hobbes granted the status of moral virtues to all of the natural laws, it appears to be primarily the third through the tenth laws he had in mind as the components of his science of virtue and vice. These are the ones that expressly prescribe some rules of conduct—justice, gratitude, complaisance, equity, and mercy—and forbid others—revenge, contumely, pride, and arrogance. The sum of this science of virtue and vice, as Hobbes rendered it, is as intelligible as it is familiar to the seventeenth-century English multitude: "Do not that to another, which thou wouldest not have done to thy selfe."[35]

To the extent that these Hobbesian natural laws have been treated as moral virtues and not just as prudential maxims of a self-interested agent, they have usually been collapsed into the remaining nineteen and explored in terms of the ethical life of the moral individual.[36] Thus, for example, A. E. Taylor begins his famous essay on "The Ethical Doctrine of Hobbes" by establishing as fundamental the question, "what ought a good man to do?"[37] From there, he proceeds to investigate the character of the natural laws as moral, deontological principles that underlie Hobbes's argument regarding obligation. For Taylor and many others who have addressed the origin and nature of Hobbes's natural laws in these terms, the question ultimately boils down to a philosophical and ethical one; hence, the natural laws are examined from the standpoint of a doctrine of moral obligation. What I suggest, however, is that by casting the natural laws in such a way, we tend to overlook Hobbes's principal aim in articulating the science of virtue and vice. That aim is not so much philosophical and ethical as practical and political: to craft the means of civil peace and so forestall within a citizenry the emergence of pernicious dispositions that would threaten to dissolve the commonwealth. If we remember the centrality of this aim, then the science of virtue and vice (i.e., the true doctrine of the natural law) is best read not as an abstract account of the ethical life of the moral individual but rather as the promulgation of a code of virtuous conduct which Hobbes hoped would fashion the life of the subject as (dutiful) citizen. In other words, what a purely philosophical and ethical analysis of the natural laws, informed by a doctrine of moral obligation, neglects is what we might call the Hobbesian citizen's "civic repertoire": the qualities or virtues that distinguish people as citizens of the commonwealth. Taylor's suggestion notwithstanding, we might better comprehend the principal question worth investigating in Hobbes's "true moral philosophy" as not "what ought a good man to do?" but rather "what qualities should the dutiful citizen develop?"[38]

We can find evidence for reading the third through the tenth natural laws as public, political qualities rather than private, ethical attributes in what Hobbes himself acknowledged in *Leviathan*. Although he called the natural laws "morall lawes," he also emphasized that the ones he set forth "onely concern the doctrine of Civill Society," that is, the procurement of civil peace.[39] He admitted that the failings of "particular men"—drunkenness or intemperance, for instance—are covered by the law of nature, but significantly, he said these failings are not at issue in his doctrine of civil society and are therefore "not necessary to be mentioned, nor are pertinent enough to this place."[40] Unlike the schoolmen and Christian humanists, Hobbes was not inclined to articulate a whole panoply of moral virtues in his account of what obliges a person. (One is reminded here of A's often repeated claim in *Behemoth*, that the end of moral philosophy is to teach men their duty to the public and not to deal in matters of spiritual conscience or the "estate of man's soul.") Thus, not only are temperance, moderation, and sobriety missing from Hobbes's science of virtue and vice, so too are some prominent Christian virtues—love, hope, and faith; meekness, compassion, and humility (with its practice of turning the other cheek). The exclusivity of Hobbes's science is dictated by the specific aim of the science itself—to demonstrate only those virtues conceptually and causally connected to civil peace. Like Machiavelli, Hobbes was interested in mobilizing private virtue for public ends; accordingly, the virtues he emphasized are those conducive to the stability and maintenance of the state and not the "attaining of an eternall felicity after death."[41]

If my analysis is correct, we are best advised to regard the laws of nature concerning justice, gratitude, modesty, equity, and mercy as those civic attributes that reveal the kind of person the Hobbesian citizen is or should be. They are, moreover, the qualities that ensure a citizenry's willing acquiescence to the civil law and to the rights of the sovereign. As such, these natural laws ground obedience far more securely than either the threat of punishment or the rational calculation of long-term gain, because they constitute neither an external condition nor an instrumental mode of reasoning but an intrinsic way of being—a "civic personality." Submission is thereby transformed into allegiance, and simple obedience becomes "duty to the public." Hobbes made this point explicitly in chapter 30, where he addressed the "grounds" of the "essential Rights of Soveraignty" and argued that the people need to be diligently and truly taught because they cannot be maintained by any Civill Law or terrour of legal punishment. For a Civill Law, that shall forbid Rebellion (and such is all resistance to the essential Rights of Soveraignty) is not (as a Civill Law) any obligation, but by vertue onely of the Law of Nature, that forbiddeth the violation of faith; which naturall obligation if men know not, they cannot know the Right of any Law the Soveraign maketh.[42]

My emphasis here is not upon the important and complex Hobbesian claim that the law of nature creates a natural obligation antecedent to civil society, but rather upon Hobbes's observation that a civil law in and of itself does not give rise to obligation. Obligation, it seems, emerges only as a result of the inculcation of a certain code of conduct—in this case, it is the injunction against violating faith of the sort that coheres a voluntary promise, or contract, that the citizen must value and be taught to observe. Hobbes's point, in other words, is that the civil law, the rights of the sovereign, and the commonwealth itself are secured only when the people have a sense of duty that springs "naturally" from the cultivation of certain qualities, such as the keeping of faith. The commonwealth that takes no care for the people's instruction in these civic attributes is destined to "relapse into disorder," for without a virtuous populace, the essential rights of the sovereign cannot be sustained. Leaving for a moment the citizens' instruction in these civic virtues, let us focus more explicitly upon some of the virtues Hobbes demonstrated as laws of nature, to see which qualities he thought the common people need to cultivate in order to exercise their duty to the public.

Justice is the civic virtue Hobbes singled out above all. As we have seen, this is so central a quality that in *Behemoth*, teacher A characterizes the science of virtue and vice simply as "the science of just and unjust." Justice is comprehended in the third law of nature, "That men performe their Covenants made" and do not act in violation of faith.[43] To do otherwise is to be unrighteous, for the just and the righteous man are one and the same. The person who is unrighteous is the civic equivalent of those sinners cast into darkness; he "cannot be received into any Society, that unite themselves for Peace and Defense . . . if he live in Society, it is by the errours of other men."[44] The relevant attendant quality to justice—that which "gives more relish" to humane actions—is a certain "Nobleness or Gallantnesse of courage" that leads a man to scorn fraud and breach of promise and hold to a higher standard of contentment. Justice is, in a word, the disposition that makes obedient subjects virtuous citizens; it grounds obedience to the government in a moral commitment to stand by one's own consent and contract. Therefore, justice or good faith is the quality that must be instilled in every member of the commonwealth if the rights of the sovereign and civil peace are to be secured.

Another quality indispensable for civic peace is gratitude: "That a man which receiveth Benefit from another of meer Grace, Endeavour that he which giveth it, have no reasonable cause to repent him of his good will."[45] Indeed, gratitude is second only to justice in Hobbes's articulation of the code of conduct that is the means toward peace. A grateful citizenry is one where "benevolence or trust" as well as "mutuall help" can take root; for if givers enjoy the gratitude of receivers, they will be inclined to proffer assistance again on future occasions. Likewise, those who receive will recognize that their gratitude makes giving rewarding and will be inclined to give in their turn. "No man giveth, but with intention of Good to himselfe," and gratitude is the good the benevolent man reaps. It is literally the reward that inclines the giver to keep on giving. Mutuality and the reconciliation of one man to another is the result.

Hobbes made gratitude a *civic* virtue because it is the quality that keeps men disposed toward mutual reciprocity; it is the linchpin that sustains the contract.[46] A citizenry that lives within an atmosphere of mutual trust and reconciliation, fostered by the practice of gratitude, is one that will be eager to keep its covenant. Although justice may be the disposition that formally inclines citizens to keep their word out of a righteous commitment, gratitude is what makes them *want* to do so, since it promotes a quality of life and collective interaction that reinforces the reasonableness of not breaching faith. If, in other words, justice is the cement that secures the contract, gratitude is the ground underneath; it gives to the commonwealth not just peace but a kind of *civic culture* citizens will want to promote and preserve, as an extension of peace.

The inculcation of complaisance—"that every man strive to accommodate himselfe to the rest"—is also necessary to civil peace. It reinforces the mutual trust generated by gratitude. Once more Hobbes singled out a virtue that lends itself to the keeping of covenants; for what better way to sustain the contract than by teaching citizens to despise the "insociable" behavior that distinguishes men who are given to breach of faith? The latter are like rough and irregular stones unfit for the building of an edifice, which the builders "cast away as unprofitable, and troublesome."[47] To lack complaisance is generally to lack the basic quality of a commodious public life; it is the virtue that the common people need to cultivate if they are to fulfill successfully the second clause of the fundamental law of nature—to seek peace *and follow it.*

Even in the commonwealth where sociability is the norm, however, there are bound to be people who will act in defiance of its conventions and commit offenses that will threaten civil peace. In the aftermath of such cases, the citizen must be prepared to respond in ways that will ease hostilities, not exacerbate them. Accordingly, Hobbes prescribed two more civic virtues: on the one hand, the facility to pardon, which favorably disposes men toward those who have committed offenses but asked for forgiveness and repented; and, on the other, the capacity to look not to revenge of things past, but to "the greatnesse of the good to follow" in inflicting punishment upon evil-doers.[48] Revenge works in much the same way as gratitude, only to the opposite effect: it is likely to instill in the receiver a desire to respond in kind, setting in motion a series of reciprocal interactions that will envelop the entire community and ultimately destroy it. Thus Hobbes counseled that the citizen be taught to despise cruelty that countenances revenge, for "to hurt without reason [i.e., without the security of the future in mind], tendeth to the introduction of Warre."[49] Following naturally from this is the injunction against contumely, or insult—those "deeds, words, countenances, or gestures" by which men declare hatred or contempt of one another.[50] This maxim bolsters the fifth law of nature by reinforcing within the citizen the importance of sociable behavior, and it reconfirms the seventh by rendering those dispositions and deeds that facilitate revenge as vices contrary to the establishment of personal contentment and civil peace.

The ninth and tenth virtues are, like the eighth, injunctions against vice. They proscribe pride and arrogance, respectively. With them, Hobbes attempted to enlist his science as a weapon in his war against seditious men and ambitious elites, by labeling the proud and arrogant as enemies of the civic culture constituted by contract and protected by the sovereign. If, Hobbes wrote in the ninth law against arrogance, "men require for themselves, that which they would not have to be granted to others, they do contrary to the precedent law . . . and therefore also against the law of Nature."[51] The "precedent" law against pride encourages every man to accept his fellows as "his Equall by Nature."[52] The Hobbesian citizen is thereby taught to view with suspicion those who take themselves to be more talented or wiser than the rest. As we have already seen, Hobbes believed that the activities of ambitious elites, fueled by pride and tended by arrogance, invariably lead to disorder, if not civil war. So these laws of nature may be taken as the disposition of the commons intended to check or control the selfish behaviors of the nobility and aristocracy. In short, they ensure that "ambitious persons could never [have] the hope to disturb their government after it had been once settled" because the government thrives amidst a civic culture and a citizenry that reward modesty and punish the excesses of pride.[53]

It bears repeating that Hobbes recommended the aforementioned personal qualities, not out of a republican love of civic virtue per se, but because once constituted within the common people, they provide the most secure foundation for the structures of the state. Justice, gratitude, modesty, and the rest of these civic virtues are those qualities that give fixity and depth to the subjects' obedience and hence guarantee the longevity of Leviathan itself. Indeed, upon close inspection, it appears that the "science of virtue and vice" is the fundamental key to maintaining sovereign power, since its precepts facilitate the creation of modest, sociable, peace-loving subjects who are suspicious of arrogant elites, yet slow to anger and averse to cruelty and revenge. Above all, they are faithfully committed to the terms of the contract, which, by their consent, created the commonwealth, and ever grateful to the power sovereign, donor of the "free-gift" of peace.

In light of this interpretation of some of the natural laws, I think we can profitably read Hobbes's science of virtue and vice as attempting not simply to contain subjects but to *reconstitute* them as citizens. Since war is far less likely in a public realm where justice, gratitude, and mercy are the rule, the inculcation of civic virtue is in the interest of both sovereign and subject. Hobbes, flush with the possibilities of his new science, did not hesitate to present his "Theoremes of Morall doctrine" in hope that this "Truth of Speculation" may be converted into the "Utility of Practice."[54]

But the question of how this conversion is to take place remains. The problem is not one of opportunity—as Hobbes observed in *Leviathan*, "the Common-people's minds . . . are like clean paper, fit to receive whatsoever by Publique Authority shall be imprinted in them."[55] Nor is it one of possibility; "if Whole Nations can be brought to *acquiesce* in the great Mysteries of Christian Religion," Hobbes continues, then the instruction of the people in the "Essentiall Rights (which are the Naturall and Fundamentall Lawes) of Soveraignty," poses no difficulty.[56] The problem is by what *means* the reconstitution of a citizenry can be accomplished, and Hobbes's science made accessible, so that the common people will develop in demonstrable ways, and their obedience constitute a thoroughgoing ethic of civic life.

Hobbes answered by introducing a civic code that meets three necessary criteria: it is grounded in the science of virtue and vice; it is easily promulgated through existing organs of popular culture (primarily the pulpit); and most important of all, it is readily accessible to the "Common-people's minds" because it is articulated in an idiom in which they are already well versed: the Holy Scriptures. Thus, Hobbes sought to ensure the people's duty through the promulgation of ten civic "Commandements," as he called them, designed to sustain the power of his "Mortall God."

IV

In chapter 18 of *Leviathan*, Hobbes included among the many rights the sovereign possesses the right "to be Judge of what Opinions and Doctrines are averse, and what Conducing to Peace," as well as on "what occasions, how farre, and what, men are to be trusted withall, in speaking to Multitudes of people."[57] But not until chapter 30 did he make explicit the *content* of the doctrine every sovereign ought to cause to be taught and "contained in publique Instruction" for the "Defence, Peace and Good" of the people.[58] To do this, Hobbes introduced a powerful biblical exemplar, by advising the sovereign to teach ten particulars of civic instruction in the form of civic commandments. In one bold stroke, Hobbes captured the most pervasive cultural idiom of his age—the biblical language of Scripture—gave it civic content, and deployed it toward a specific political end: to educate the common people in the requirements of civic duty. Just as Jews and Christians look back to the biblical Ten Commandments as the foundation of their religious faith and covenant with the immortal God, so the citizens of the Hobbesian commonwealth must be instructed to look upon the civic ten commandments as the foundation of their faith in that "Mortall God," the sovereign Leviathan. As Hobbes would have it, the summons to conform to the requirements of the science of just and unjust is to be continually reiterated throughout the history of the commonwealth, in the form of civic commands delivered from the pulpit of the sovereign's ministers.[59]

To put all of this slightly differently, Hobbes recognized the political necessity of translating his "demonstrable" science from a lengthy exercise in deductive logic into comprehensible, teachable shorthand. So he presented to the sovereign a civic code of justice, rooted in the language of the Old Testament and open to dissemination from the pulpit. He appreciated, we might say, the importance of "thinking with the learned and speaking in the vulgate." This is not simply because speaking the vulgate is more efficient or less given to "fearful prolixity" but because it is a political necessity for the sovereign whose power depends upon the active support of the multitude.[60] Thus it is also absolutely necessary for the political philosopher who advises the sovereign to consider the ways in which a theoretically demanding science can be translated into a simple and compelling practical discourse. This Hobbes did, and the civic commandments, which draw so vividly upon the biblical Scriptures, are the result.

The first table of the civic commandments consists of ordinances concerning the "love of Soveraign." The first commandment takes its significance from the first biblical one: "*Non habebis Deos alienos*— Thou shalt not have the Gods of other Nations." Likewise, in the civic realm, the common people "ought not to be in love with any forme of Government they see in their neighbor Nations, more than with their own."[61] Hobbes drew from this admonition to patriotism a corollary: the people should also resist the "desire of change." The second commandment instructs the subjects not to defer to their fellows, however much they "shine" in the commonwealth, since any "obedience," "honor," or "admiration" is owed to the sovereign only. It resembles the counsel of the second biblical commandment, "You shall make no graven images" (Deut. 5:8). The third commandment, like its biblical parallel, warns against speaking evil of the sovereign representative or using his name irreverently. And the fourth calls for a day of civic instruction so the people can assemble and "(after prayers and praises given to God, the Soveraign of Soveraigns) hear those their Duties told them, and the Positive Lawes . . . read and expounded."[62] Thus through the creation of a "civic sabbath," Hobbes institutionalized the practice of civic socialization.

The second table of civic commandments concerns the subject's love of others. The fifth commandment also follows its biblical counterpart and counsels children to be obedient to their parents, "through externall signes of honour" and "(as gratitude requireth)."[63] The next four commandments are subsumed under the general directive to justice, "to cause men to be taught not to deprive their Neighbours, by violence or fraud, of any thing which by the Soveraign Authority is theirs."[64] Here Hobbes recapitulated the "Thou shalt nots" of the biblical commandments—against violence, against the "violation of conjugall honour," against "forcible rapine, and fraudulent surreption of one anothers goods," as well as against bearing "false Judgement."[65] The summation of this table—Hobbes's civic version of Leviticus 19:18—is the tenth commandment: "Thou shalt love thy neighbour as thy selfe."[66]

Like the natural laws, the civic commandments are best taken not as guidance for the good man but rather as directives for the dutiful citizen. The natural laws (understood as civic virtues) are themselves contained within these civic commandments, insofar as the commandments either implicitly presume the personal qualities advanced in the laws of nature or explicitly reinforce (or forbid) them. For example, the fifth commandment that counsels children to obedience reinforces the duty of gratitude (the fourth law of nature), a virtue, as we have seen, vital to the maintenance of a sociable commonwealth. And the final commandment, with its admonition to "mutuall Charity," is simply the fifth, sixth, and eighth natural laws—for complaisance and forgiveness and against contumely—condensed into a precept that people can follow, independent of time, place, or circumstance. So ends the science of virtue and vice, transformed into a lesson in civil religion and civic identity.

Not coincidentally, Hobbes recognized that in order for the practical discourse of civic virtue to be effective, there must exist "means and conduits"—cultural modes of political communication—through which the people can receive it. Thus he concluded his discussion of the civic commandments by considering "the use of universities." Here again, his primary concern is not with the learned, except to the extent that the learned (and particularly the divines in the pulpit) are those who teach the people. The universities are of central political importance to Hobbes because control of their doctrine means control of the people, and control of the people (i.e., their instruction in the true moral philosophy) will bring civil peace. Hobbes, ever cognizant of how political ideas are culturally produced and socially distributed, summed this up by observing that the majority of men

receive the Notions of their duty, chiefly from Divines in the Pulpit, and partly from such of their Neighbours, or familiar acquaintance, as have the Faculty of discoursing readily, and plausibly, seem wiser and better learned in cases of Law and Conscience, than themselves. And the Divines and such others as make shew of Learning, derive their knowledge from the Universities. . . . It is therefore manifest, that the Instruction of the people, dependeth wholly, on the right teaching of Youth in the Universities.[67]

In order to be effective, then, the science of just and unjust—the basis of popular obedience to the law of the commonwealth—must first become the subject of instruction within the universities. Only then will the preachings of the divines and the orations of the lawyers, both "seasoned against the Civill Authority," be silenced and the way be cleared for the inception of a new political culture steeped in the civic commandments of dutiful citizenship.[68]

V

From this discussion of Hobbes's civic code, we might draw one final interpretive alternative to some of the conventional readings of Hobbesian civil philosophy. This possibility responds both to Keith Thomas's argument that Hobbes's "ethical ideal" is aristocratic, informed by standards of chivalry and nobility nearly obsolete in the seventeenth century, and to the opposite view, advanced by Leo Strauss, C. B. Macpherson, and others, that Hobbes's ethical ideal is essentially bourgeois and directed toward a merchant middle class.[69]

Although in opposition regarding the social origins of Hobbes's moral philosophy, both Thomas and Strauss share an emphasis upon fear as a central feature of Hobbes's "new morality." Thus, Thomas argues that in the face of rising mass politics and a decaying aristocratic ethic that maintained a code of honor, Hobbes found his only recourse in an argument for obedience through fear.[70] And Strauss contends that, "in the movement from the principle of honour to the principle of fear, Hobbes's political philosophy comes into being."[71] Whatever their differences, both Thomas and Strauss downplay the significance of the common people in their political analysis: Thomas by suggesting that Hobbes's perception of "the limits to popular capacity" lead him to emphasize fear as the root of obedience, and Strauss by arguing that the middle class holds Hobbes's interest and that his argument concerning fear is a way of checking the potentially fatal bourgeois tendency to complacency and self-satisfaction.[72] In closing, I shall argue briefly that neither of these views pays proper attention to the role the common people play in Hobbes's thought. As a result, both Thomas and Strauss miss something important about Hobbes's new civil philosophy; namely, that it lays the groundwork for a popular code of civic virtue.

Clearly, to suggest that Hobbes championed civic virtue in order to render fear obsolete would be untenable and would rob Hobbesian theory of one of its crucial distinguishing elements. As Thomas reminds us, the role fear plays in the obedience of the multitude cannot be lightly dismissed. Yet by the same token, as I hope I have shown, fear is not all there is to Hobbes's discussion of the obedience of the common people. We need to place it within a broader context and ask who the "great majority" is *after* the fear of violent death has done its work. In this regard, we should remember that Hobbes sought more than "bare Preservation of life" in his vision of civil society. Likewise, we may presume that he imagined the majority of citizens as more than a cowed mass constantly threatened by the sovereign's swift sword and a fear of violent death. I suggest that we accept, with Thomas, the primacy of fear in Hobbes's philosophy of mass politics but that we not take it as *the* defining characteristic of the Hobbesian citizenry. Once fear has done its work—the passions are stilled, the contract extracted, the sovereign in place—the people are in a position to be schooled in the finer qualities requisite for their civic duty (including, of course, the fearful consequences of not following it). The political virtues of what Hobbes called a "strong and lusty" citizenry may in this way be understood as held hostage to fear, but not as synonymous with it. To put this otherwise, Hobbes was as interested in the "*civil*ization of obedience" as he was in the simple extraction of it through fear.[73]

Strauss's reading of Hobbes's new morality as "the morality of the bourgeois world" raises a different problem. Although he pays proper attention to Hobbes's recognition of the expanding urban populace and a growing commercial environment populated by men of trade, Strauss ignores the possibility that Hobbes's civil philosophy may be a response to a political problem and not simply an alternative social ethic. The problem, of course, is the recovery of civil peace and how to sustain popular obedience to the sovereign government. Hobbes, knowing full well that the heroic code of Grand Tew was a decaying ethic, was forced to consider an alternative: a new code of political obedience for an age that was beginning to witness, as Christopher Hill puts it, "the seething mobility of forest squatters, itinerant craftsmen and building labourers, unemployed men and women seeking work, strolling players, minstrels and jugglers, pedlars and quack doctors, gipsies, vagabonds, [and] tramps"—the common people on the move.[74] But granted that the common man and woman could not be made in the mold of the noble Godolphin, they could (so Hobbes seemed to believe) at least be instructed in, and so internalize, some basic civic virtues— gratitude, mercy, justice, complaisance—and be guided by a set of readily accessible commandments, rooted in the popular idiom of the Bible and the pulpit. Thus, as Strauss argues, Hobbes's "new moral philosophy" was indeed intended to function as a code of nonaristocratic virtue, but not merely for the reasons Strauss suggests. It is not just because Hobbes was bourgeois in his instincts or driven to articulate the moral virtues of the rising middle class that he developed his new moral philosophy but, equally important, because he was intent upon constructing a solid foundation for the political obedience of the multitude.[75] Accordingly, he set out to demonstrate a science of virtue and vice, based on a set of simpler but no less virtuous principles than the old heroic code, in which the "plainer sort of men" could be instructed and which they could practice as dutiful citizens every day. Strauss notwithstanding, I believe Hobbes's science of virtue and vice can best be understood as "civic" and not just bourgeois, and as directed, with political intent, toward the common people and not simply as a sociological reflection of the rising middle class.[76]

A final, cautionary note. My reading of Hobbes as a theorist of civic virtue—however persuasive I hope it is—can nonetheless take us no farther than his theory of sovereign absolutism allows. We may now agree that Hobbes's subject is a more fully constituted being, instructed in the virtues compatible with civic peace, than previously thought and that *Leviathan* provides a richer doctrine of civic virtue than has generally been noticed. But this still leaves Hobbes a far distance from a conception of civic virtue as we have come to understand it in its classical republican guise. Whatever his qualities, the Hobbesian citizen exhibits precious few of the attributes that equip him for a life of participatory self-government, the performance of public service, and the cultivation of political liberty. Indeed, insofar as the virtues of Hobbes's citizen cultivate a disposition toward obedience to Leviathan, they conspire to deprive the citizen of precisely the sort of liberty that distinguished classical republicanism—a liberty Hobbes deemed specious. That Hobbes was neither a Machiavellian nor a Harringtonian goes without saying. But his vision of a citizen-subject suggests that the argument for civic virtues need not be the exclusive possession of the classical republican.[77]

NOTES

For their insights, comments, and helpful suggestions, I thank James Farr, Jeffrey Isaac, and Dana Chabot.

1. Quentin Skinner, "The Context of Hobbes's Theory of Political Obligation," in *Hobbes and Rousseau*, ed. Maurice Cranston and Richard S. Peters (Garden City, N.Y.: Doubleday & Company, 1972), p. 117.

2. Thomas Hobbes, *Leviathan*, ed. C. B. Macpherson (Harmondsworth, Middlesex: Penguin, 1968), ch. 18, p. 237. All subsequent references to *Leviathan* will be to this edition.

3. Ibid., ch. 18, p. 238.

4. Hobbes himself seemed to fear that the relationship he established between the sovereign and its subjects would be interpreted badly. In *Leviathan* he wrote, "A man may here object, that the Condition of Subjects is very miserable; as being obnoxious to the lusts, and other irregular passions of him, or them that have so unlimited a Power in their hands" (ch. 18, p. 238). He continued, however, to recall the "dissolute condition of masterlesse men" and to suggest that, in submission to a "coercive Power," subjects find peace and are secure from the "horrible calamities that accompany a Civill Warre" (ch. 18, p. 238).

5. *Leviathan*, ch. 31, p. 395.

6. Thomas Hobbes, *The History of the Grecian War Written by Thucydides*, in *The English Works of Thomas Hobbes*, ed. William Molesworth, 11 vols. (London: John Bohm, 1839–1845), 8:xvii.

7. Thomas Hobbes, *Behemoth*, vol. 6 in *The English Works*, pp. 166, 169. All references to *Behemoth* will be to this volume.

8. *Leviathan*, ch. 17, pp. 224–25.

9. Ibid., ch. 17, p. 227.

10. Ibid.

11. Ibid., ch. 17, pp. 227–28.

12. Throughout this essay I will use "man," "he," "him," etc., because Hobbes confined himself to this gender-laden language. Like most political theorists of his time, he associated the domain of political action with men—and "men" in a specific, not the so-called generic sense of the term.

13. Hobbes made this even more explicit in *Leviathan*, ch. 30, where he wrote that by "the safety of the people" he meant not "a bare Preservation, but also all other Contentments of life, which every man by lawfull Industry, without danger, or hurt to the Commonwealth, shall acquire to himselfe" (p. 376).

14. *Behemoth*, p. 184; *Leviathan*, ch. 30, p. 376.

15. *Behemoth*, p. 192.

16. Ibid.

17. See, in particular, Deborah Baumgold's essay in this volume and her *Hobbes's Political Theory* (Cambridge: Cambridge University Press, 1988).

18. *Behemoth*, p. 166.

19. Ibid., p. 235.

20. Ibid., p. 211.

21. Ibid., p. 212.

22. Ibid.

23. Ibid., p. 219.

24. Ibid., p. 220.

25. In *Leviathan*, Hobbes made a similar point by distinguishing the sovereign from the commonwealth and arguing that the former should always act in ways to ensure the latter. His particular subject is the disbursement of money and reward. Hence, "it belongeth to the Office, and Duty of the Sovereign, to apply his Rewards alwayes so, as there may arise from them benefit to the Common-wealth: wherein consisteth their Use, and End; and is then done, when they that have well served the Common-wealth, are with as little expence of the Common Treasure, as is possible so well recompenced, as others thereby may be encouraged, both to serve the same as faithfully as they can, and to study the arts by which they may be enabled to do it better" (p. 390). It is worth noting that in this passage and others, Hobbes's conception of political order seems to encompass more than the sheer maintenance of sovereign power. It extends to a more substantive conception of the peace of the country, one that requires the government to promote the welfare of its inhabitants and to avoid "making ill impressions in the mindes of the People" (ibid.).

26. *Behemoth*, p. 367.

27. Ibid., p. 212.

28. Ibid., p. 213.

29. Ibid., p. 252, emphasis added.

30. Hobbes also voiced his concern about ambitious men in *Leviathan*, where he counseled the sovereign, "It is therefore against the Duty of the Soveraign, to whom the Publique Safety is committed, to Reward those that aspire to greatnesse by disturbing the Peace of their Country, and not rather to oppose the beginnings of such men, with a little danger, than after a longer time with greater" (p. 391). Not coincidentally, this warning appears in chapter 30, where, as we shall see, Hobbes was concerned to advance and defend a program of "publique instruction" which Leviathan should present to the common people.

31. *Behemoth*, p. 213.

32. *Leviathan*, ch. 26, p. 314, emphasis added.

33. Ibid., ch. 15, p. 216.

34. Ibid., ch. 15, p. 214.

35. Ibid.

36. For the most systematic defense of the natural laws as prudential maxims, see J. W. N. Watkins, *Hobbes's System of Ideas: A Study in the Political Significance of Philosophical Theories* (London: Hutchinson University Library, 1965). My concern in this essay is not with the *form* of the Hobbesian natural laws (i.e., with whether they are best understood as prudential maxims, "assertoric hypotheticals," deontological principles, etc.) but rather with their substantive *content*. I do not think my view of some of the natural laws as civic virtues presupposes that they are of one particular form rather than another; but in any case, I will not pursue that argument here. What I do want to emphasize is the collective political significance of the natural

laws and, accordingly, Hobbes's understanding of civil society as not merely a collection of strangers pursuing individual ends but a commonwealth of mutually engaged and unavoidably social beings living under a powerful sovereign.

37. A. E. Taylor, "The Ethical Doctrine of Thomas Hobbes," in *Hobbes Studies*, ed. K. C. Brown (Cambridge, Mass.: Harvard University Press, 1965), p. 36.

38. As Ian Shapiro points out in *The Evolution of Rights in Liberal Theory* (Cambridge: Cambridge University Press, 1986), since Hobbes, theories of consent have become increasingly more abstract and individualist. Thus, in post-Kantian liberal theory, "the 'normal' or 'essential' human condition in civil society is conceived as both asocial and apolitical" (p. 287). Given this, it is not surprising that post-Kantian interpreters of Hobbes have, in turn, read both deontological and apolitical assumptions back into *Leviathan*. For reasons I have articulated in reference to the Hobbesian natural laws, I think such a reading is problematic.

39. *Leviathan*, ch. 15, p. 214.

40. Ibid.

41. Ibid., ch. 15, p. 205. Hobbes's affinities with Machiavelli do not extend to an agreement on what virtues count as important civic dispositions, however. The virtues Machiavelli (and many other classical republicans) celebrated are, for example, rendered in decisively masculine terms and are linked to masculine activities: courage in arms-bearing, valor in battle, prudence in the calculation of military activities and their outcomes, temperance in statesmanship, etc. By contrast, many of the virtues Hobbes emphasized—mercy, sociability, modesty, charity, gratitude—have traditionally been linked to feminine sensibilities, although Hobbes certainly did not present them in these terms. Still (and ironically) it seems that his authoritarian politics issues in virtues that some feminists would find more appealing, if not less gender-laden, than civic republican ones. But then Hobbes's primary concern *is* the attainment of civic peace, also a feminist emphasis, and not the defense of citizen liberty and purposeful self-government. For an interesting discussion of the relationship between gender and civic republican virtues, see Ruth H. Bloch, "The Gendered Meanings of Virtue in Revolutionary America," *Signs: Journal of Women in Culture and Society* 13 (1987): 37–58.

42. *Leviathan*, ch. 30, p. 377.

43. Ibid., ch. 15, p. 201.

44. Ibid., ch. 15, p. 205.

45. Ibid., ch. 15, p. 209.

46. Bernard Gert makes a different but equally interesting argument concerning gratitude when he suggests that "free gift" is actually the origin of sovereign power, insofar as "Hobbes's social contract is not primarily a covenant, but a free gift of one's right to decide what is best for one, *by the subject to the sovereign*" (emphasis added). Thus the sovereign should also observe this law of nature because it is the beneficiary of the subject's giving. See Gert's review of Gregory Kavka, in *Political Theory* 16, no. 1 (1988): 162. I am suggesting—more consistent with Protestant theology, from which the notion of God's "free gift" of grace emerges—that we can also read this relationship the other way around and see the sovereign (the "Mortall God" who offers the free gift of peace) as the benefactor to whom subjects are obliged to show gratitude.

47. *Leviathan*, ch. 15, p. 209.

48. Ibid., ch. 15, p. 210.

49. Ibid.

50. The eighth natural law against contumely—and the ninth and tenth, against pride and arrogance—also reveal Hobbes's animus toward the offensive aspects of the aristocratic code and many of its conventions, such as the insult, which more often than not led to conflict and internecine civil strife. Thus, in addition to being civic virtues, the natural laws I am considering may also be read as evidence of Hobbes's effort to challenge and reconstitute some of the tacit aristocratic conventions of his age.

51. *Leviathan*, ch. 15. p. 212.

52. Ibid., ch. 15, p. 211.

53. *Behemoth*, p. 252.

54. *Leviathan*, ch. 31, pp. 407–8.

55. Ibid., ch. 30, p. 379.

56. Ibid.

57. Ibid., ch. 18. p. 233.

58. Ibid., ch. 30, pp. 376, 377.

59. Implicit in my argument is the idea that Hobbes, like Machiavelli, promulgated a "civil religion" distinct from a theologically Christian one. That does not mean that he ignored the latter; in fact, unlike Machiavelli, he was most concerned to articulate some of the doctrinal elements of Christian "publique worship" of the immortal God as well (*Leviathan*, ch. 31, pp. 401–5). But note how Hobbes's doctrine of public worship works to shore up or reinforce the ten civic commandments that, in full, counsel obedience to the state. As always, Hobbes recognized the complex interrelationship between religious and political culture and sought to advance doctrines in both that would lead to a mutually reinforcing result: public unity and obedience to the law.

60. This is actually a paraphrase of Watkins, who is quoting Agostino Nifo's observation that the reductionist will "think with the learned, and speak with the vulgar" (*Hobbes's System of Ideas*, p. 84). I have substituted "vulgate" not only to underscore Hobbes's concern with everyday speech but also to call up that other Vulgate—the popular edition of the Bible used in the Roman Catholic Church.

61. *Leviathan*, ch. 30, p. 380.

62. Ibid., ch. 30, p. 381.

63. Ibid., ch. 30, p. 382.

64. Ibid.

65. Ibid., ch. 30, p. 383. It may be worth repeating that by describing Hobbes's moral philosophy as "civic," I do not mean to suggest that *Leviathan* itself was aimed directly at the common people. Nevertheless, I think that the common people were meant to be the beneficiaries of the science of virtue and vice Hobbes "demonstrated" therein.

66. Ibid.

67. Ibid., ch. 30, p. 384.

68. We should note that, as concerned as he was with the doctrinal and thus "ideological" manifestations of civil obedience, Hobbes was also aware that particular material conditions are conducive to the subjects' allegiance to the sovereign and need to be created. In *De Cive*, for example, he stressed that "grief of mind arising from *want*" disposes subjects to sedition and that their grievances are often just. "Burthens" of the realm should not be unequally imposed upon subjects; taxes and labors should be equally born by all. See *De*

Cive, translated by Hobbes as *Philosophical Rudiments concerning Government*, ed. Bernard Gert, *Man and Citizen* (Gloucester, Mass.: Peter Smith, 1978), pp. 263–64. In *Leviathan*, he wrote: "To Equall Justice, apperraineth also the Equall imposition of Taxes; the Equality whereof dependeth not on the Equality of riches, but on the Equality of the debt, that every man oweth to the Common-wealth for his defence" (ch. 30, p. 386). And he made a case for a state welfare: "Whereas many men, by accident unevitable, become unable to maintain themselves by their labour; they ought not to be left to the Charity of private persons; but to be provided for . . . by the Lawes of the Common-wealth" (ch. 30, p. 387). Although Hobbes did not go so far as to argue that certain economic and social conditions could ensure the subject's obedience in the *absence* of a particular political doctrine, he clearly thought that instruction in the civic commandments alone was also not enough to ensure allegiance to the commonwealth or obedience to sovereign power. We should not overlook, however, that it is the eleventh law of nature, prescribing "equity," and the twelfth, advising "equall use of things Common," that provide the "civic ideological" basis for the social policies Hobbes recommended above.

69. See Keith Thomas, "The Social Origins of Hobbes's Political Thought," in Brown, *Hobbes Studies*, pp. 185–236; Leo Strauss, *The Political Philosophy of Hobbes: Its Basis and Genesis* (Chicago: University of Chicago Press, 1952); and C. B. Macpherson, *The Political Theory of Possessive Individualism, Hobbes to Locke* (Oxford: Oxford University Press, 1962).

70. Thomas notes, "Despite his origins, therefore, Hobbes's ethical ideal remained an aristocratic one. Although he considered that it was only the leisured minority of the population who were likely to cause trouble by their obsession with honour and reputation, he also thought that it was from their numbers that the most public-spirited citizens were likely to be drawn. . . . [The] great majority could only be governed by fear" ("The Social Origins of Hobbes's Political Thought," pp. 202–3).

71. Strauss, *Political Philosophy of Thomas Hobbes*, p. 128.

72. Ibid., pp. 122–3. In fact, in his account of Hobbes's sociology, Strauss pays only fleeting attention to the common people and instead sets up the tension in Hobbes's "new morality" only in terms of the aristocracy and the middle class.

73. In addressing many of these same issues, Michael Oakeshott refers to Hobbes's attempt to achieve "the moralization of pride." He argues that Hobbes defended "the morality of the tame man" and so the endeavor for peace, but he stops short of considering Hobbes a theorist of civic virtue, and he says nothing of the civic commandments. See Michael Oakeshott, "The Moral Life in the Writings of Thomas Hobbes," in *Rationalism and Politics* (London: Methuen Press, 1962), pp. 288–89.

74. Christopher Hill, *The World Turned Upside Down: Radical Ideas during the English Revolution* (New York: Penguin, 1972), pp. 48–49.

75. As the following passage in *Leviathan* reveals, Hobbes clearly did not limit himself to an understanding of "the people" as "the middle class": "The safety of the People, requireth . . . that Justice be equally administered to all degrees of People; that is, that as well the rich, and mighty, as poor and obscure persons, may be righted of the injuries done them; so as the great, may have no greater hope of impunity, when they doe violence, dishonour, or any Injury to

the meaner sort, than when one of these, does the like to one of them" (ch. 30, p. 385).

76. The thrust of my argument in this section owes much to Jeffrey Isaac's insightful treatment of John Locke, in "Was John Locke a Bourgeois Theorist? A Critical Appraisal of Macpherson and Tully," *Canadian Journal of Political and Social Theory* 11 (1987): 107–29.

77. Shortly after completing this essay, I discovered Alan Ryan's article, "A More Tolerant Hobbes?" in *Justifying Toleration,* ed. Susan Mendus (Cambridge: Cambridge University Press, 1988). Ryan observes that those scholars who charge Hobbes with "the destruction of the public realm" go too far. As a defender of toleration, he argues, Hobbes gave the classical conception of civic virtue "courteous handling," while the fanaticism of Puritan individualism "receives the reverse" (p. 58). And Ryan makes the same argument concerning toleration that I offer with regard to civic virtue: namely, that Hobbes defended it not "on principle" but as a utilitarian measure directed toward strengthening allegiance to the sovereign and the commonwealth. However, even though he recognizes that Hobbes's case for toleration is circumscribed by his political, utilitarian ends, Ryan can still find him a tolerationist—much as I can still find him a theorist of civic virtue.

7

Political Psychology in Hobbes's *Behemoth*

Stephen Holmes

Although cast as a dialogue, *Behemoth* is unmistakably Hobbesian in style as well as theme. The explosiveness of the language reflects the crotchety impatience of the author's mind. As his perverse contribution to the "act of oblivion" of 1660, meant to inhume twenty years of animosity (p. 203),[1] Hobbes skewered all parties in the English Civil War: lawyers, merchants, soldiers, city-dwellers, Commons, Lords, bishops, Presbyterians, king's advisers, and of course, the people. Stupidity and corruption are ordinary human failings, but seldom have they seemed so effortlessly combined. His censorious, although nonpartisan, approach reveals Hobbes's modest talents as a coalition builder. It also helps explain Charles II's reluctance to license prompt publication of the work.

Completed in manuscript around 1668, *Behemoth* represents Hobbes's mature understanding of political breakdown and the reestablishment of authority. This time his theory of "human nature in general" (p. 29) is not filtered through a set of political recommendations. Instead, it is expressed in a description of the way human beings behave—not the way they might behave under imaginary or ideal conditions, but the way they actually did behave in England between 1640 and 1660.[2] Not surprisingly, an anatomy of disorder is more realistic than a blueprint for order. Particularly noteworthy is *Behemoth*'s fine-grained account of human motivation. The psychological assumptions inspiring its historical narrative may not be totally consistent, but their richness and subtlety are compelling.

OPPORTUNISM

Sometimes Hobbes struck a cynical pose. When writing in this vein, he depicted rational and affectless advantage seeking as the principal or sole motor of human behavior. Even in matters of religion, the scramble for money and power is uppermost. The reason people call themselves "godly," for example, is to acquire more land (p. 161). Beneath the surface, the devout are "just as other men are, pursuers of their own interests and preferments" (p. 29). Despite appearances, religious controversies boil down to "questions of authority and power over the Church, or of profit, or of honour to Churchmen" (p. 63). The sole rationale behind theological doctrines is to redirect "towards the clergy" obedience due to the Crown (p. 71).[3] Even the king's Anglican allies opposed sedition only with an "eye to reward" (p. 63).

Presbyterian ministers in particular are "impious hypocrites" (p. 26) who seek power in order "to fill their purses" (p. 89). They claim to interpret the Bible better than others only "for their advancement to benefices" (p. 90). They focus on blasphemy and adultery, neglecting "the lucrative vices of men of trade or handicraft" in order to win merchant support and for the sake of their own "profit" (p. 25). They are shameless frauds and play-actors: "No tragedian in the world could have acted the part of a right godly man better than these did" (p. 24). But the charge of hypocritical advantage seeking is not aimed exclusively at Protestants. Under the reign of Charles I, courtiers converted to Catholicism for "hope of favour from the Queen" (p. 60). Regardless of denomination, in fact, "ambitious clergy" (p. 13) are mountebanks who don "the cloak of godliness" (p. 26) to peddle snake oil at a profit.[4]

One consequence of this reductionist approach to human motivation is a tendency to exaggerate the calculative powers and foresight of the rebels. From the very beginning, apparently, the Presbyterians and their allies in Parliament "were resolved to take from [the king] his royal power, and consequently his life" (p. 102).[5] These prescient revolutionaries did not stumble backwards into civil war, pursuing a redress of grievances that only slowly escalated into radically antiroyalist demands. Their appetites were not gradually whetted by successive concessions. At the very outset, instead, the clear-eyed "design of the Presbyterian ministers" was "to change the monarchical government into an oligarchy" (p. 75).

If this sort of conspiracy thinking were dominant, then *Behemoth*'s psychological portraits would be wholly unrealistic. Fortunately, Hobbes was not biased toward consistency. His account of motivation is much more complicated than his occasional stress on rational and affectless opportunism would lead us to expect.

SELF-FULFILLING PROPHECIES

To gain an initial sense of the psychological intricacy of Hobbes's theory, consider the fascinating passage in dialogue 4, where he strikingly asserted that "prophecy" is "many times the principal cause of the event foretold" (p. 188). Despite his physicalism, Hobbes was committed to the idea that, in some circumstances, the unreal controls the real. Equipped with imagination and language, human beings respond to the possible as well as to the actual, to the dreaded or anticipated future as well as to the experienced present. If the yet unreal future had no causal power, human beings could never be moved by threats of punishment or fear of violent death.

Hobbes introduced his analysis of self-fulfilling prophecies with a discussion of the "dreams and prognostications of madmen." These rantings can seriously injure the commonwealth because human beings always suffer anxiety from "the uncertainty of future time." Ideas in the head control behavior. More specifically, "foresight of the sequels of their actions" shapes what people subsequently do (p. 188). But how does this curious process work? If a prophet could convincingly "predict" that Oliver Cromwell was doomed to be defeated, then most people (supposed, for the sake of argument, to be rational and affectless opportunists) would desert his party, thus weakening it and ensuring its defeat. Contrariwise, if a fortune-teller persuaded the majority that Cromwell's party was certain to win, then people would rush to join his coalition, making its victory inevitable. The struggle for sovereignty is fought on a battlefield of wholly unreal imaginings or rationally unjustifiable assumptions about the future. Whoever controls the future (or the idea people have of the future) has unstoppable power.

This passage has interesting implications for Hobbes's theory of authority. It presupposes, of course, that people are basically advantage-seekers, that they will always join the winner and desert the loser in order "to deserve well" (p. 188) of the victorious party. But it also attributes an important causal role in the chain of social events to ideas, fantasies, and baseless mental attitudes. The outcome of a civil war may depend on something as intangible as the capacity to dishearten foes and embolden allies. You cannot *explain* (much less foresee) social outcomes by reference to the postulate of universal self-interest. Human behavior, no matter how self-interested, remains unpredictable because it is guided partly by assessments of the future—assessments that, in turn, result from irrational traits of the mind (naive trust in prognostications, a gloomy disposition, etc.), not from the calculations of a rational maximizer. On inspection, moreover, human aspiration often turns out to be "sottish ambition" (p. 145): not clear-eyed or self-serving, but drunken, foolish, whimsical, stupid, and self-defeating.

FOLLY

The behavior of passionless and calculating opportunists is ultimately controlled by less than rational or even preposterous assumptions about the future. But this modest qualification of rational-actor theory is not Hobbes's last word on the subject. Indeed, the notion that human beings are, by nature, relentless pursuers of their own advantage conflicts wildly with *Behemoth*'s fabulous chronicle of human folly. Impulsiveness and compulsions, hysterical frenzy and aimless drifting—these are more characteristic of mankind's history than eye-on-the-ball purposiveness, thoughtful self-preservation, or the sober cultivation of material interests. Students of "the prisoner's dilemma" assert that individually rational behavior can be socially irrational. A cool aversion to being suckered wreaks havoc on social cooperation. Although Hobbes argued this way in a few scattered passages, he emphatically did not assume that society's problems result from too much rationality on the part of individuals. In most cases, the irrationality of behavior has its origin in the irrationality of an individual's motives—notably, in an unreasonable skittishness about insult and public humiliation. If people were rational, they would (for they easily could) develop thick skins against gratuitous signs of undervaluing. But they do not do this. They do not do it because they are *irrational* fools.

Even when stressing the opportunism of fanaticism (p. 25), Hobbes did not paint a flattering picture of mankind's capacity for clear-headedness. Cromwell's fetishism about his lucky day (3 September) (p. 183), and the king's appointment of Arundel to lead an army into Scotland merely because his "ancestor had formerly given a great overthrow to the Scots" (p. 30–31), reveal the elementary incapacity of human minds to learn from experience or absorb the most obvious truths about natural causality. No rational actor would be as narcotized as most people patently are by such "foolish super-stition" (p. 31). It is another major "infirmity of the people" that they "admire nothing but what they understand not" (p. 96). Human be-ings in general can be easily conned "with words not intelligible" (p. 164). Widespread gullibility has massive historical effects. For centu-ries, people admired the arguments of Catholic theology "because they understood them not" (p. 17). They applauded these arguments not despite but because of their unintelligibility.

Deference, conformism, and group-think are further irrational re-flexes of the human mind. Men are sheep.[6] By a natural obsequious-ness and need to be told what to do, "inferior neighbours" follow "men of age and quality" (p. 54). Soldiers are "addicted to their great officers" (p. 189), while subjects in general heed their "immediate cap-tains" (p. 39), be they preachers, gentlemen, or officers. Personal loy-alty, a quasi-erotic identification with local notables, has a tremendous grip on most subjects. The English people do not hate Catholicism be-cause that religion is false; they are too ignorant and stupid to tell the difference between a true and a false religion. No, they hate Catholi-cism because their preachers tell them it is detestable (p. 60), and they docilely parrot whatever their superiors declaim. Ordinary subjects also think that "boldness of affirmation" (p. 69) is a proof of the thing affirmed. The more self-assured an orator's tone of voice, the more persuasive he becomes. It is only because most people are credulous dupes that ecclesiastical imposture succeeds so well. Indeed, a pa-thetic incapacity for individual advantage seeking has always charac-terized the greater part of humanity: "What silly things are the com-mon sort of people, to be cozened as they were so grossly" (p. 158).

Even without schoolmasters, people will acquire their opinions by osmosis rather than by critical reflection—by being dunked in "the stream" (p. 112) of public opinion. Within a group, a person can be "passionately carried away by the rest," which explains the paradox that "it is easier to gull the multitude, than any one man amongst them" (p. 38) Almost all people are "negligent" (p. 17). *L'homme copie* irrationally imitates the beliefs and behavior-patterns of those around him, failing to notice what he is doing. He acts with-out thinking about it, not in order to save time as economists might imagine, but from mindlessness, distraction, inveterate slovenliness, poor moral character, and an inborn monkey-see-monkey-do system for forming preferences.

Dreamily indulging their wildest fantasies about the distant fu-ture, most people lack the gumption to think causally two steps ahead. Hobbes emphasized this nearly universal myopia: "All men are fools which pull down anything which does them good, before they have set up something better in its place" (p. 155).[7] Rebels will overthrow an unsatisfactory regime only because they give no thought to the tyranny or anarchy that is bound to follow. Such everyday thoughtlessness (or failure to calculate) is not limited to commoners. In the early stages of the Civil War, the Lords themselves proved stupendously obtuse. They did not understand that weakening the king would expose their own order to an attack by the Commons. The reason for this "folly in the Lords" (p. 155) is most instructive. Great peers closed their eyes to the middle-range future, acquiescing in the Commons' assault on the Crown "for fear of violence" (p. 88) at the hands of London crowds. Squeamishness about a violent death clouds the mind and promotes irrational, short-sighted, and self-defeating behavior.

Failure to think causally about the probable consequences of one's actions has woeful results. An amusing exception confirms this rule. Parliament's army was more successful than it should have been because its soldiers were heedless half-wits. They would have quaked spinelessly at danger "approaching visibly in glistering swords." But "for want of judgment, '' they "scarce thought of such death as comes invisibly in a bullet, and therefore were very hardly to be driven out of the field" (p. 114). If you have not absorbed the latest technological advance, if you are irrationally prone to overestimate your good luck, or if, in the heat of action, you simply fail to think ahead, the threat of violent death ceases to operate as a sobering deterrent.

Hobbes's preoccupation with the sources of human irrationality clashes rudely with the rational-actor approach that many commentators project into his works. Despite a few memorable and citable passages, he did not conceive of man as an economic animal, engaging in preemptive strikes. The pitiful and snarled mess that is the human mind cannot be painted with such a monochrome palette. To help us disentangle the complexities of Hobbes's position, I would suggest, at least provisionally, a tripartite scheme. Human behavior is motored not by self-interest alone, but rather by *passions, interests,* and *norms.*[8]

NORMS

Throughout *Behemoth*, Hobbes invoked norms rhetorically. He spoke in favor of honesty, oath keeping, debt repayment, fair play (p. 11),[9] gallantry (p. 38), civility (p. 125), decency, and loyalty.[10] With palpable sincerity, he denounced not only "wicked Parliaments" (p. 154) but, more generally, "impudence and villainy" (p. 86), flattery (p. 110), "drunkenness, wantonness, gaming," and even "lewd women" (p. 147). More seriously, he lashed out repeatedly against cruelty[11] and tyranny.[12] His stomach was particularly churned by the Judas-like sale of the king, first to Parliament by the Scots (p. 134) and subsequently to the Independents by the Presbyterians (p. 155).

This is all quite touching. For our purposes, however, Hobbes's moral sentiments are beside the point. As he said, "What one calls vice, another calls virtue" (p. 45). And a value-subjectivist can scarcely propose his own values as commitments readers are rationally compelled to accept. Of course, if he employs morally charged language, he may be assuming that it will strike a chord. Hobbes invoked Christian and martial values to vilify merchants.[13] From this rhetorical maneuver, we can conclude nothing about his own values. We can say with some certainty, however, that he thought readers would respond sympathetically to traditional moral codes.

Of interest is Hobbes's empirical, rather than normative, approach to norms. Norms are *effective*. They are not simply rationalizations that can be peeled away to discover someone's single-minded obsession with personal advantage. People not only should, but actually do honor their plighted word, even when the personal costs of doing so are quite high. Motives that remain irreducible to self-interest are especially powerful in complex choice-situations where considerations of advantage do not clearly privilege one decision over another.

Despite his torrent of jibes about religious hypocrisy, Hobbes straightforwardly asserted that the queen's Catholicism was genuine and disinterested (p. 61). Indeed, he assumed that people naturally believe what they are taught to believe as children.[14] The passivity of primary socialization alone belies an exclusively instrumental interpretation of religion. Crafty prelates can use religion to serve their interests only because most subjects, indoctrinated from infancy, have a habitual or uncritical (that is, noninstrumental) attitude toward their faith.

The presence of nonopportunistic behavior can be inferred even from Hobbes's most cynical-sounding claims. The assertion that "there were very few of the common people that cared much for either of the causes, but would have taken any side for pay or plunder" (p. 2) implies that the loyal few, devoted to either king or Parliament, would have been somewhat less susceptible to monetary rewards. Moreover, Hobbes's remark about "men that never look upon anything but their present profit" (p. 142) refers not to most people but solely to those who have grown rich through trade and craft.

Hobbes's most arresting example of norm-driven behavior is this: members of the Commons passionately hated Wentworth *because he had once been a parliamentary leader* (p. 68). Such seething hatred cannot be reduced to the self-interest of the enraged party. Their animosity was not fueled by anticipated advantage. It was engendered instead by an implicit norm: deserters are intrinsically worse than people who have always been enemies, even if their behavior is the same. Much more loathsome than any damage he did to Parliamentary interests while in the king's service was Strafford's heinous defection, his breach of a taboo. Equally noisome, perhaps, was his all-too-rapid rise from knight to earl, which although not injuring parliamentary interests, violated a prevailing sense about how the status system was supposed to work. Hobbes explicitly invoked status anxiety to explain why the Scottish nobility cooperated in the abolition of episcopacy: "Men of ancient wealth and nobility are not apt to brook, that poor scholars should (as they must, when they are made bishops) be their fellows" (pp. 29–30).[15] A compulsive attachment to inherited place, fused with trepidation about change, explains patterns of hostility unintelligible from the standpoint of rational self-interest alone.

Consistency is another causally effective norm. Having first protested against irregular royal taxes, Parliament eventually imposed irregular taxes of its own. It should thus have been hoisted with its own petard (p. 85). But such apt punishment is not merely a hope; it can also be a fact. Priestly licentiousness before Henry VIII's break with Rome actually undermined clerical power: "the force of their arguments was taken away by the scandal of their lives" (p. 18). The normative trespassing of priests, monks, and friars helped disgrace the church and prepared the way for the English Reformation.

Norms exhibit their greatest causal force in the swaying of fence-sitters. The moral principle that *the aggressor is in the wrong* seems to be a case in point. To win the cooperation, or at least compliance, of uncommitted moderates, the rebels worked hard "to make it believed that the King made war first upon the Parliament" (p. 36). Similarly, the Dutch "wisely" (p. 176) made it seem that English ships attacked *them* (even though, in general, potential allies will consult their own advantage and ignore the justice of the struggle).

NAMES

Throughout *Behemoth*, Hobbes also stressed the politics of name calling and, especially, of name-avoidance. Even when not backed up by the sword, "words" and "breath"[16] possess enormous political force. This is a little-explored dimension of Hobbes's nominalism: people react more emotionally to names than to facts. Cromwell did not dare assume the name of *king* (p. 109) for fear of awakening the latent envy of subordinates. Aware that the treason laws were draconian, supporters of Parliament anxiously explained that they were not *rebels*. It was "Parliament's artifice" (p. 67), on the other hand, to affix the epithet *traitor* on anyone it aimed to kill. The label of treason has a particularly profound effect on waverers and temporizers. Thus, the capture and publication of the king's correspondence with France (about the possibility of introducing French troops into England) swelled parliamentary ranks. And, of course, you can destroy an enemy by making him "odious to the people" (p. 161). To this end, the Presbyterians smeared the king's party with the label of *episcopalian* (p. 89), and the Anglicans, in turn, with the name of *papists* (p. 83). Recrimination with the tongue cannot be waived aside as a mere "externall thing."[17]

Public opinion is politically decisive. Hobbes called Parliament's claim to be *King-in-Parliament* a "university quibble" (p. 124), but he never doubted its subversive effect. To curry popular favor, Parliament cleverly presented itself as the *guardian of English liberties*. The Rump, in turn, confiscated the name of *Parliament* because, "being venerable amongst the people" (p. 157), this nomenclature served their cause. Veneration attaches to names, and veneration is an important source of power. Vilification, too, requires a shrewd application of labels. By rhetorical skill, "the Parliament had made the people believe that the exacting of ship-money was unlawful" (p. 60). They assailed ship-money, which was financially a very light tax, as a form of *illegal oppression* (p. 37). Given the gracious receptivity of the human mind, flung mud tends to stick.

Hobbes's account of the Hampden affair assumes that most people are relatively indifferent to the monetary cost of taxation. The raucous to-do about ship-money arose not from damage to material interests but from ideologically induced hysteria—from the assumption that extraparliamentary taxation was a form of *tyranny*. The Commons was able "to put the people into tumult upon any occasion they desired" (p. 69); that is, it could drive the people into actions contrary to their real interests. Few names were more useful in this regard than the name of *tyrant*. In reality, "no tyrant was ever so cruel as a popular assembly" (p. 23). But the readers of Greek and Roman history propagated the fiction that "popular government" was *free*, while monarchical rule was *tyrannical*.[18]

Right and might are far from identical. In *Behemoth*, surprisingly, the practical exchange of obedience for protection seems overshadowed by Stuart legitimacy. The dynastic right to rule is apparently valid without any real power to keep the peace. The possibility that Charles I might have forfeited his right to rule when he became unable to protect his subjects is mentioned but not taken seriously (p. 146). This curious twist in the argument might be dismissed as Hobbes's servile attempt to ingratiate himself with the restored Stuarts. But notice his causal claim. Mere names, such as king or Stuart, sway the popular mind. The right to rule cannot be inherited, but words do govern the world. Dynastic right thus has a potential for powerfulness independent of any actual military strength. Residual "reverence" for the Crown was an important factor in the king's capacity to raise an army without parliamentary support (pp. 35–36). True, *Behemoth* is not completely consistent on this point. Parliament's seizure of the power of self-perpetuation accomplished "a total extinction of the King's right" (p. 74). Yet, somewhat later, Hobbes said: "The right [to rule] was certainly in the King, but the exercise was yet in nobody" (p. 135).[19] Legitimate authority, in any case, is not automatically transferred to the wielder of superior military force. After the king's execution, a non-coincidence of right and might became apparent: "If by power you mean the right to govern, nobody [here] had it. If you mean the supreme strength, it was clearly in Cromwell" (p. 180).

Hobbes's deceptively positive attitude toward the Stuart "right to rule" implies nothing about his own theory of just authority. It shows only that he believed most people were outfitted with conventional minds. Custom, inertia, habit, and the enduring grip of ideas imbibed in infancy ensure that "a rightful king living, an usurping power can never be sufficiently secured" (p. 131). The very *name* of Stuart has a power to attract resources and allies far out of proportion to its bearer's current capacity to impose his will by force. The intangible power attached to family pedigree explains why, inevitably, "usurpers are jealous" (p. 184) and also why the Stuarts returned with a mysterious ineluctability to the throne.

Norms and names can be tools for some because they are not tools for all. Hypocrisy would be wholly pointless if everyone was fraudulent and no one was sincere. At one point, Hobbes claimed that sects and fanatics were "Cromwell's best cards" (p. 136) in the card game for sovereignty. The distinction, implicit here, between the calculating and the noncalculating, between the players and the played-with, is consistently drawn. Broadly speaking, there are two types of human beings: the cynic and the dupe.[20] Dupes vastly outnumber cynics. As a result, norms and names will always exert a decisive influence over the train of events.

TEACHINGS

Free speech and freedom of the press concerned Hobbes not as promises but as threats. The rebellion was driven by ideas that vexed the mind and distorted people's perception of their own advantage. These "dangerous doctrines" (p. 71), in turn, crept into English heads by way of books and public speech. To a large extent, "this late rebellion of the presbyterians and other democratical men" (p. 20) was a *reader's revolt*, an uprising led by unsupervised students of the Bible, on the one hand, and of Greek and Roman history, on the other.[21] As disruptive as the printed word were sermons from pulpits, "harangues" in Parliament, and "discourses and communication with people in the country" (p. 23). England's problems were wrought by a joint looseness of pen and tongue. Lawyers "had infected most of the gentry of England with their maxims" (p. 119), promulgating the notion of fundamental law which was nothing but an invitation to regicide. Even the king's advisers had caught the doctrinal plague, falling "in love with *mixarchy*" and thus being irrationally "averse to absolute monarchy" (p. 116).[22] This intellectual contagion had significant effects on the king's closest allies. Disastrously, it "weakened their endeavour to procure him an absolute victory in the war" (p. 114–115).

Hobbes reserved some of his bitterest criticisms for the two great centers of learning. He even claimed that "the core of rebellion . . . are the Universities" (p. 58). From the universities, Presbyterians dragged their theology into the churches and gentlemen carried their politics into Parliament (p. 23). It was Laud's great mistake "to bring . . . into the State his former controversies, I mean his squabblings in the University about free-will, and his standing upon punctilios concerning the service-book" (p. 73). In a healthy society, these "unnecessary disputes" (p. 62) would have remained quarantined within the ivory tower.

The universities were originally established as a trojan horse for papal power in England, as outposts for inculcating "absolute obedience to the Pope's canons and commands." University indoctrinators supported papal supremacy by employing "verbal forks," "distinctions that signify nothing" (p. 41), and "unintelligible distinctions to blind men's eyes" (p. 40). If one overlooked their dastardly political purpose (to erode secular authority), then Duns Scotus and Peter Lombard would seem to be "two of the most egregious blockheads in the world, so obscure and senseless are their writings" (p. 41).

Those who first pitched theological dust into the eyes of readers were not themselves unseeing. By Hobbes's own day, however, university theologians had come to compose treatises "which no man else, nor they themselves, are able to understand" (p. 17). The worst feature of the doctrines transported from the universities into the polity is that they are so opaque as to be endlessly "disputable" (p. 55). Reasonable people will always disagree about what they imply. Thus, "the babbling philosophy of Aristotle . . . serves only to breed disaffection, dissension, and finally sedition and civil war" (p. 95). Doctrines are politically dangerous because disagreements are politically dangerous. Intellectual discord engenders civic discord because parties coalesce around ideas. To introduce theological conflict into the public domain through the universities is "an excellent means to divide a kingdom into factions" (p. 14). faced with Anglican-Puritan or Arminian-predestinationist squabbles, Laud was disastrously wrong to think "that the state should engage in their parties, and not rather put them both to silence" (p. 62).

Norms, names, and doctrines are politically crucial. This is especially true because "the power of the mighty hath no foundation but in the opinion and belief of the people" (p. 16). Frequently neglected, this remarkable pronouncement highlights an essential feature of the Hobbesian theory of power. To explain human behavior, appeals to self-interest are insufficient because, quite simply, "the Actions of men proceed from their Opinions."[23] Man may be a pleasure/pain machine, but he is pained by a flung insult or pleased by the burning down of a rival church depending on his beliefs, not on his nerve-endings. The opinions that guide and misguide people's lives are not themselves the products of a rational pursuit of private advantage. Beliefs are not tools to be picked up or dropped as strategic rationality decrees. A person does not ordinarily adopt opinions because they promote his or her self-preservation or material advantage; few opinions are so rational. Pascal, a younger contemporary of Hobbes's, argued as follows: "Toute opinion peut être préférable à la vie, dont l'amour paraît si fort et si naturel."[24] The love of life seems strong, but in fact, people are willing to die for almost any belief, however illogical. This was Hobbes's dismayed conclusion as well.[25]

PASSIONS

The rebellious Presbyterians and parliamentarians were driven to rebellion not only by ambition and love of gain but also by *malice* and *envy* (p. 23). Such turbulent passions also complicate attempts to offer a rational explanation of human behavior. They cannot be smoothly inserted into the utility bundle of a rational maximizer because, at the extremes, they fluster and de-compose the mind, making the weighing of costs and benefits next to impossible. At one point, Hobbes threw up his hands: "What account can be given of actions that proceed not from reason, but spite and such-like passions?" (p. 169) Pascal's claim that the love of life, apparently so strong, can be overcome by almost any opinion, is nicely complemented by an earlier remark of Francis Bacon: "There is no passion in the minds of man, so weake, but it Mates, and Masters, the Feare of Death."[26] Man is not a rational actor because his intellect is not a "dry light." On the contrary, "affections colour and infect the understanding."[27] The bewitching passions that regularly override the desire for self-preservation include revenge, love, honor,[28] shame, grief, fear, pity, and boredom.[29] Having acted as Bacon's amanuensis during the composition of his *Essays*, Hobbes was thoroughly persuaded of the motivational power of mind-clouding emotions.

Consider boredom. Many "seditious blockheads" are "more fond of change than either of their peace or profit" (p. 113). They seek a "change of government" (p. 38) for its own sake. Restlessness, fidgetiness, cabin fever, or love of novelty are the contraries of inertness, homesickness, and dread of change. None of these motives is particularly rational, none is selected for its instrumental value, and none can be reduced to self-interest.[30] For some people, change is simply tastier than material advantage, and boredom is more frustrating than material deprivation. A few lunatics even consider tedium to be worse than anarchy. Their taste for innovation explains why, quite irrationally, rebels will tear down a government before giving the least thought to what they can erect in its place (p. 155).

Many of the passions to which Hobbes attributed causal force are rooted in vanity or in the irrational desire for applause. People yearn to be thought superior, and they resent it bitterly when others forget their names. For example, the Marian exiles were apparently satisfied with the status of the clergy in England before the dispersal. But when they observed the Presbyterians in Geneva, they experienced the psychological trauma of relative deprivation. Not hard interests but anxieties about comparative prestige led them, on returning home, to escalate their demands. They wanted "the same honour and reverence given to the ministry in their own countries" (p. 22) as they had observed in Geneva. As a result, they "have endeavoured, to the great trouble of the Church and nation, to set up that government here, wherein they might domineer and applaud their own wit and learning" (p. 136).

Emotions divert the mind unhealthily from material concerns. For example, "*Envy* is grief for the prosperity of such as ourselves, arising not from any hurt that we, but from the good that they receive."[31] This other-regarding passion is socially rampant. Ministers envy bishops, whom they think less learned than themselves, while gentlemen envy privy councillors, whom they consider less wise (p. 23).[32] Subordinate commanders envy victorious generals, which is why Cromwell could not safely assume the name of king (p. 109). Envy at the level of states, "the emulation of glory between the nations" (p. 30), has incalculable consequences. English dominion of the seas was "envied by all the nations" (p. 176),[33] while English merchants envied Dutch prosperity (p. 4). For the outcome of the Civil War, no emotion was more decisive than the envy harbored by the Scots toward the English.[34] Among neighboring nations, even when their interests coincide, "the less potent bears the greater malice" (p. 32). An irrational obsession with comparative status explains the explosive energy of the less powerful.

Although it sickens the envier, envy may gratify the envied. Indeed, the consumption of envy (a subtle variation on the consumption of praise) is one of mankind's most fatuous and common amusements. Even the charm of political participation stems from a foolish desire to consume the envy of nonparticipators. Like recent self-realization theorists (but without their naively approving tone), Hobbes advanced a narcissistic theory of participation. Under Presbyterianism, "every minister shall have the delight of sharing in the government" (p. 89); that is, shall enjoy a positional good from which most others are frustratingly excluded.

All people, of course, "think highly of their own wits" (p. 23), a form of intellectual vanity that is dangerously exacerbated by a university education. This vanity proved terribly damaging to the king's cause.[35] The parliamentary party rapidly gained the support of gentlemen who had been passed over for office, who believed their talents had gone unrecognized by the king (pp. 27, 155–56). Because man is the only animal obsessed with the adjectives attached to his name, stable government requires gag rules to stifle mutual insult,[36] as well as an artful distribution of immaterial resources, especially status and prestige.

In his abridged "translation" of *Rhetoric*, Hobbes departed from Aristotle's original by adding intriguingly that people have a tendency "to hate" anyone "whome they have hurt."[37] Hatred, anger, contempt, and malice are even more irrational than moral psychologists have traditionally assumed. The Hirschmanian distinction between interests and passions, in fact, is beautifully illustrated by Hobbes's contrast between covetousness and malice. The Presbyterians sought political power in order to "satisfy not only their covetous humour with riches, but also their malice with power to undo all men that admired not their wisdom" (p. 159). References to "malice" (p. 25) abound. For example, the king's soldiers were stout, but "their valour was not sharpened so with malice as theirs were on the other side" (p. 114).[38] This was no negligible defect, because "spite" is "more conducing to victory than valour and experience both together" (p. 110). If people pursue power "farther than their security requires,"[39] they also pursue malice to irrational excess, being "more spiteful . . . than revenge required" (p. 165). Ill nature outruns advantage seeking and even surpasses the needs of retaliation. Discussing Parliament's "spiteful" veto against royal pardons, Hobbes again contrasted opportunism and malice: "All the rest proceeded from ambition, which many times well-natured men are subject to; but this proceeded from an inhuman and devilish cruelty" (p. 107).

The need to have one's vanity massaged is the flip side of the need to avoid humiliation and "affront" (p. 97). The pointless Dutch decision to insult some English ambassadors resulted in a military debacle (p. 174). Names are especially potent politically when they resonate with contempt. Thus, "the Irish nation did hate the name of subjection to England" (p. 79), just as Parliament could not "endure to hear of the king's absolute power" (p. 33). Essex agreed to lead the parliamentary army because his wife's too-public dalliance had humiliated him at court, calling his manliness into question and exposing him to the disagreeable reputation of a cuckold.[40]

Power may be valued as an instrument for acquiring wealth or extorting praise. But it may also be desired for its own sake, as a consummatory not instrumental good. *Libido dominandi*, or the desire to "domineer" (p. 136), is no more rational than the desire to be told what to do. It is just another semicomical passion with potentially anarchical consequences.[41] The Parliamentarians wanted to be "the people's masters" (p. 164). Similarly, "Presbyterians are everywhere the same: they would fain be absolute governors of all they converse with" (p. 167). Perversely enough, they find enjoyment in "a severe imposing of odd opinions upon the people" (p. 169). In these passages, the great advocate of uncritical obedience fanned resentment against mastery and subordination.

THE PERILS OF RELIGION

Despite a concern for earthly self-preservation, Hobbes was well informed about the relish for martyrdom and otherworldly rewards. He introduced his history of the Long Parliament with an extensive excursus on transubstantiation, auricular confession, celibacy, and the medieval struggles between emperor and pope. He did so because he saw religion as a potent amalgam of opinion and passion, with an almost irresistible power to shape and misshape human behavior.

Modern Christianity is especially dangerous. That, at least, is the message conveyed by the frontispiece of *Leviathan*, where the weapons of the church are displayed as distressingly equal to the weapons of the state. Religious civil war is singled out as Christianity's chief contribution to political development. Nothing similar ever occurred in the ancient world (pp. 63–64).[42] Moreover, "the cause of all our late mischief" (p. 55) was the spillover of abstruse theological disputes into the public realm. Christian authorities never forgot that "the tongue is the instrument of domination."[43] They thus poured enormous resources into the diffusion of sermons. As for the causes of rebellion, "The mischief proceeded wholly from the Presbyterian preachers, who, by a long practised histrionic faculty, preached up the rebellion powerfully" (p. 159).[44] Here lies the uniqueness of Christianity: "only in Christendom" is "liberty . . . given to any private man to call the people together, and make orations to them frequently, or at all, without first making the state acquainted." The "heathen Kings" committed no such mistake, because they "foresaw, that a few such orators would be able to make a great sedition" (p. 16).[45] Practice is a continuation of theory by similar means: "the doctrine of the Presbyterians" was "the very foundation of the then Parliament's treacherous pretensions" (p. 82); and, of course, the king "was murdered, having been first persecuted by war, at the incitement of Presbyterian ministers" (p. 95).[46]

As a book-centered religion, Christianity suggests anarchically that it is "lawful . . . for subjects to resist the King, when he commands anything that is against the Scripture" (p. 50); that is, against any one person's interpretation of Scripture.[47] The "doctrine" that moral obligations disclosed by private reading may override the duty to secular authority is calamitous and "divides a kingdom within itself." Moreover, the preachers "who in the pulpit did animate the people to take arms in the defence of the then Parliament, alleged Scripture, that is, the word of God, for it" (p. 50). A book-based and freely sermonizing religion will necessarily promote anarchy. Certain passages of the Bible imply that kings should lay down their sovereignty and submit themselves to ecclesiastical authority (p. 6). But no realm can be stable so long as subjects may "resist the King, when he commands anything that is against the Scripture, that is, contrary to the command of God" (p. 50). Unruliness becomes endemic once "private interpretation" (p. 22) of the Bible becomes common—once subjects themselves become "judge of the meaning of the Scripture" (p. 50).[48] The promulgation of "evil principles" (p. 204) by "seditious ministers" (p. 50), "pretending to have a right from God" (p. 2), provoked Hobbes's shocking remark, "How we can have peace while this is our religion, I cannot tell" (p. 57).

THE PAPAL TRADITION

As bishop of Milan toward the end of the fourth century, Ambrose wrote saucily to Emperor Theodosius: "I prefer God to my sovereign."[49] The anarchical strain in Christianity thus long predated the Reformation. Scanning the past for dangerous precedents, Hobbes interpreted the execution of Charles I as a Protestant adaptation and implementation of the Jesuit doctrine of regicide. Atabalipa of Peru discovered that Catholic ecclesiastics will murder kings "when they have power" (p. 11). Charles I learned the same lesson about their reformed counterparts.

In the Middle Ages, the papacy "encroached upon the rights of kings" (p. 40), overturning the power of lay investiture.[50] Aware of the power of propaganda, the pope multiplied sermons and dispatched "preaching friars" (p. 15) throughout Europe to spread his authority. With these unarmed battalions alone, the church "found means to make the people believe, there was a power in the Pope and clergy, which they ought to submit unto, rather than to the commands of their own Kings, whensoever it should come into controversy" (p. 13). They taught "that we ought to be governed by the Pope, whom they pretended to be the vicar of Christ" (p. 3)—a clever formula, for everyone knew that "Christ was King of all the world" (p. 12). Most important of all, the pope claimed "a power of absolving subjects of their duties, and of their oaths of fidelity to their lawful sovereigns" (p. 7). The natural result was an unstably divided sovereignty: the centuries-long conflict between the *sacerdotium* and the *imperium*, which Hobbes saw revived or reenacted in the battle between the king and a religiously inspired Parliament.

There "was never such another cheat in the world" (p. 21) as the pope. From early times, the occupant of the Holy See was uncannily shrewd, parlaying the "pretence of his power spiritual" (p. 11) into real political power by a series of deft tactical maneuvers. By making marriage a sacrament, he gained a "monopoly of women" (p. 7) and control over a question crucial for every king—legitimate succession. Even more cunning was the papal decision to impose celibacy on the clergy itself. By this seemingly self-abnegating move, the pope ensured that secular rulers, needing heirs, could never be priests and thus could never personally benefit from the indelible aura of sacerdotal authority. Priestly celibacy made every king *politically* impotent, depriving him of "the reverence due to him from the most religious part of his subjects" (p. 13).

The Anglican bishops remained loyal to the Crown during the Civil War. But their loyalty provides no evidence for the usefulness of Anglicanism to kings. Indeed, they refrained from personally decapitating His Majesty only because they were hostile to the rebels and very unpopular with the common people (p. 95). The bishops shared the delusion, common to all Christian clergy and inherited ultimately from the pope, that they were not meant to be creatures of the king (p. 89). They, too, claimed to exercise jurisdiction autonomously, "in the right of God" (p. 19). They heartily approved when Henry VIII abolished the pope's power in England, but only because, by sheerest coincidence, they discovered divine right in themselves. The unnerving conclusion to this attack on Anglicanism is that "the doctrine taught by those divines which adhered to the King . . . may justify the Presbyterians" (p. 49). Anglicanism itself vindicates regicide by disgruntled subjects.[51]

To B's idealistic suggestion that arms and force count for nothing because soldiers will never fight against their consciences, A replies, with a touch of cynicism, that religiously based power is strong enough to foment rebellion; but "if they have money" (p. 18) kings can always rout such opponents. Money can tip the balance against inspiration because "there are but few whose consciences are so tender as to refuse money when they want it" (p. 18). In this respect, money is no different from religion. Religion, too, is an especially powerful force when the scales otherwise rest in delicate equilibrium. (As mentioned, this is true for norms and names as well.) The power of religiously legitimated actors depends on the overall power situation in which they find themselves: "The great mischief done to kings upon pretence of religion is when the Pope gives power to one king to invade another" (p. 18). The pope survived because kings, driven by irrational envy of rivals, "let his power continue, every one hoping to make use of it, when there should be cause, against his neighbour" (p. 21). The power of religion does not cancel, but does seriously qualify, the authority of money and arms.

A FATE WORSE THAN DEATH

What is the secret of religious authority? How did "so many poor scholars" (p. 21) acquire so much power? Hobbes frequently suggested that the sole source of power is the ability to inflict physical pain; that is, the capacity to deliver a believable threat to crush rivals by force in cases of conflict. For example, "he that is master of the *militia*, is master of the kingdom" (p. 98). This statement raises an obvious question, however. If a government imposes its authority by means of the police and the army, "what shall force the army?" (p. 59). How can a sovereign gain "the power of pressing and ordering soldiers" (p. 79)? How can he attain authority *over* his own authority-enforcing machine?[52] The sovereign's "right" to control the army "signifies little" if the soldiers entertain "seditious" opinions (pp. 27–28). If force were the only source of authority, then state building (or militia building) could never get off the ground. Luckily, there is another source of social power: fraud.[53] A king can govern his subjects by the psychological manipulation of his soldiers' beliefs.

Mankind's *summum malum*, according to Augustine, is not violent death but eternal damnation.[54] The belief that damnation is worse than death obviously weakens the deterrent power of secular punishments. The crucial biblical passage on this theme is Matt. 10:28: "Fear not them which kill the body and after that have power to do naught; but rather fear Him who after He has killed the body, has power to condemn to hell."[55] Taken literally, this advice would

cripple the peace-keeping state and swell the power of rebellious ecclesiastics: "As much as eternal torture is more terrible than death,
so much [the people] would fear the clergy more than the King"
(pp. 14–15). A says he would rather obey the king who can inflict
real punishment than religious authorities who fulminate about the
afterlife. Qualms about excommunication, B responds, hinge on the
premise that salvation and damnation are controlled by the church:
"Which supposition, it seems, you believe not; else you would
rather have chosen to obey the Pope, that would cast your body and
soul into hell, than the King, that can only kill the body" (p. 8).[56]

At times, Hobbes denied that anyone "when his life is in extreme danger . . . will voluntarily present himself to the officers of
justice" (p. 50). But he cited with approval a contrary claim from
Diodotus Siculus concerning the extraordinary power priests can
wield in civil affairs. In ancient Ethiopia, people would voluntarily
submit themselves to capital punishment by the order of religious
officials (p. 94). This zombielike self-sacrifice testifies to the entranc-
ing power of theological beliefs. Most amazing of all, priests issued
orders for kings themselves to commit suicide; and the monarchs
would submissively take their own lives. They complied because
they were men of simple judgment and "educated in an old and indelible custom (p. 94). Thus, Diodotus concluded, "in former times
the Kings did obey the priests, not as mastered by force and arms,
but as having their reason mastered by superstition" (p. 94). Mind-
mastery and custom are sources of power sharply distinct from the
capacity to employ force.[57]

EXCURSUS ON THE SOURCE OF POWER

Power belongs to those who can plausibly threaten to crush rivals by
physical force. But it also flows, according to Hobbes, toward those
who can plausibly threaten to withdraw their cooperation when it is
most needed.[58] The theory of power implicit in *Behemoth* is complex.
Hobbes's insistence that rulers must be "skilful in the public affairs"
(p. 70) certainly implies that no one can rule by monopolizing force
alone. Kings need cooperation. In particular, they need "money,
men, arms, fortified places, shipping, counsel, and military officers"
(p. 110) adequate to their political aims. Such resources cannot be
wrung from subjects by force. This is the secret behind a lament
about "that unlucky business of imposing upon the Scots, who were
all Presbyterians, our book of Common-prayer" (p. 28).[59] Acknowl-

edging the independent causal power of religious ideas, Hobbes stressed the self-defeating character of attempts to change people's minds by brutal means: "Suppression of doctrine does but unite and exasperate, that is, increase both the malice and power of them that have already believed them" (p. 62). This is a stunning admission from a champion of unlimited sovereign power.

Regret about the prayer-book episode is the closest Hobbes came to admitting that royal misgovernment, rather than insubordination among miseducated subjects, led to the breakdown of authority. In the abstract, he was committed to the notion that the "private interest" of an absolute monarch automatically coincides with the interest of "the publique."[60] But this claim was historically implausible. The rebellion began not with parliamentary disobedience but with a series of annoying royal coups. Charles I extorted money in unconventional ways from influential subjects and persecuted religious nonconformists. These arrogant actions alienated important people from his dynasty and barred his access to "the purses of the city of London" (p. 2). In other words, unlimited power can be self-weakening and even self-destructive. When the Scots army invaded the country, Charles found himself all alone, literally help-less. As a result of his absolutist ambitions, the nation went on a tax strike. The king would have been more powerful if, having submitted himself to parliamentary limitations, he could have counted on parliamentary cooperation.

Hobbes admired the Romans for their capacity to win power through strategic concessions (pp. 33–34). They gained obedience by offering not merely protection but also status and the right to influence policy. By restricting their own arbitrary discretion, they gained useful cooperation and support. Limited power, they recognized, was more powerful than unlimited power. A flickering awareness of the self-defeating character of unconstrained authority explains an obscure sentence of the preface to *Leviathan* in which Hobbes claimed to advocate a middle way between "too great Liberty" and "too much Authority."[61] How can there be too much authority for Hobbes? The answer lies here: authority is excessive when it is self-defeating, when it undermines itself by alienating potential cooperators.[62]

This train of thought also explains the surprising passage in *Behemoth* where Hobbes stated categorically that not all commands of the sovereign can be considered laws. Laws are only those commands that attain a high level of generality, naming no names: "By disobeying Kings, we mean the disobeying of his laws, those his laws that were made before they were applied to any particular person" (p. 51). A bill of attainder, by this standard, would not be a valid law. To his prohibition on retroactive laws, [63] Hobbes added a clear affirmation of the person-office distinction: the sovereign "commands the people in general never but by a precedent law, and as a politic, not a natural person" (p. 51). The requirement that laws be general and published in advance is an obvious limitation on the discretion of the king. But it is also useful as a means for winning cooperation, not merely compliance, from proud subjects.

GATEKEEPER-PRIESTS

We are now in a position to answer more fully the question about the origins of clerical power. Priests insinuate themselves with the sick and dying, bilking them of money in order to build religious houses. Before "women and men of weak judgment" (p. 16), clergymen pose as magicians able to transform bread into Christ's flesh, claiming "at the hour of death to save their souls" (p. 15). Similarly, "When they shall have made the people believe that the meanest of them can make the body of Christ; who is there that will not both show them reverence, and be liberal to them or to the Church, especially in the time of their sickness, when they think they make and bring unto them their Saviour?" (p. 41). Ecclesiastics successfully present themselves as gatekeepers to heaven, as intermediaries between man and God. Such mind-mastery pivots upon their threat to *withdraw cooperation* from those who would forego eternal damnation and taste eternal bliss. Imagining what it would be like to confront churchmen holding the key to salvation, B exclaims: "For my part, it would have an effect on me, to make me think them gods, and to stand in awe of them as of God himself, if he were visibly present" (p. 15). More crudely, if people believe they cannot be saved without a priest's help, they will probably do whatever he requests. [64]

Such subservience is based on emotion as well as opinion. The principal passion favoring church authority is fear. But religious apprehension is distinct from the rational fear that induces obedience to a sovereign's laws. It is more like hysteria or, to use Hobbes's word, *anxiety*. Emotional turmoil afflicts a person who is "over provident," that is, who "looks *too far* before him" and is irrationally obsessed with possible future calamity. Such a person is "gnawed on" by anxiety. [65] He suffers from a form of shrieking misery and near dementia especially easy for clerical merchants of repose to exploit.

RECHANNELING THE POWER OF RELIGION

Christianity is dangerous to the state. But it is "not in man's power to suppress the power of religion" (p. 82).[66] Thus, a prudent sovereign will attempt to monopolize the pretense of spiritual power along with the reality of physical force. Although subversive in the wrong hands, the ability to threaten damnation can be useful if controlled exclusively by the king. By wrapping himself in a religious mantle, the monarch can acquire a bit of divine legitimacy, obtaining the "reverence" (p. 13) due to God's agent. If he can manage to make the content of religion "indisputable" (p. 43) within his kingdom, he will have repulsed the main danger posed by religion to civil concord. As the noncelibate archbishop of England, he can have "the laws of England" read from the pulpits once a week (p. 16). Following the pope's example, he can use the universities as *his* trojan horse, as a vehicle for indoctrinating his subjects into Hobbes's "science of *just* and *unjust*" (p. 39).[67] An appeal to divine authorization, indeed, is essential for stable monarchy. Subjects who think "of this present life only" are almost impossible to control (p. 54).

Although he obviously respected the papacy's no-translation policy, Hobbes conceded that having the Bible in the vernacular can prove useful to secular authority. True, the disobedience passages can never be wholly eclipsed by the obedience passages. But the greatest source of anarchy is pride; and (as Pascal showed) there is no mythology more effective in attacking pride than the mythology of sin and redemption. Society would certainly be more peaceful if both "glory" and "vengeance" could be reserved to God, as Scripture says they should be. It is no accident that Hobbes lifted his central metaphor—the state as the king of the children of pride—from the Bible. And his insistence that *inoboedientia* stems from *superbia* shows the degree to which he was indebted to an old Christian, even papal, tradition. If military training inculcates a willingness to "dare" (p. 45) and even to die with one's boots on, Christian training does the opposite. The notion that the last shall be first, that the meek shall inherit the earth, sedates the soul into "a quiet waiting for the coming again of our blessed Saviour" (p. 58). So valuable is this unmanning or dis-couragement to the state that the appalling risks of a book-based religion must be run.

According to Bacon, "it often falls out, that *Somewhat* is produced of *Nothing*: For Lies are sufficient to breed Opinion, and Opinion brings on Substance."[68] Hobbes emphatically concurred. Religion solves the problem of how to create political power in the first place, how a ruler can initially gain control over a staff that will, in turn, enable him to impose his authority by force. Indeed, this is the central example of self-fulfilling prophecy in Hobbes's theory: if people believe someone is a (immortal) god, that person will be a (mortal) god. Power is based on nothing more substantial than a "reputation" for power (p. 95). Fiction becomes reality.[69] If a person can cajole others into believing that he or she has power, that person *will* have power.[70] Authority cannot be stably based on either reason or force; it depends, ultimately, on a sleight of hand.[71] A social *creatio ex nihilo* presupposes the gullibility of most people. By a primitive bootstrapping operation, political institutions can be created even though no one possesses, at the outset, visible political resources. Thus priests have challenged the authority of secular rulers; thus political society originally emerged from the war of all against all.

Hobbes hoped to confiscate the intangible power of religious fraud from dangerous clergymen and bestow it safely on the king. He therefore asserted that legal positivism should *not* be the official doctrine of the Crown. Indeed, the sovereign must pretend "that the civil laws are God's laws" (p. 58). To admit that law is exclusively man-made is to expose its contingent or might-have-been-otherwise character to public view. The king can increase his power only if he conceals it to some degree. For one thing, less apparent power will provoke less real envy. The claim that *auctoritas non veritas facit legem*—that authority, not truth, makes the law—gives only a partial picture of Hobbes's approach to lawmaking power. When publicly professed, positivism implies precisely the kind of liberal responsibility and accountability for legislation that he hoped to avoid.

SEXUAL GUILT

Like the Grand Inquisitor, Hobbes believed that "it is the desire of most men to bear rule" (p. 193). But the inborn need to be told what to do can be powerfully reinforced by clever manipulation of circumstances. By spreading confusion and bitter disagreement, power seekers can create a pent-up need for a higher authority able to settle disputes by fiat. As Richelieu, Hobbes's one-time protector in France, purportedly said; "Le désordre fait partie de l'ordre." Occasional doses of anarchy will help remind subjects of why they should obey their king. Similarly, Aristotle's writings "puzzle and entangle men with words, and . . . breed disputation, which must at last be ended in the determination of the Church of Rome" (p.

42).[72] This guileful divide-and-rule strategy is based on the assumption that dispute and discord are psychologically intolerable.

Divisions can be introduced *within* the person. A distaste for autonomy and desire to be ruled can be increased by bifurcating people's minds, making them feel nauseated at themselves. The traditional Christian ploy was to teach people that sexual attraction to a member of the opposite sex, with no untoward action whatsoever, was a disgrace before God, that "the delight men and women took in the sight of one another's form" was "a sin" (p. 26).[73] Thus, power-hungry ecclesiastics "brought young men into desperation and to think themselves damned, because they could not (which no man can, and is contrary to the constitution of nature) behold a delightful object without delight." By inducing guilt and self-hate, the clergy increased prodigiously the need for a rescuing authority: "By this means they became confessors to such as were thus troubled in conscience, and were obeyed by them as their spiritual doctors in all cases of conscience" (p. 26). The mechanism here is partly this: inner divisions make people feel disoriented, unable to govern their own actions and therefore in need of authoritative instruction to get them through the day. When a person feels faint, he or she reaches for a crutch. But the psychological dependency created in this way can also be interpreted in a more rationalistic vein as an extremely subtle version of the obedience-for-protection exchange, assuming rational advantage seeking on everyone's part. The Christian clergy implants a fictive danger in the minds of the people: the danger of burning in hell for experiencing sexual desire. After inculcating a sense of peril, they sell their protection from this phantom threat for the price of total obedience. That, at least, might be a rational-choice reconstruction of the opium of the people.[74]

CONCLUSION

Although acutely aware that norms and passions can derail the opportunistic pursuit of personal advantage, Hobbes sometimes described people as "never meditating anything but their particular interest" (p. 39). But why does he lapse into this apparent inconsistency? Why does he flirt with motivational reductionism even though, as I have amply documented, his portrait of the human psyche is actually rich and unparsimonious? An answer to this question is fairly complex. For starters, invocations of sinister interest are essential to the technology of exposé. To say that people follow their particular interests is to say that they ignore "their duty to the public" (p. 39). It is rhetorically useful, as well as psychologically plausible, to attach the label of opportunism to a ruling faction that claims hyperbolically to *be* the nation. Hobbes exploded the *pars pro toto* pretension that "the Parliament is the people" (p. 154) by accusing its leaders of concealing a desire for oligarchy behind a smokescreen of democracy (p. 75). Motivational reductionism attracted Hobbes, even though it is descriptively unrealistic, because it helped him pillory his political foes.

In a normative vein, Hobbes sometimes argued that particular interests and the common good are the same. It is always in one's interest to obey the law (p. 44). Submission to authority is instrumentally rational because "calamities ever follow disobedience" (p. 144). Tax chiselers chisel only because they *fail* to discern their true interests. Such homilies are unconvincing, however.[75] All deviations from self-interest cannot be explained by cognitive defects alone. More realistic is the assumption (shared by Bacon, Pascal, and others) that unruly emotions and abstract principles can override self-interest and *thereby* unleash political calamities. In addition, a normative bias against dangerous passions and norms helps explain Hobbes's occasional lapses into motivational reductionism. In an ideal world, people would pursue self-preservation alone. Paradoxically, the postulate of universal self-interest is not merely cynical and disparaging; it is also eulogistic and utopian.

Hobbes exaggerated the relative importance of self-interest for another reason as well. Political theorists traditionally divided humanity into two groups: a vast majority, motivated by lowly self-interest, and elites, propelled by higher ideals such as glory or the common good.[76] When Hobbes wrote of universal self-interest, he meant the stress to fall on *universal*. He was universalizing, so to speak, the morality of the common man. His disproportionate emphasis on self-preservation was profoundly egalitarian or majoritarian.[77] The goals of traditional elites, such as the desire to rule or taste superiority, are stiffly rebuffed. Hobbes probably believed that most people were pitiable chumps, but he wrote sincerely on their behalf. He allied himself unswervingly with the "anti-violence interest group" comprising the vast majority of the population.[78]

Politically, Hobbes proved a poor guide to the future. Anarchy will result, he predicted, if "the great affairs of the kingdom be debated, resolved, and transacted only in Parliament" (p. 105). Order cannot be restored unless representatives again become mere couriers to the Crown, delivering word of popular grievances without interfering in governmental policy (p. 78). It turned out, however, that semiconstitutional restraints do not automatically hurl a nation into civil war. To limit government is not necessarily to destroy government. Parliamentary discussion does not inevitably inflame passions and produce political deadlock. Freedom of thought does not invariably compel people to murder everyone their consciences describe as immoral. Hobbes's dire forebodings proved unrealistic and alarmist. His political prescriptions were born obsolete. Delightfully unshaken, by contrast, are his insights into the subversion of rationality—into discombobulating passions, intoxicating doctrines, imposing names, and mesmerizing norms.

NOTES

1. All in-text citations refer to Thomas Hobbes, *Behemoth or the Long Parliament*, 2d ed., ed. Ferdinand Tönnies (London: Frank Cass and Co, 1969).

2. Hobbes himself, it is worth recalling, lived in exile in France during the 1640s.

3. The Augustinian invocation of free will, meant to solve the dilemma of theodicy, was also designed to increase ecclesiastical power: "Because there must be some ground for the justice of the eternal torment of the damned; perhaps it is this, that men's wills and propensions are not (they think) in the hands of God, but of themselves; and in this also I see somewhat conducing to the authority of the Church" (p. 42). The sly clerical attempt to attain power by inducing irrational guilt is discussed below.

4. Here are some nonreligious examples of Hobbes's cynical perspective on human nature: London merchants supported the rebellion because they thought a change in government would increase their profits (p. 4); many other participants "longed for a war" for the sake of riches and land, as if warfare were a private business deal as well as a distracting escapade (pp. 4, 115); the Scots did not invade England in response to political grievances (e.g., Laud's imposition of the Anglican prayer book) but solely "with a promise of reward and hope of plunder" (p. 31). Similarly, "There were in the army a great number (if not the greatest part) that aimed only at rapine and sharing the lands and goods of their enemies" (p. 136). Taking precautions against free riders (in a literal sense), "the plundering foot" at one siege "kept the gates shut, lest the horse should enter and have a share of the booty" (p. 171).

5. Similarly, the Parliamentarians "were resolved to take from [the King] the sovereign power to themselves" (p. 83).

6. Only if human beings are blank pieces of paper on which a legislator can write whatever he chooses can Hobbes himself hope to solve the problem of civil war by indoctrination.

7. On the characteristic human folly of destruction without construction, see also pp. 78–79, 109, 192.

8. To this usefully simple list can be added religious or political *doctrines* and psychological *identification* with leaders or groups.

9. Interestingly, Hobbes expressed moral revulsion at Pym for his "knavery and ignoble shifts" (p. 38), that is, for being a calculator.

10. Parliament hoped to dishonor the king by forcing him publicly to betray his friends (p. 81).

11. "They were Presbyterians," he explains, "*id est*, cruel" (p. 133); the gunpowder plot was "the most horrid act that ever had been heard of before" (p. 20); Cromwell's executions in Ireland were "horrid" (p. 163); and "condign punishment" (pp. 86–88) is just "cruelty" well liked.

12. Even though he elsewhere defined tyranny as but monarchy misliked, Hobbes here expressed indignation about both the "Pope's tyranny" (p. 172) and "Presbyterian tyranny" (p. 169). Nothing could be worse, it seems, than "a tyranny over a king" (p. 81). Once Parliament has the sovereignty, it will tyrannize over England, he said, implying that sovereign tyranny and tyrannical sovereignty are perfectly cogent ideas (p. 88).

13. The "only glory" of merchants is "to grow excessively rich by the wisdom of buying and selling" (p. 126). They become wealthy, moreover, "by making poor people sell their labour to them at their own prices" (p. 126). These asides, of course, do not prove that Hobbes was a devotee of *martial* glory or that he lost much sleep over poverty.

14. But note the touch of cynicism in this passage: "For what other cause can there bee assigned, why in Christian Common-wealths all men either beleeve, or at least professe the Scripture to bee the Word of God, and in other Common-wealths scarce any; but that in Christian Common-wealths they are taught it from their infancy; and in other places they are taught otherwise?" (*Leviathan*, ed. C. B. Macpherson [Harmondsworth, Middlesex: Penguin, 1968], ch. 42, p. 614).

15. Cf. "The reason why we conceive greater *indignation* against new than ancient riches, is that the former seem to possess that which is none of theirs, but the ancient seem to have but their own: for with common people, to have been so long, is to be so by right" ("The Art of Rhetoric," in *The English Works of Thomas Hobbes*, ed. Sir William Molesworth, II vols. [London: John Bohn, 1839–1845], 6; 463).

16. *Leviathan* ch. 18, p. 231.

17. Ibid. ch. 42, p. 527.

18. Hobbes's concept of "liberty" is not altogether clear. He defined it in at least three different ways: first (scoffingly), as "a liberty of everyone to govern himself" (p. 38), fulfilling people's desire "to do what they list" (p. 157); second (approvingly), as an arrangement giving people "their voice in the making of laws" (p. 34), such as the union which made the Scots "free" because it "gave them equal privilege with the English" (p. 172); and third (with dictatorial insistence that this is the one true meaning), as freedom from private power (p. 38)—men enjoy "liberty" when they enjoy "an exemption from the constraint and insolence of their neighbors" (p. 59).

19. The king had "the right of defending himself against those that had taken from him the sovereign power" (p. 108).

20. After first denouncing the common people as one of the "seducers" of the commonwealth (pp. 2, 4), Hobbes shifted to accusing them of being one of the commonwealth's "distempers" (p. 20). This is a switch from active to passive, from craft to disease, from player to played-with.

21. Ancient political works taught "a great many gentlemen" to love "pop-

ular government" (p. 23), even though such an arrangement would obviously damage their material interests. But why did Hobbes refer to Aristotle as a radical democrat who viewed all kings as ravenous beasts (p. 158)? The answer seems to be, first, that he cared less about what Aristotle actually wrote than about the ways he was then being read. Second, Aristotle viewed good monarchy as a utopian dream. He spoke favorably of participation and advocated a mixed constitution. Despite some tough criticisms, he also considered democracy to be the *best* of the bad forms of government. And third, Aristotle's "natural" morality (as opposed to a "conventional" morality based on the say-so of the sovereign) was a weapon any revolutionary could seize. Equally dangerous was his irresponsible use of that perilous smear word, *tyranny*.

22. People will fight for what they think England *is*. If they incorrectly believe it to be a *mixed monarchy*, they will fight on the wrong side, less for personal profit than from an irrational addiction to the perceived status quo—a motive Hobbes was willing to exploit, of course, when it redounded to the king's advantage.

23. *Leviathan*, ch. 18, p. 233.

24. Blaise Pascal, "Pensées," *Oeuvres complètes*, ed. Jacques Chevalier (Paris: Pléiade, 1954), p. 1129.

25. He also concluded that to govern human beings you must govern their opinions; and if you cannot do this by force or threat of force, you must find other means.

26. Francis Bacon, "Of Death," *The Essayes or Counsels, Civill and Morall*, ed. Michael Kiernan (Cambridge, Mass.: Harvard University Press, 1985), pp. 9–10.

27. Bacon, *The New Organon*, ed. Fulton Anderson (Indianapolis: Bobbs-Merrill, 1960), p. 52.

28. Pascal was no less sensitive to "la douceur de la gloire" than Bacon or Hobbes: "Nous perdons encore la vie avec joie pourvu qu'on en parle" (*Oeuvres complètes*, pp. 1128–29).

29. Bacon, "Of Death," *The Essayes*, p. 10.

30. The contrast between self-preservation and other motives appears in Hobbes's account of Ergamenes' anticlerical coup: he killed the priests "for the safety of his person," while they had killed his predecessors "out of ambition, or love of change" (p. 94). (See also n. 57.)

31. "The Art of Rhetoric," in *English Works*, 6: 464.

32. The bishops, he repeated elsewhere, faced "the envy of the Presbyterians" (p. 89).

33. Unlike other European nations, Hobbes's country swims freely in the ocean, "the dominion of the seas belonging to the English" (p. 176). England is an island, a naval power, a large ship, even a large fish—perhaps a Leviathan. Previously trapped by papal fishermen, "we broke out of their net in the time of Henry VIII" (pp. 43–44).

34. Hobbes expressed bewilderment at ethnic identification and cultural animosity: "I think they were mistaken, both English and Scots, in calling one another foreigners" (p. 35). Yet the identification of an individual with a group that may survive his or her death obviously helps solve the problem of mobilizing subjects to protect their protector (*Leviathan*, Review and Conclusion, pp. 718–19). As is well known, Hobbes opted for the implausible idea that dying in war is the wage subjects pay their sovereign for preserving their lives (ibid., ch. 30, p. 386). His entire approach prohibits any appeal to group loyalty. His aim, one

might even say, was to put the sting back into mortality by blocking the projection of individual identity onto the group. His individualism may have been partly formulated in opposition to an ethics of revenge that drove avengers to risk their lives for a larger and more enduring social unit.

35. He even claimed, reductionistically, that quarrels about opinions are actually quarrels "about who has the most learning" (p. 90)—a piquant assertion, given Hobbes's own outrageous vanity.

36. Public recollection of civil war presents a double problem. People tend to forget the horrors of civil war too quickly; they are therefore prone to relapse into insubordination (p. 39). But they also tend to harbor personal grudges too long, which is why Hobbes, despite his petulance against groups, carefully refrained from naming individual names (p. 117), thus sanitizing memories of the conflict in order to avoid rekindling quiescent hatreds. The state of nature may be an attempt to solve both problems at once, making quasi-permanent a *depersonalized memory* of civil war.

37. "The Art of Rhetoric," in *English Works*, 6: 475. One might also speculate on the contrary proclivity: the irrational tendency to love those whom we have helped, simply *because* we have helped them.

38. Similarly, Parliament's soldiers were driven partly by a desire for booty; but equally important was the irrational spite they felt toward flatterers, papists, and fortune-seekers (p. 110).

39. *Leviathan*, ch. 13, p. 185.

40. Hobbes expressed this point more euphemistically: "The unfortunateness of his marriages had so discountenanced his conversation with ladies, that the court could not be his proper element" (p. 112).

41. One of the peculiar characteristics of Hobbes's theory (in contrast, say, with Augustine's) is an assumption that the sovereign himself never seeks dominion. Needless to say, this premise is hard to reconcile with his general views about human nature.

42. B says, with some despair, "For aught I see, all the states of Christendom will be subject to these fits of rebellion, as long as the world lasteth" (p. 71). Christianity did not make Europeans more *moral* than the inhabitants of pagan antiquity (p. 63), only more prone to shed blood for religion.

43. Augustine, *The City of God*, trans. William Chase Greene, 7 vols. (Cambridge, Mass.: Harvard University Press, 1960), 5: 29.

44. Similarly, "our rebels were publicly taught rebellion in the pulpits" (p. 144).

45. In the same spirit: "I confess also, that considering what harm may proceed from a liberty that men have, upon every Sunday and oftener, to harangue all the people of a nation at one time, whilst the state is ignorant of what they will say; and that there is no such thing permitted in all the world out of Christendom, nor therefore any civil wars about religion; I have thought much preaching an inconvenience" (pp. 63–64).

46. Because the Presbyterians were the one dissenting group to survive as an active force into the 1660s, Hobbes may have somewhat magnified their role in the Civil War in order to discredit them politically.

47. "The most frequent prætext of Sedition, and Civill Warre, in Christian Common-wealths hath a long time proceeded from a difficulty, not yet sufficiently resolved, of obeying at once, both God and Man, then when their Commandements are one contrary to the other" (*Leviathan*, ch. 43, p. 609).

48. Hobbes had written suggestively that "the Independency of the Primitive Christians . . . is perhaps the best" (*Leviathan*, ch. 47, p. 711). Yet in *Behemoth* he took a radically antidisestablishmentarian line (p. 46). He made one positive reference to the Independents. The Rump "plucked out the sting of Presbytery" (p. 169) by voting liberty of conscience and this incapacitation of the Presbyterians was welcome. But, in general, he feared religious anarchy so much that he praised the pope's no-translation policy (p. 21), stated that the king should monopolize communication with God, and denounced the priesthood of all believers. He disliked a situation in which "every man became a judge of religion, and an interpreter of the Scriptures to himself" for the simple reason that private interpretation is "the cause of so many several sects" (p. 22). He wanted a near-total "subordination of the Church to the civil state in the things of Christ" (p. 172), to guarantee that the commands of God never conflict with the commands of the sovereign. Toleration spells chaos, a religious state of nature wherein people are "assured of their salvation by the testimony of their own private spirit, meaning the Holy Ghost dwelling within them" (p. 25).

49. *The Letters of Ambrose* (Oxford: James Parker and Co., 1881), p. 329.

50. The pope succeeded in the pernicious erosion of imperial authority only because the emperor had haughtily refused to "descend into the obscure and narrow mines" (p. 13) of Catholic theology, ignoring the indispensability of religion for the stability of political power.

51. Hobbes's specific charge is that the distinction between passive and active disobedience, set forth in *The Whole Duty of Man*, is a distinction without a difference, meant to distract from the quite seditious implications of Anglican theology, which outrageously justifies rebellion (pp. 47–50).

52. This is not merely a philosophical question but also a practical one, which, as is well known, plagued and eventually destroyed the Long Parliament (p. 109).

53. The two cardinal virtues in war, including civil war, are force and fraud (*Leviathan*, ch. 13, p. 188).

54. The "ultimate good is eternal life, and . . . the ultimate evil is eternal death" (Augustine, *City of God*, 6: 122).

55. Cited at *Leviathan*, ch. 43, p. 610.

56. Hobbes notoriously suggested that people fear invisible spirits more than death (*Leviathan*, ch. 29, p. 371). He also advanced the following pertinent but frequently neglected claim: *fear* is wired into human nature, but *the object of fear* is a variable, depending on individual constitution and education (ibid., Introduction, p. 83). It is the purpose of Hobbes's "science" to manipulate the object of fear, to reeducate people to dread violent death more than dishonor or damnation. If he were to succeed in this aim, he would have cut the root of civil war.

57. Physical violence can be used effectively *against* priests, of course. Having praised Henry VIII for his "nature quick and severe in the punishing of such as should be the first to oppose his designs" (p. 19), Hobbes offered Machiavellian advice to Charles II, encouraging him (although only by implication) to "fall upon" and "destroy" (p. 58) religious subversives, to cut them off as did Hercules the heads of Hydra (p. 73). A prince worth imitating is Ergamenes, the Ethiopian king educated in philosophy, who daringly murdered all the priests in his land. This was a cruel act, but one less cruel than letting them live (pp. 94–95). Hobbes concluded, on the same Machiavellian note, that it would have been

best for the English monarchs to have killed the one thousand or so Presbyterian ministers "before they had preached" (p. 95).

58. Power has numerous other sources as well, e.g., the possession of embarrassing information.

59. The pope's stupid decision to vex Henry VIII in his marriage designs (p. 19) is another good example of the self-destructiveness of "absolute" power.

60. *Leviathan*, ch. 19, p. 241.

61. Ibid., Epistle Dedicatory, p. 75.

62. That Hobbes did not fully integrate this insight into his theory is obvious. He presumably understood the factors that contributed to the outbreak of the Civil War. Yet he still defended the king's absolute right to levy as much money as he liked (*Leviathan*, ch. 30, p. 377).

63. Ibid., ch. 27, p. 339.

64. The set of requests that he may decently make, presumably, are limited by the norm of consistency as discussed above.

65. *Leviathan*, ch. 12, p. 169, emphasis added.

66. The seeds of religion, Hobbes said, "can never be so abolished out of humane nature, but that new Religions may againe be made to spring out of them" by ambitious cultivators (*Leviathan*, ch. 12, p. 179).

67. Hobbes suspended his usual hard-headedness when he optimistically suggested that the problem of social disorder can be solved "by mending the Universities" (p. 71). It seems that the entire course of human history can be permanently changed if the universities begin to teach "infallible rules . . . for the common people to take notice of" (p. 70). In politics, science is more important than native intelligence (p. 70, 159). Luckily, Hobbesian science is idiot-proof, and truth can never serve sinister ambitions (p. 96); that is, a good theory cannot be misused. These are extraordinary claims for a student of rhetorical manipulation to make.

68. Bacon, "Of Vaine-Glory," *The Essayes*, p. 161.

69. This magical transformation of the ethereal into the solid may have something to do with Hobbes's odd decision to describe sovereignty as the "Soul" of the commonwealth (*Leviathan*, Introduction, p. 81), even though, in the human case, he considered the soul a theological fiction.

70. In one well-known passage, he said that "the Religion of the Gentiles was part of their Policy" (*Leviathan*, ch. 12, p. 178). That is, "the peace of the Commonwealth" is enhanced by religious myths: "The first Founders, and Legislators of Common-wealths amongst the Gentiles, whose ends were only to keep the people in obedience, and peace, have in all places taken care; First, to imprint in their minds a beliefe, that those precepts which they gave concerning Religion, might not be thought to proceed from their own device, but from the dictates of some God, or other Spirit; or else that they themselves were of a higher nature than mere mortalls, that their Lawes might the more easily be received. . . . Secondly, they have had a care, to make it believed, that the same things were displeasing to the Gods, which were forbidden by the Lawes" (ibid., ch. 12, p. 177).

71. The beginnings of commonwealths can never be morally justified (*Leviathan*, Review and Conclusion, p. 722). What is true for foundation by conquest is equally true for foundation by religious deception.

72. Contrariwise, disagreement *among* religious authorities encourages dangerous moral autonomy among subjects.

73. Hobbes sometimes objected to this sort of guilt-inducement on humanistic grounds: "The Desires, and other Passions of man, are in themselves no Sin" (*Leviathan*, ch. 13, p. 187).

74. Hobbes approved of government by guilt, so long as this tactic is monopolized by the secular sovereign. People are "lesse apt to mutiny against their Governors" (*Leviathan*, ch. 12, p. 178) if they blame their misery on themselves. Fear of having neglected the gods apparently cripples subjects, making them feel recreant and unwilling to rebel.

75. They also provoke suspicions of rhetorical deception—as if Hobbes were trying to entice subjects into lawfulness by disguising the common good as a mere instrument of personal advantage.

76. For example, Richard Hooker, *Of the Laws of the Ecclesiastical Polity*, 2 vols. (London: Everyman's, 1969), 1: 192.

77. The first law of nature takes the unusual form of a *conditional imperative*, distinct from both the categorical and hypothetical imperatives described by Kant. Namely, *if* all others put down their weapons, *then* you must put down yours as well. More precisely, you must put down your weapons if *almost* everyone else does so too—and the state should then forcibly disarm the diehards. At what percentage of compliance, short of universal cooperation, the first law of nature becomes morally obligatory remains perhaps intentionally obscure in Hobbes's presentation of the argument. This self-exemption taboo or universalistic norm of fairness can be understood neither as a convention established on the say-so of the sovereign, nor as a subjective preference, nor as a mere maxim of prudence. The minority of diehards who pursue goals incompatible with peace, and who refuse the Hobbesian program of reeducation, must be exiled from the state or killed (*Leviathan*, ch. 15, p. 209; ch. 18, p. 232). To them, obviously enough, the first law of nature cannot possibly be a maxim of prudence. In any case, state-enforced cooperation will make not everyone, but only *almost* everyone, better off than they would have been under conditions of noncooperation. As a consequence, Hobbes's theory is not universalist, but supermajoritarian.

78. Arthur Bentley, *The Process of Government* (Bloomington, Ind.: Principia, 1935), p. 361.

8

Hobbes and Locke on Toleration

Richard Tuck

Ever since Peter Laslett published his edition of Locke's *Two Treatises of Government* in 1960, it has been customary to follow his lead and to suppose that there is little of historical interest to be found in a comparison of Hobbes and Locke. Laslett argued that the *Two Treatises* were written in 1680, as a contribution to the exclusion debate, and that Locke's actual as well as ostensible target in both treatises was Sir Robert Filmer and not, as had sometimes been supposed by earlier writers, Hobbes. Locke, Laslett observed, did not even have in his possession a copy of *Leviathan* when he wrote the treatises; and though Hobbesian ideas may have been part of the general intellectual air that Locke breathed, his object in writing the work was utterly different from Hobbes's object in writing *Leviathan*. Laslett summed up this difference by saying that the *Two Treatises* "contained just that ingredient which *Leviathan* lacked—policy; statement of guidance of what men will accept, respond to and pursue, of the limits of their loyalty and the possible extent of generalization about their behaviour."[1] Hobbes, Laslett believed, was a political rationalist, concerned to produce a complete philosophical system with political implications, while Locke deliberately separated the *Two Treatises* from his own philosophical works and sought to appeal to a wider audience than the one that would have understood and appreciated his *Essay*.

Though scholarship on both Locke and Hobbes has moved on since 1960, there has been no attempt yet properly to revise Laslett's views in this area. Since the work of writers such as James Tully in the late 1970s,[2] we have grown more used to situating Locke in the intellectual context in which such European contemporaries as Jean Barbeyrac unhesitatingly placed him—the "modern" school of natural law founded by Hugo Grotius, a school in which they also placed Hobbes. But the relationship between Hobbes and Locke within this tradition is complex and involves issues which, as Laslett recognized, are far removed from many of the particular political matters with which Locke was concerned in 1680. The belief that Hobbes and Locke were concerned in their political writings with different *policy* issues would, I think, still command assent from most scholars. It is, however, this belief that I want to call into question and to replace with the suggestion that the actual politics of Hobbes and Locke during the 1660s and 1670s were much closer than has ever been properly recognized. There is an exception to this, namely, the works by Mark Goldie and John Marshall on Restoration political thought[3]; but even there, I shall suggest, the true character of both Hobbes's and Locke's politics has been misunderstood.

An appropriate starting-point is the record of what was probably the closest encounter between the two men. In February 1673 John Aubrey (the author of *Brief Lives* and a close friend of Hobbes) wrote to Locke as follows:

> I cannot but present you my thanks for your great Humanity and kindnes to me; as also for the honour you doe me to peruse my Scriblings. I was at your lodgeing twice to have kiss't your hands before I came out of Towne—to have recommended a MSS or two (worthy of your perusall) of my old friend Mr Th: Hobbes. One is a Treatise concerning the Lawe, which I importun'd him to undertake about 8 yeares since. . . . In this treatise he is highly for the Kings Prerogative. Oh: Just: Hales haz read it, and very much mislikes it; is his enemy and will not license it. Judge Vaughan haz perusd it and very much commends it, but is afrayd to license for feare of giving displeasure. . . . When you goe by the Palsgrave-head Taverne be pleasd to call on mr W: Crooke at the green dragon and remember me to him . . . and he will shew it to you. I have a conceit that if your Lord sawe it he would like it. You may see likewise his History of England from 1640 to 1660 about a quire of paper, which the King haz read and likes extremely, but tells him there is so much truth in it he dares not license for feare of displeasing the Bishops. The old gent is still strangely vigorous (85) if you see him

(which he would take kindly) pray my service to him. God graunt length of dayes to our Illustrious Lord Chancellor, who seriously deserves a Statue for the good he haz already begin.[4]

We do not know if Locke actually called on Hobbes, who was then living at Little Salisbury House in London. But Aubrey's letter reveals a clear expectation that both Locke and Locke's patron the earl of Shaftesbury (the Lord Chancellor) would approve of the two manuscripts which were available at Crooke's, Hobbes's publishers. (The manuscripts referred to were those known later as *A Dialogue of the Common Laws of England* and *Behemoth*.) So the first question to ask about the relationship between Hobbes and Locke is, why should a well-informed observer like Aubrey have believed that the two men would sympathize with one another's views in February 1673—only seven years before Locke wrote the *Two Treatises*?

To answer this question, we first need to understand the character of the government which was in power at the time, of which Shaftesbury was a leading member and for which Locke worked. This was the government known subsequently as the "Cabal," an acronym for the five leading ministers—Clifford, Arlington, Buckingham, Ashley Cooper (i.e., Shaftesbury), and Lauderdale. The Cabal ministers came to power in November 1667, after the impeachment of the earl of Clarendon. They had all enjoyed government office before Clarendon's fall, but from 1667 until 1673, they were able to act as a reasonably cohesive group with a number of common policies, foremost among which was the intention of modifying the religious settlement arrived at after the Restoration.

That settlement was always associated with Clarendon and was indeed termed the "Clarendon Code," though Clarendon himself may not originally have wanted such a resolutely Anglican set of measures. Leaving aside the more limited Corporation Act of 1661, the code fell in effect into two sections, separate both in character and date. The first section was the Act of Uniformity of 1662, which essentially reconstituted the Church of England on the basis of the old Book of Common Prayer and which removed from their livings any clergymen who would not declare their assent to "all and everything" contained in the prayer book. This act left ejected clergymen, and indeed all other people, free to preach and to gather to worship outside the ancient parish churches of England. In this respect, it was no more intolerant than the ecclesiastical order in England today; indeed, the act has never been repealed in its entirety.

More important from the point of view of all political theorists were the acts in the second section, the Conventicle Act of August 1664 and the Five Mile Act of October 1665. The former proscribed all unauthorized meetings for the purpose of religious worship ("conventicles") by more than four people (apart from a household), while the latter forbade anyone found guilty of preaching in a conventicle from coming within five miles of a corporate town. These were the truly persecutory statutes, reminiscent of laws passed against dissenters by all intolerant regimes. But (though historians have virtually never remarked on this) the acts had a built-in time limit, for the Conventicle Act laid down that "this Act shall continue in force for Three yeares after the end of this present Session of Parliament, and from thence forward to the end of the next Session of Parliament after the said Three yeares and noe longer" (16 Car. 2, c. 4., art. 20). Its expiry would clearly also nullify the Five Mile Act, since that drew its force from the proscription of conventicles. "This present Session" ended on 20 August 1664, so after that date the act was virtually a dead letter unless it could be renewed in the course of the next session of Parliament. Again, by providing for an expiry date, the acts suggest those types of modern legislation that have taken away civil liberties in the face of considerable public protest.

This time limit meant that Clarendon was ousted at just the moment when the question of toleration was once again urgently on the political agenda. If the act simply died, then England would have no repressive legislation about religion on the statute books, for all prewar measures enforcing religious uniformity on the *population* (as distinct from the beneficed clergy) had been rescinded. The medieval laws against heresy had been repealed at the Reformation, and High Commission, the executive device used by Queen Elizabeth and her successors to discipline the lay population in religious matters, had been abolished by the Long Parliament and not revived at the Restoration. New statutes had thus to be passed if the Anglican hegemony was to be maintained.

Hard-line Anglicans wanted the Conventicle Act renewed and, if possible, strengthened, to force the population as a whole into a church defined by the existing Act of Uniformity. More moderate Anglicans, and most Presbyterians, wanted "comprehension"; that is, a looser Act of Uniformity which would readmit Presbyterians to the national church but which would not necessarily imply any toleration for the more radical sects such as Quakers or Baptists (or Catholics). The Presbyterians, heirs to the prewar English Calvinists, wanted to establish something like Calvinist church government, with its policing of lay religion and morals, within the interstices of a broadened Church of England. The comprehension scheme put before Parliament in October 1667 would have defined the doctrine of the church (in terms originally laid down in a statute of Elizabeth I) as the articles agreed upon in the first four councils of the primitive Church—thus excluding Socinians and other "heretics." Many of the supporters of comprehension were enthusiastic advocates of persecution for such heresies.[5]

On the other hand, former Independents and other theological radicals from the Civil War years, who had seen their dreams of congregational church government triumph in 1649 and fade in 1660, wanted toleration and were not particularly concerned with how exclusive the Church of England made itself, as long as it did not exclude other churches from the national life. The Independents, therefore, alone of the three great religious groupings, would have been happy to let the Conventicle Act expire and to pass no new legislation, for they alone had no desire to discipline the general population in religious matters. It was to the debate about these new statutes, and what form (if any) they should take, that Hobbes and Locke made remarkably similar contributions, in the shape of unpublished advice to ministers of Charles II urging (in effect) the Independent point of view.

Hobbes himself fell victim to the first attempt by the antitolerationist members of the House of Commons to supplement the Conventicle Act with something stronger and more lasting. In October 1666, as part of the hysteria after the Great Fire of London, a bill was introduced against "Atheism and Prophanity," which was discussed in both houses down to the prorogation of Parliament in February 1667. The bill was revived in a stronger form during the next session, in October 1667, when it was discussed on and off (principally in the House of Lords) until finally being dropped in August 1668. Hobbes himself was caught up in these discussions after the Commons' committee considering the bill was empowered on 17 October 1666 to collect information specifically about *Leviathan*; he was also summoned before a committee of the House of Lords in 1667. In its stronger version, the bill would have made the following punishable by imprisonment or banishment: the denial of "the essence, powers or attributes of God the Father, Son or Holy Ghost, given to them in Scripture, or the omnipotency, wisdom, justice, mercy, goodness or providence of God in the Creation, Redemption or Governance of the world"; the denial of "the divine authority of any of the canonical books contained in the Old and New Testaments, received in the Church of England"; and the denial of "the immortality of men's

souls, the resurrection of the body, and the eternal rewards in
Heaven or eternal terments in Hell."[6] Almost all of these were opinions that Hobbes apparently held in *Leviathan*.

Much more than atheism was thus proscribed: All religious beliefs other than those of orthodox Trinitarian Christianity would
have been made criminal offenses (including Judaism and Islam as
well as Christian heresies such as Socinianism and other unitarian
doctrines). Compared with that proposal, the Conventicle and Five
Mile Acts paled into some insignificance. Moreover, the bill kept being reintroduced; when in February 1674 a bill for comprehension of
Anglicans and Protestant dissenters was introduced into the House
of Lords, it incorporated a reworking of the 1667–68 proposal—a neat
illustration of how comprehension and toleration might pull in very
different directions. Although the new bill failed at the prorogation
later that month, the 1667–68 proposal reappeared in November
1675, failed again at a prorogation in January 1678, and made a last
appearance in December 1680, to disappear once more at the prorogation of January 1681. So the goal of an intolerant, orthodoxly
Christian regime was kept constantly before the public gaze from
1666 to 1681.[7]

Aubrey recorded in his life of Hobbes that "there was a report
(and surely true) that in Parliament, not long after the King was
setled, some of the Bishops made a Motion to have the good old
Gentleman burn't for a Heretique."[8] This is probably a garbled
memory of the fact that the 1674 and 1675 bills were referred by the
House of Lords to a subcommittee composed of the bishops, but it
also illustrates that the church authorities were in general very keen
on the bills. Indeed, despite the fact that none of the bills actually
became law, the ecclesiastical authorities were prepared to behave as
if they had been carried. Thus at Cambridge in March 1668 a Fellow
of Corpus, Daniel Scargill, was deprived of his fellowship and
ejected from the university for holding "Hobbist" opinions. Although he made a famous recantation the following year, he was
never readmitted to his fellowship.[9]

The struggle over the atheism bills and his own involvement in
Parliament's proceedings gave Hobbes a most unpleasant shock,
which colored the rest of his life and forced him into a remarkable
burst of writing. The first product was probably the *Dialogue of the
Common Laws*, which (as we saw earlier) Aubrey told Locke he had
asked Hobbes to write "about eight years" before 1673. About half
the book is concerned specifically with the English law on heresy,
and it is likely that Hobbes in fact composed it in 1666 rather than

1665.[10] Sir Edward Coke, the great early seventeenth-century lawyer, was the prime butt of this book, largely because he had expressed the opinion in 1612 that there was a common law offense of heresy[11]; Hobbes replied by showing that the common law could not be of such a character that it could contain a law against heresy and that the repeal of the old statutes left no such law in force.

In addition to the *Dialogue*, Hobbes published in 1668 at Amsterdam a collection of his Latin works with a Latin translation of *Leviathan*, to which were appended some extensive notes on heresy. During that same year, he wrote *An Historical Narration concerning Heresy* as well as a defense of Scargill; before the end of 1670, he had composed *Behemoth*, in which the theme of heresy also bulks large.[12] In addition, he probably composed during these years the note on heresy that Samuel Mintz published from a Chatsworth manuscript in 1968,[13] and he is also likely to have written his verse *Historia Ecclesiastica* at about this time. So between 1666 and 1670 Hobbes wrote seven works, two of which (the *Dialogue* and *Behemoth*) were quite substantial: an astonishing achievement for a man who was seventy-eight in 1666 and a testimony to the terror into which he was plunged by the events of 1666-68.

These works were not written simply as a defense of himself against Parliament: *Behemoth* was dedicated to Lord Arlington, one of the Cabal ministers, who had intervened on Hobbes's behalf when he was summoned before the House of Lords. Hobbes also sent him the *Historical Narration* for his comment.[14] Hobbes clearly intended his views to be used in the political debates of 1666-70 about toleration, and indeed Edward Seymour (a strong supporter of toleration and opponent of comprehension) quoted Hobbes in support of his position in a debate of March 1668. Seymour's position, indeed, was probably very close politically to Hobbes: He opposed comprehension because he saw it as bringing into power an association of Presbyterians and Anglicans, the two most intellectually intolerant groups. He remarked of the comprehension proposal that "three Presbyterians did endeavour to be three bishops" and that instead "he would have every man to wear his coat after his own fancy."[15] Hobbes's arguments about the law of heresy in the *Dialogue*, moreover, seem to have influenced the judges. Asked for their opinion by the House of Lords committee considering the atheism bill in April 1668, they ruled that matters of this kind were not "of temporal cognizance."[16] It was presumably on this occasion that Hale and Vaughan read the *Dialogue*.

At the heart of all these works by Hobbes of 1666-70 were two claims, one explicit and the other implicit but nevertheless clear enough. The former was that there was currently no law against heresy or the public enunciation of heterodox opinion in England, and the latter was that there should not be. As he said in the *Dialogue*, "At this day there is neither Statute, nor any Law to punish Doctrine, but the ordinary Power Ecclesiastical, and that according to the Canons of the Church of *England*, only Authorized by the King."[17] The "Power ecclesiastical," given the demise of High Commission, could be exercised only on beneficed clergy of the Church of England; and though laymen could be excommunicated by church courts for a wide range of moral offenses, the only consequential civil penalties would be such things as loss of municipal office rather than criminal sanctions.

The obvious questions arising from these claims are, what did Hobbes understand by "heresy," and why did he hold that it should in general go unpunished by the civil sovereign? To answer fully requires at least a summary account of Hobbes's earlier views about authority in religious matters—views which were less straightforward than has often seemed to be the case.

All that Hobbes had to say about religion in his major works took place against the background of a fundamental distinction between "faith" and "reason." Reason was the province of the philosopher, and only those propositions which were beyond dispute could be admitted into it. One of these propositions, Hobbes believed, was that the world has had a first cause: Something started the mechanical processes which have continued down to our own time, but we can in principle know nothing whatsoever about what it was that did so, nor can we meaningfully predicate anything of it. Philosophically speaking, this is what "God" means: "By the word *God* is to be understood *the cause of the world*" (*De Cive*, chap. 15, sec. 14).[18] Nevertheless, if we believe that we owe our existence to such a first cause, it is natural, Hobbes argued, to honor it in some way, for such a cause must be more powerful than anything we can possibly imagine and has ultimately given us life itself. So there is a natural religion, consisting essentially in the worship of the first cause but finding expression in all the practices which men customarily use to honor whatever they take to be supremely good and powerful. This natural religion is described in some detail in chapter 15 of *De Cive* and with rather less detail in chapter 31 of *Leviathan*. Hobbes's ideas about it belonged broadly to the same tradition as Grotius's in *De Veritate Religionis Christianae* and Edward Lord Herbert's in his *De Veritate* and *De Religione Gentilium*.

Also like Grotius, Hobbes did not believe that the natural rationality of religion implied that an atheist could not grasp the laws of nature which constitute moral conduct. An atheist was like an incompetent mathematician who had failed to see something that was clearly true in a mathematical proof; however, such incompetence in a particular case did not imply that the person concerned would be ignorant of or would deny the force of the general laws of nature. Hobbes made precisely this point in one of his explanatory footnotes to the second edition of *De Cive* in 1647 (chap. 14, sec. 19), and he went on to argue that any punishment of an atheist is justifiably performed in the first instance by God, on the grounds that the atheist is an enemy to God, and only in the second instance by a civil magistrate acting in effect on behalf of God. He was always careful to avoid saying that an atheist should be punished because (for example) he would not keep his contracts; in the Latin *Leviathan*, he argued that "it is essential to every commonwealth [*civitas*] that contracts are kept, especially if they are confirmed by oaths. Since an atheist cannot be bound by an oath, he should be banished from the republic, not as a criminal, but as a danger to the public" (p. 352).[19] What is striking about this passage is that it was the *oath* and not the *contract* which the atheist could not be bound by; it is also worth noting that earlier in the work, he had denied that oaths add anything to the force of contracts. Only when the existence of God is *expressly* an issue of political importance (as in the maintenance of the system of natural religion, or as in the case of oaths) might an atheist appear to be a danger to the public.

Hobbes believed that this natural religion was the basis of the particular and local religions of all human societies but that those local peculiarities must be seen as purely a matter of *faith*. The truths of Christianity (other than the initial proposition that there is a God) fell into this category, and Hobbes devoted much intellectual effort to explaining the relationship between Christian faith and natural reason in the political and ethical spheres. It was in this area that one of the most significant changes occurred in his thought between his first two books on politics and *Leviathan*.

In all three books, Hobbes argued that Christianity depends upon a faith that the Scriptures, which record the doings of Christ and his prophets, are true—a faith for which there can be no natural evidence. Because the Scriptures are a text, they require interpretation, so the actual content of Christianity is determined exclusively by the interpretations given to the text. Whose interpretations are authoritative is thus a crucial question for establishing the very being of the religion. In the *Elements of Law* and *De Cive*, Hobbes gave a different answer to this question from the one he gave in *Leviathan*. His early views are set out most clearly in *De Cive*; in the context of the Christian religion,

> to decide questions of faith, that is, *about God*, which are beyond human capacity, we need a divine blessing derived from CHRIST himself through the *laying-on of hands*, in order to prevent us going wrong at least on necessary points. Since we are tied to a supernatural doctrine if we are to gain eternal salvation (a doctrine which can consequently not be understood), it would contradict equity if we were to be left to go wrong on these points. Our Saviour promised this *Infallibility* (in things which are necessary to salvation) to the *Apostles* until the Day of Judgement; that is, to the *Apostles* and the *Pastors* succeeding the Apostles and consecrated by the *laying-on of hands*. So the sovereign over the commonwealth [*civitas*] is obliged, insofar as he is a Christian, to interpret the Holy Scriptures (when any question is raised about the *mysteries of faith*) through properly-ordained *Clergymen*. (chap. 17, sec. 28)

Hobbes went on in the next chapter to answer the doubts of those who were uncertain that what the sovereign and the church said was *in fact* true. Citizens "know what Kings and a Church assembly [*ecclesia congregata*] command, but they do not know whether *what* they command is against the commands of God" (chap. 18, sec. 1). His answer was that there is only one instruction from God which is indubitably contained in the Scriptures and which therefore no interpretation of prince or church can contravene, namely, that "Jesus is the Christ"—that the belief that Jesus existed and has a special role in the history of man's relations with God will in itself ensure salvation. It is important to stress that the purpose of this minimal Christianity for Hobbes was to reassure citizens that they would have no adequate grounds for questioning whatever interpretation, more or less, of Scripture was offered to them by the church through the prince. Its purpose was not to suggest that this was *all* that the citizens should in fact believe.

Thus Hobbes in these early works was a reasonably orthodox Anglican. The actual content of our Christianity is to be determined by the Apostolic Church, and unless that church abandons the notion that Jesus is the Christ, its doctrines will be intellectually binding. The sovereign (if he is a Christian) must promulgate the doctrine established by the church, and if he is not a Christian, his Christian subjects must turn to their church alone as the source of authoritative interpretation (cf. *De Cive*, chap. 18, sec. 13). All the Christian heresies outlawed by the Apostolic Church were thus rightly outlawed, and only the creed laboriously constructed during the first centuries of Christianity and formulated finally at Nicea contained authentic doctrine. Hobbes had some slight trouble at this point fitting his general materialist metaphysics into the Nicene Creed and Scripture. However, in the *Elements* (where the matter is most fully discussed), he argued that there was no commitment laid upon orthodox Christians to believe in the *immateriality* of the soul, only its *immortality* ("The Resurrection of the dead, And the life of the world to come" being the final words of the Nicene Creed). And the immortality of the soul is then duly asserted as an article of Christian faith (*Elements*, pt. 1, chap. 2, sec. 5).[20]

All this changes in *Leviathan*, and the change was the principal occasion for the hostility harbored toward Hobbes after 1651 by many Anglicans who had been his close friends earlier and who had admired his first books. In *Leviathan*, as is well known, Hobbes handed the sole power of interpreting Scripture over to the civil sovereign, and he went into some detail to show that the apostolic succession through the laying-on of hands was of no particular significance. The *ecclesia congregata* ceased to have any distinctive role in the elaboration of doctrine, and by a natural consequence, the doctrines which it had elaborated over the centuries as Christian orthodoxy ceased to have any special purchase upon the Christian citizen. It remained true that the defining characteristic of a Christian was the belief that Jesus is the Christ; but all other beliefs were now to be determined solely by the civil law of the Christian's commonwealth.

In principle, that law could simply restate the Nicene Creed as the public doctrine of the commonwealth, but Hobbes emphasized in chapter 47 of *Leviathan* that orthodox Christianity had been bound up with a particular ecclesiastical history, in which power over opinion had gradually come to be concentrated in the papacy. The overthrowing of such power meant that there was no particular reason for the doctrines historically associated only with one tradition of Christianity to be imposed upon an entire population. In the most passionate defense of toleration to be found in the book, he praised the decentralized ecclesiastical order of the new republic in England:

So we are reduced to the Independency of the Primitive Christians to follow Paul, or Cephas, or Apollos, every man as he liketh best: Which, if it be without contention, and without measuring the Doctrine of Christ, by our affection to the Person of his Minister, (the fault which the Apostle reprehended in the Corinthians,) is perhaps the best: First because there ought to be no Power over the Consciences of men, but of the Word it selfe, working Faith in every one, not alwayes according to the purpose of them that Plant and Water, but of God himself, that giveth the Increase; and secondly, because it is unreasonable in them, who teach there is such danger in every little Errour, to require of a man endued with Reason of his own, to follow the Reason of any other man, or of the most voices of many other men; Which is little better, then to venture his Salvation at crosse and pile. Nor ought those Teachers to be displeased with this losse of their ancient Authority: For there is none should know better then they, that power is preserved by the same Vertues by which it is acquired; that is to say, by Wisdome, Humility, Clearnesse of Doctrine, and sincerity of Conversation; and not by suppression of the Naturall Sciences, and of the Morality of Natural Reason. (English *Leviathan*, p. 711)

In the Latin *Leviathan*, this tactless defense of Independency was eliminated, and the Restoration praised, but with no explicit reference to the ecclesiastical settlement. In chapter 2 of the appendix, moreover, Hobbes went into some detail to illustrate that since the Restoration there had been no laws prescribing any particular Christian doctrine and especially the Nicene Creed. In the dialogue form of the appendix, B utters Hobbes's own views:

A. Surely the fact that the Creed is published in the Common Prayer Book is a sufficient enactment of a law against heresy?
B. Yes, if it had been written into the law. But there is no mention in the law of the Nicene Creed.[21]

Chapter 1 of the appendix examined the creed itself and concluded that "what the Fathers say outside the Holy Scriptures as particular explanations of their Faith does not oblige Christians."[22] The particular stumbling block in the creed was now its declaration of faith in the immortality of the soul: In both the English and Latin editions of *Leviathan*, Hobbes insisted that the soul was not only corporeal but also mortal and that any other view could not be squared with his a priori metaphysics. He also cast doubt on the Trinity, both by denying the possibility of a Holy Ghost or Spirit and by asserting that Christ was the same person as God only in the sense in which Moses was also: "Our saviour therefore, both in Teaching, and Reigning, representeth (as Moses did) the Person of God; which God from that time forward, but not before, is called the Father; and being still one and the same substance, is one person as represented by Moses, and another Person as represented by his Sonne the Christ" (English *Leviathan*, p. 520). Effectively, therefore, Hobbes had declared himself both an Arian and a mortalist, each a heresy denounced by the early church.

It is important to stress that the idea that the civil law will in general be tolerant arises naturally, not just from this history but also from Hobbes's fundamental theory. As he repeatedly said, our natural right is to use our own judgment about what will *preserve* ourselves, not to do anything which we might just *want* to do. In the note to *De Cive*, chapter 3, section 27, he gave as examples of things we might choose to do in the state of nature, but would have no *right* to do, "drunkenness" and "cruelty" (i.e., "revenge which does not have a future good as its object"). By the same token, what we transfer to the sovereign is the right to exercise judgment about what will preserve us (at least in cases where there may be some dispute; in other cases, such as when we are being directly and indubitably attacked, we retain the right to use our own judgment). Consequently, the sovereign has no right to do anything unless he sincerely believes that it will conduce to the preservation of his subjects and himself. It is true, of course, that if he acts without right his subjects have no right to resist him, unless their survival is at stake; but Hobbes was primarily concerned with delineating the *rights* of the sovereign and the citizen, and not with considering what might happen if either acted without right. (His view here seems to have been, as he said in *Leviathan* chapter 31, that the "Negligent government of Princes" leads to rebellion, and rebellion to "Slaughter.")

It follows that the sovereign would have no right to impose doctrines on his citizens unless he sincerely believed that doing so would preserve them; and, Hobbes implied, it was highly unlikely that such circumstances would arise. It is because the sovereign has this constricted responsibility, compared with the unlimited power of a church to decide dogma, that *Leviathan* is a defense of toleration, and *De Cive* a defense of religious repression. All that a Christian sovereign was likely to impose upon his subjects was the doctrine which defined Christianity—namely, Jesus is the Christ—but even that imposition cannot be straightforwardly extracted from the theory of *Leviathan*, except by way of natural religion. In chapter 31 Hobbes repeated what he had said in *De Cive* about the natural religion and also repeated something he had said there about the need for uniformity of worship: It was this, and this alone, that gave a general justification for a sovereign's imposing any religious views on his subjects whatsoever (though particular justifications, arising from what the sovereign believed in particular cases about the political necessities of the situation, were always possible).

The reason for this dramatic change in Hobbes's ideas between 1647 and 1650 (when news of what he was doing leaked out to disconcerted friends) puzzled contemporaries, and they resorted to explanations based on Hobbes's rough handling by the Anglican divines at the exile court of St. Germains.[23] There may have been some truth in that, but it is more likely that Hobbes both saw the inconsistency of his earlier theory and welcomed the new ecclesiastical regime in England. *De Cive*'s anomaly that the church could have a right of interpretation independent of the civil sovereign was fairly obvious, and *Leviathan* presented a much more integrated theory.

We can now see why Hobbes was so anxious about the question of heresy in 1666–70, and what kind of laws on religion he envisaged. There is nothing in his writings to suggest that he favored comprehension on the basis of the Nicene Creed (the same basis proposed for the comprehensive church in 1667–68), and much to suggest that he would have been bitterly opposed to it. For this reason, I think that Mark Goldie's or John Marshall's assimilation of Hobbes to the "latitudinarian" Anglicans who wanted comprehension is misleading, at least if it is Hobbes the author of *Leviathan* who is under consideration.[24] Hobbes the author of *De Cive*, on the other hand, *was* a plausible champion of comprehension, for the theory of *De Cive* implied that the body of clergymen who had been apostolically ordained should "congregate" to decide church doctrine—and that body included many ministers who had been excluded under the Act of Uniformity (and would have included still more had the 1667–68 comprehension bill been passed). It is therefore no accident that Edward Stillingfleet, one of the great latitudinarians, who advocated comprehension but firmly opposed toleration, should have drawn on *De Cive*.[25] It was their use of this aspect of Hobbes which led to the latitudinarians often being branded "Hobbists." Anglican use of *De Cive* rather than *Leviathan* should come as no surprise; as we have seen, it was a book read with appreciation by Anglicans at the time it was written, and it was only *Leviathan* that led to the breach between Hobbes and his old friends.

The advice Hobbes gave to Arlington and the other Cabal ministers in 1667–70 was thus to not pursue comprehension within a framework in which other more obviously heretical opinions were persecuted (the only framework, in general, which made comprehension a position distinct from toleration). In other words, he appeared as a radical tolerationist, a fact recognized by contemporaries. The Anglican Samuel Parker, writing in 1669, attacked "the Consequences that some men draw from Mr. Hobs's Principles in behalf of Liberty of Conscience."[26] In this respect he was identical to Locke, who was then writing advice for another Cabal minister.

Locke's position on toleration is far better known than Hobbes's, but it is worth emphasizing that the views of both Locke and Ashley Cooper in 1667–69 were that the Conventicle Act should not be renewed and that there should be no further legislation on religious matters. In his essay on toleration which he wrote in 1667, Locke assumed throughout that there was *not* doctrinal uniformity in the English nation, and he argued against those who thought that it ought to be "restored."[27] The beliefs that (in his opinion) ought to be tolerated extended well beyond those that would have been permitted within a comprehensive church and included all the matters with which Hobbes had been concerned. Locke even praised the Japanese, except with regard to their persecution of Christians; and even that persecution, he claimed,

> was not to set up uniformity in religion (for they tolerate seven or eight sects, and some so different as is the belief of the mortality or immortality of the soul; nor is the magistrate at all curious or inquisitive what sect his subjects are of, or does in the least force them to his religion), nor any aversion to Christianity, which they suffered a good while quietly to grow up among them, till the doctrine of popish priests gave them jealousy that religion was but their pretence, but empire their design, and made them fear the subversion of their state.[28]

Locke after all shared that same fear about the Roman Catholic priesthood.

Locke had long believed that the magistrate could if *politically* necessary outlaw any doctrine or practice, other than the fundamental worship of God. (This was the theme of his early, apparently antitolerationist writings, christened by Philip Abrams the "two tracts." He differed from Hobbes in this area only on one issue, and that issue had at this time little practical significance. Locke never believed that the test of whether a sovereign was right in promulgating laws is his *sincerity* in judging that the laws would preserve his citizens; he always believed that it is possible to argue about the reasonableness of any policy and to convict the sovereign of a mistake in his judgment. But in practice (at least in the 1660s) this distinction obviously amounted to little, for both Hobbes and Locke were at that time addressing the sovereign, urging him *not* to believe that such measures as the atheism bill were necessary for the preservation of his people. Moreover, the sovereign was prepared to listen to them and in most respects agreed with them; not until King Charles's treachery (as it seemed to Ashley Cooper and Locke) in yielding to Anglican pressure and allowing the Test Act to be passed on the fall of the Cabal in 1673 did the sovereign commit himself to an exclusively Anglican order. Furthermore, in 1667 Locke, like Hobbes, argued that if the sovereign *did* act outside his rights and enforce unnecessary doctrines upon his people, then the citizens must submit and not resist, even at the cost of their own life or property: "Certainly he is a hypocrite, and only pretends conscience, and aims at something else in this world, who will not, by obeying his conscience and submitting also to the law, purchase heaven for himself and peace for his country, though at the rate of his estate, liberty, or life itself."[29]

We can now see more clearly why early in 1673 John Aubrey should have supposed that Locke would be interested in reading Hobbes's *Dialogue* and *Behemoth* and in meeting their author. Even the discussion of prerogative in the former work would not have repelled Locke, for in 1672 he had drafted for Shaftesbury a justification of Charles II's Declaration of Indulgence toward dissenters. Despite some theoretical differences, their *policies* (to return to Laslett's distinction and terminology) were virtually identical. Sixteen seventy-three was probably the last time that was true; as the 1670s progressed, Locke became increasingly willing to espouse theories of resistance, which were on the face of it far removed from the ideas of *Leviathan*, and to believe that a sovereign could be *forced* by his subjects to introduce toleration. Toleration remained absolutely central to his thought: It is now clear that the *Two Treatises* were composed at the same time as a lengthy attack on Stillingfleet's proposals for comprehension without toleration.[30]

But even during the Exclusion Crisis of 1679–81, it is striking how far Hobbes and Locke could agree politically. The Whigs in the crisis wanted Parliament to pass an act excluding Charles's brother the Duke of York from the throne. The eldest son of the Earl of Devonshire, in whose household Hobbes lived, was a member of the 1679 Parliament and took the side of exclusion. (He later helped the prince of Orange and was rewarded with the dukedom of Devonshire.) Among the Hobbes papers at Chatsworth is a manuscript (originally published by Quentin Skinner), discussing the question of whether the legitimate heir to a king can be excluded by the current sovereign and answering in the affirmative (with the proviso that the sovereign cannot be *forced* to do so).[31] This was precisely what the Whig exclusionists in 1679 were trying to arrange through a bill in Parliament, and this short note must be reckoned Hobbes's contribution to the exclusion debate, as well as his last piece of political writing. Once again, he was politically on the same side as Locke.

Leviathan was a book that sought to persuade its readers of two things: First, that there was no source of moral or religious judgment in a commonwealth independent of the sovereign; and second, that the very lack of such a source implied toleration. Each aspect of the book was argued for with power and imagination, and it is hard when reading it to know exactly how Hobbes would have reacted to the spectacle of a sovereign seeking to enforce upon his subjects doctrines thought up by, and of importance only to, one particular church. This was the issue with which Locke had to grapple after 1673, and coping with it led him into a theory which appears very different from that of *Leviathan*. In particular, he had to abandon the belief he had shared with Hobbes—that the absence of right on the part of a sovereign does not imply a right to resist on the part of a subject. Rather, the need to protect the principle of toleration from the attacks by Anglicans or Presbyterians turned out to be paramount in Locke's thought. A precisely similar trajectory can be traced in the career of Henry Stubbe, who had been a friend of Locke's at both school and college and a protégé of Hobbes's in the 1650s when he began to translate *Leviathan* into Latin.[32] Considering Hobbes's own experiences at the hands of those two religious groups, it is tempting to suspect that he might have undergone a similar transformation, had he been as close to the issues of the 1670s as Locke. Locke's reticence on the subject of Hobbes in the *Two Treatises* is far less surprising seen in this light: Why should he have attacked someone who in many respects had been his ally in the struggle for toleration?

NOTES

1. John Locke, *Two Treatises of Government*, ed. Peter Laslett (Cambridge: Cambridge University Press, 1960), p. 104.

2. James Tully, *A Discourse on Property* (Cambridge: Cambridge University Press, 1980).

3. Mark Goldie, "John Locke and Anglican Royalism," *Political Studies* 31 (1983): 86–102; idem, "Sir Peter Pett, Sceptical Toryism and the Science of Toleration in the 1680s," in *Persecution and Toleration*, Studies in Church History Vol. 21, ed. W. J. Scheils (Oxford: Basil Blackwell, 1984), pp. 247–73; idem; "The Civil Religion of James Harrington," in *The Languages of Political Theory in Early-Modern Europe*, ed Anthony Pagden (Cambridge: Cambridge University Press, 1987), pp. 197–222; John Marshall, "The Ecclesiology of the Latitude-men 1660–1689: Stillingfleet, Tillotson and Hobbism," *Journal of Ecclesiastical History* 36 (1985): 407–27.

4. *The Correspondence of John Locke*, ed. E. S. de Beer (Oxford: Oxford University Press, 1976), 1:375–76.

5. The best account of the comprehension proposals, and of all this debate, is Norman Sykes, *From Sheldon to Secker* (Cambridge: Cambridge University Press, 1959), ch. 3.

6. For this story, see the *Journals of the House of Commons* VIII, pp. 632, 687; *Historical Manuscripts Commission*, 8th Report I, pp. 111–12. The parliamentary diarist John Milward, who was absent on 17 October, recorded that "I was informed that it was moved in the House that certain atheistical books should be burned, among which Mr. Hobbes's *Leviathan* was one." *The Diary of John Milward Esq.*, ed. Caroline Robbins (Cambridge: Cambridge University Press, 1938), p. 25.

7. *Historical Manuscripts Commission*, 9th Report II, pp. 43, 67, 98; 11th Report II, p. 257.

8. John Aubrey, *Brief Lives*, ed. Oliver Lawson Dick (Harmondsworth, Eng.: Peregrine Books, 1962), p. 235.

9. Samuel I. Mintz, *The Hunting of Leviathan* (Cambridge: Cambridge University Press, 1962), pp. 50–52.

10. Aubrey's remark, incidentally, was unknown to the *Dialogue*'s most recent editor, Joseph Cropsey, who could not date the work. Thomas Hobbes, *A Dialogue between a Philosopher and a Student of the Common Laws of England*, ed. Joseph Cropsey (Chicago: University of Chicago Press, 1971), p. 2.

11. Ibid., p. 129.

12. The Scargill piece is mentioned in Mintz, *Hunting of Leviathan*, p. 52; *Behemoth* is dated by Crooke's remark recorded in *Behemoth*, ed. Ferdinand Tönnies (London:.Cass and Co., 1889), p. vii.

13. Samuel I. Mintz, "Hobbes on the Law of Heresy: A New Manuscript," *Journal of the History of Ideas* 29 (1968): 409–14. Mintz has wrongly dated the manuscript to 1673, by mistaking the dating of Charles II's regnal years.

14. *Calendar of State Papers, Domestic, 1667* (London, 1866), p. 163; *Calendar of State Papers, Domestic, 1667–68* (London, 1893), p. 466.

15. Anchitel Grey, *Debates of the House of Commons 1667–1694* (London, 1763), 1:103; Robbins, *Diary of John Milward*, p. 221.

16. *Historical Manuscripts Commission*, 8th Report I, p. 112.

17. *Dialogue*, pp. 131–32.

18. *De Cive: The Latin Version*, ed. Howard Warrender (Oxford: Oxford University Press, 1983), p. 226. Given that the existing English translation (*De Cive: The English Version*, ed. Howard Warrender (Oxford: Oxford University Press, 1983) is not by Hobbes and is very inaccurate in places, I shall use my own translations of *De Cive* throughout this paper. See my "Warrender's *De Cive*," *Political Studies* 33 (1985): 308–15.

19. All citations of the English *Leviathan* in this paper are from the edition by C. B. Macpherson (Harmondsworth, Eng.: Penguin, 1968).

20. Thomas Hobbes, *The Elements of Law*, 2d rev. ed., ed. Ferdinand Tönnies (London: Frank Cass and Co., 1969), 55.

21. Thomas Hobbes, *Opera Philosophica* (Amsterdam, 1668), 2:357.

22. Ibid., p. 346.

23. See particularly the letters from Robert Payne to Gilbert Sheldon, in "Illustrations of the State of the Church during the Great Rebellion," *The Theologian and Ecclesiastic* 6 (1848): 161–75.

24. Marshall, "Ecclesiology of the Latitude-men"; Goldie, "Sir Peter Pett," pp. 263–64.

25. Marshall, "Ecclesiology of the Latitude-men," p. 413 n. 26.

26. Samuel Parker, *A Discourse of Ecclesiastical Polity* (London, 1670), heading of chap. 5.

27. H. R. Fox Bourne, *The Life of John Locke* (London, 1876), e.g. 1:193.

28. Ibid.

29. Ibid., p. 181.

30. Richard Ashcraft, *Revolutionary Politics and Locke's "Two Treatises of Government"* (Princeton, N.J.: Princeton University Press, 1986), pp. 490ff.

31. Quentin Skinner, "Hobbes on Sovereignty: An Unknown Discussion," *Political Studies* 13 (1965): 213–18; cf. also (in apparent ignorance of Skinner's article) Arnold A. Rogow, *Thomas Hobbes* (New York: Norton, 1986), pp. 253–54.

32. See James R. Jacob, *Henry Stubbe, Radical Protestantism and the Early Enlightenment* (Cambridge: Cambridge University Press, 1983).

9

Atomes of Scripture:
Hobbes and the Politics
of Biblical Interpretation

James Farr

The world was falling apart before the very eyes of seventeenth-century Englishmen. The specter of disintegration and atomization transfixed the vision of poets and political philosophers alike. John Donne felt that Nature herself was crumbling to bits under the doubting gaze of the "new Philosophy."

> And freely men confesse that this world's spent,
> When in the Planets, and the Firmament
> They seeke so many new; they see that this
> Is crumbled out againe to his Atomis.
> 'Tis all in pieces, all cohaerence gone.[1]

Some years later, Sir Robert Filmer feared a more troubling, if less metaphysical, incoherence in parliamentary politics. The people's representatives, he charged, "are constrained to epitomize and sub-epitomize themselves so long, till at last they crumble away into the atoms of monarchy, which is next to anarchy."[2] Filmer sought order and wholeness in, among other places, the dictates of Scripture. But Thomas Hobbes espied disintegration and atomization there, too, especially when Holy Writ was interpreted by the enemies of peace and truth. Seeking their own advantage, they obscured everything by "casting atomes of Scripture, as dust before mens eyes."[3]

What would put the world back together again? Hobbes certainly had some ideas regarding Scripture—not to mention politics and the new philosophy. Hobbes's full passage deserves quotation, for it brings to a close his (unfortunately still neglected) account "Of a Christian Commonwealth" (part 3, *Leviathan*); and it prepares a bridgehead for his furious assaults against the "Kingdome of Darknesse" (part 4, *Leviathan*), the first chapter of which is "Of Spiritual Darknesse from MISINTERPRETATION of Scripture." It also contains a summary of what Hobbes alleged to be his own method of scriptural interpretation. He began with a glance back (at part 3), and he followed immediately with a disclaimer that is not above suspicion.

> And this much shall suffice, concerning the Kingdome of God, and Policy Ecclesiasticall. Wherein I pretend not to advance any Position of my own, but onely to shew what are the Consequences that seem to me deducible from the Principles of Christian Politiques, (which are the holy Scriptures,) in confirmation of the Power of Civill Soveraigns, and the Duty of their Subjects. And in the allegation of Scripture, I have endeavoured to avoid such texts as are of obscure, or controverted Interpretation; and to alledge none, but in such sense as is most plain, and agreeable to the harmony and scope of the whole Bible; which was written for the reestablishment of the Kingdome of God in Christ. For it is not the bare Words, but the Scope of the writer that giveth the true light, by which any writing is to bee interpreted; and they that insist upon single Texts, without considering the main Designe, can derive no thing from them cleerly; but rather by casting atomes of Scripture, as dust before mens eyes, make every thing more obscure than it is; an ordinary artifice of those that seek not the truth, but their own advantage.[4]

The careful reader—whether in the seventeenth or the twentieth century—would notice at least two things about this summary passage. First, in the course of *Leviathan* up to that point—not to mention his other works—Hobbes himself flung great dustbins full of "atomes of Scripture" before the eyes of his readers. Even in the most famous and widely read part of *Leviathan* (part 2, "Of Commonwealth"), for example, he supported "the Rights of Monarchy" by citing, in this nearly random order, verses from Exodus, Samuel, Kings, Samuel, Colossians, Matthew, Titus, Matthew, and (first coming last) Genesis.[5] In none of Hobbes's works, including *Leviathan* where Scripture receives its most sustained attention, do we find an epistle read in its entirety, a gospel faithfully reflected upon from beginning to end, a book perused for its meaning or guidance. Hobbes hurled atomes of Scripture as ably and cleverly as any pastor, presbyter, or priest.

Second, except for the truthful and even understated confession that Hobbes was writing "in confirmation of the Power of Civill Soveraigns, and the Duty of their Subjects," so very much else in the passage conflicts with what he said and did in *Leviathan* and elsewhere. The "sense" which he found in certain texts (or atomes) of Scripture is not always "most plain"; and even the distinction between "obscure" and "plain" passages fails to capture another class of metaphorical passages with which he wrestled. Insisting that interpreters seize not upon "bare Words" but upon the "Scope of the writer" sounds like an appeal, among other things, to the intentions of a particular writer as expressed in many texts. But Hobbes elsewhere observed how often "we cannot safely judge of men's intentions" within recent history, much less during the times of the Bible's composition.[6] Even then, the Bible was written and transmitted (with possible falsifications)[7] not by one writer but by many diverse writers whose collective intentions do not conspire to produce one "main Designe." Indeed the very identity of these many writers is unclear: "Who were the originall writers of the severall Books of Holy Scripture, has not been made evident by any sufficient testimony of other History, (which is the only proof of matter of fact)."[8] Finally, the whole summary passage does not appear to underwrite the often incredible interpretations of Scripture that Hobbes offered. Even the modern secular reader could be forgiven for agreeing with the Puritan minister Richard Baxter in *A Holy Commonwealth* (1659): "If any man will but read Scripture, he need no other confutation of Hobbes."[9]

If the rules expressed in Hobbes's summary passage in part 3 of *Leviathan* do not capture what he said and did when he interpreted Scripture, which implicit ones do? This question has hardly ever been posed in this way—one of the unfortunately simple and simply unfortunate consequences of the fact that Hobbes's writings on or invoking of Scripture are themselves hardly ever read.[10] And when read, they are often passed off as preserving a merely "decorous orthodoxy" and/or dismissed as a pioneering example of purely "destructive biblical criticism," as Basil Willey put it half a century ago.[11] This differs little from the reception accorded Hobbes by his contemporaries who thought him an atheist, and all the more dangerous an atheist because of his literary genius and savage wit.[12] More recently and sympathetically, David Johnston has recognized the principled and skillful way that Hobbes interpreted Scripture. But in reference to the principles articulated in the summary passage, he has surprisingly concluded that "Hobbes applies these interpretative principles to the Scriptures with relentless virtuosity."[13]

In this essay, I try to disinter the rules that *actually* underlie Hobbes's assuredly relentless interpretative practice. I also consider Hobbes's political and philosophical intentions in the matter of biblical interpretation. In short, I assay Hobbes's hermeneutical strategies in an account that is chiefly internal to his texts. To anticipate some of my conclusions, Hobbes sought to use Scripture to confirm his rationalism, his natural philosophy of body, and his political philosophy of absolute obedience; to interdict any special scriptural claims to political or ecclesiastical power on the part of churchmen;[14] and to exorcise the enthusiastic and superstitious strains in Christianity which unglued reason and undermined obedience. Read aright, Scripture served what Hobbes repeatedly called "peace and truth"[15]— though hardly a policy of civil toleration. Wildly diverse scriptural interpretations had helped to fuel the fires of civil war; and Hobbes hoped to use his own scriptural interpretation to help put them out. Should he succeed in convincing his readers—among them the sovereign—that his reading was the only one consistent with peace and truth, he would have helped to reconstitute the language and political community of his time.

PUTTING SCRIPTURE IN ITS PLACE

For a man who boasted of his timorousness and confessed that with the first "scent of civil war . . . I fled the shores of my country,"[16] Hobbes was bold and provocative in his writings, *especially* in his scriptural interpretation. This, at any rate, was his own advertisement—whether or not it does justice to his immediate predecessors. Both in the epistle dedicatory and in the review and conclusion of *Leviathan*, Hobbes called explicit attention to part 3 where "some new doctrines" are put forward. Further, these doctrines are not only new, they are offensive: "That which perhaps may most offend, are certain Texts of Holy Scripture, alledged by me to other purpose than ordinarily they use to be by others. But I have done it with due submission, and also (in order to my Subject) necessarily; for they are the Outworks of the Enemy, from whence they impugne the Civill Power."[17]

The arch-authoritarian Hobbes did not impugn the civil power, to put it mildly. Nor did he deny the truth of anything in Scripture even as he forwarded his admittedly offensive new doctrines. He did not deny, for example, that the Bible was authoritative over Christian souls, or that it contained our warrant for believing in God's existence and Christ's Second Coming, or that it should be "the rule of our actions, both public and private."[18] Hobbes's most personal religious (or irreligous) beliefs are not perfectly clear, to be sure; and subsequent debates about them refuse to be put to rest. But whatever one makes of those debates or of Hobbes's deepest convictions, it bears emphasizing that when it comes to the practice of scriptural interpretation and the politics of biblical discourse, Hobbes made a rule of not denying anything outright.

Hobbes's boldly advertised new doctrines purport to speak for "truth" as well as for "peace and loyalty."[19] Their "Novelty can breed no trouble" for an absolute sovereign or an obedient people. One surefire way to avoid trouble is to render unto the sovereign all manner of power, both ecclesiastical and temporal. Thus Hobbes allowed that among his (or its) many powers, the sovereign is the head of both church and state, commander of both law and canon.[20] Accordingly, he (or it) must be an interpreter: "There is need therefore of an interpreter to make the Scriptures canon. . . . *The word of an Interpreter of Scriptures is the word of God.*"[21] The power of interpretation adheres to sovereignty more generally. "For he to whom it belongs to interpret the controversies arising from the divers interpretations of Scriptures, hath authority also simply and absolutely to determine all manner of controversies whatsoever."[22]

This doctrine is *not* new with Hobbes, for it is the shared property of a number of early modern Erastian political theorists. If Hobbes made any novel contribution here, it is in the emphatic underscoring of the popular foundation of the sovereign's power over Scripture, as in all else. This is implied in *Leviathan* and driven home in *Liberty, Necessity, and Chance.* In response to Bishop Bramhall's view that "the positive law of the Bible, is a law without our assent," Hobbes fired back a series of rhetorical questions, to which he, naturally, provided the answers.

The Bible is a law. To Whom? To all the world? He knows it not. How came it then to be a law to us? Did God speak it *viva voce* to us? Have we then any other warrant for it than the word of the prophets? Have we seen the miracles? Have we any other assurance of their certainty than the authority of the Church? And is the authority of the Church any other than the authority of the commonwealth, or hath the head of the commonwealth any other authority than that which hath been given him by the members? Else, why should not the Bible be canonical as well in Constantinople as in any other place? They that have the legislative power make nothing canon, which they make not law, nor law, which they make not canon. And because the legislative power is from the assent of the subjects, the Bible is made law by the assent of the subjects.[23]

Having put Scripture in its *political* place under the popularly authorized power of the sovereign, the Erastian Hobbes could well have held his tongue or fled "the war between the pens"[24] in any further matters of scriptural interpretation. But this he did *not* do, even though it would have saved him the seventeenth-century accusation of being an atheist, much less the twentieth-century slur that he was a hypocrite and possibly a communist patriarch as well.[25] Although he granted to the popularly authorized sovereign the power to put interpretative controversy to rest, Hobbes himself did not rest content with rendering the Word unto the modern Caesar. If "peace" required the sovereign to interpret Scripture, "truth" required Hobbes to interpret it as well.[26] In the process, he put Scripture in its *textual* place.

Hobbes put Scripture last, at the end. This is so in a general analytical way, at least as his argument unfolds. Thus, in both *De Cive* and *Leviathan*, he listed the threefold Word of God in this order: reason, revelation, and prophecy (where the latter is "the *Voyce* of some *man*, to whom by the operation of Miracles, he procureth credit with the rest"[27]). But Hobbes noted for his contemporaries that "Miracles ceasing, Prophets cease, and the Scripture supplies their place."[28] As a matter of analysis, then, Scripture comes last. Beyond the analysis of the Word of God, Hobbes also brought Scripture to bear as a matter of literary form at the end of his various substantive discussions. This is true of whole works, such as *De Cive* (where the third and last part on "Religion" consists almost solely of scriptural interpretation) and *Leviathan* (at least if we take parts 3 and 4 together). This is also true of particular issues wherever they occur in Hobbes's works, even in the earlier parts.

Consider a brief list of examples. Having distinguished between paternal and despotical power, and having argued that by covenant the sovereign's power is absolute, Hobbes had his readers "now consider what the Scripture teacheth in the same point."[29] "Places and examples of Scripture of the rights of Government" are introduced to be "agreeable to what hath been said before."[30] Scripture also comes at the end of the analysis of natural law.[31] Hobbes belatedly cast the atome of Acts 19:40 in order to press home his argument with respect to unlawful assemblies.[32] Proverbs and Deuteronomy duly follow upon the argument that the law must be written and promulgated.[33] That men are bound to obey, though not necessarily to believe, divine positive law as dictated in a commonwealth Hobbes made "yet cleerer, by the Examples and Testimonies concerning this point in holy Scripture," where Genesis does the trick.[34] And then there is the most powerful and imaginal of Hobbes's atomes of Scripture. Having "set forth the nature of Man" up to the last paragraph in chapter 28, Hobbes looked back upon his achievement and crowned it at the end with that "comparison out of the two last verses of the one and fortieth of *Job,* where God having set forth the great power of *Leviathan,* called him King of the Proud."[35]

Scripture comes at the end for what appears to be two reasons. It functions to confirm what has come before; and it is given the last word. That is, rhetorically, Scripture "confirms"[36]—supports, justifies, rationalizes—the other forms of the Word of God which precede it, *especially reason.* Prophecy and miracles have ceased in modern England, and Scripture confirms only those reported during biblical times. Revelation hardly survives Hobbes's skepticism and humor, however, though of course it is never denied: "To say [God] hath spoken to [a man] in a Dream, is no more than to say he dreamed that God spake to him."[37] Others need believe such a dreamer even less, for God "obliges no man to beleeve . . . him that pretends it; who (being a man) may err, and (which is more) may lie."[38] In this way, Scripture functions as an "appendage" to the natural, first, and "undoubted word of God," namely reason.[39] Hobbes's rationalism, in short, finds its confirmation in Scripture.

But in this confirmation of reason, Scripture is also given the honor of being the last word. For Hobbes's Christian audience, it is that final invocation to which nothing else can or should be said. If not in the beginning, at least in the end, there is the Word.

DIVIDE AND CONQUER: THE WORD OBEDIENT

Once in place, Scripture still requires interpretation. Hobbes simply dismissed those who claim that Scripture requires no interpretation whatsoever. "Out of Holy Scripture: behold the book, read it," say the simple-minded—or those who would cozen them—in support of their self-certifying ideas. "In vain," thundered Hobbes in return.[40] All words require interpretation, whether in speech, text, law, or Scripture.[41] But there is danger here because of the degrees of freedom that interpretation allows. This is especially so of holy words, which seem particularly susceptible to wildly different and even licentious interpretations. These contributed to the "disorders" that Hobbes found around him and that occasioned his best writing.[42] In 1651, Hobbes counted that "the number of apostates from natural reason is almost become infinite. And it sprang from sick-brained men, who having gotten good store of holy words by frequent reading of the Scriptures, made such a connexion of them usually in their preaching, that their sermons, signifying just nothing, yet to unlearned men seemed most divine."[43]

In a context so confused and confusing, Hobbes took upon himself the task of interpreting the substance of Scripture. In practice, we find him dividing the words of Scripture into different sorts and then mobilizing different interpretative strategies for conquering them—or at least trying to conquer the assent of his own readers. The summary passage of part 3 of *Leviathan* signals Hobbes's demarcation of two of these sorts; those that are "plain" and those that are "obscure." Plain words virtually speak for themselves; or, rather, they are readily interpreted by those with the simplest command over any vulgar tongue into which the Bible has been translated, who will but take the time to consider the "harmony and scope of the whole Bible."[44] Obscure ones Hobbes avoided. Alas, there are some mysteries that passeth all human understanding, even Hobbes's.

In the summary passage, Hobbes did not elaborate on the plain or the obscure. He did not articulate there what messages plain texts usually convey. He neither identifies those passages whose words are obscure nor intimates any other sort of text, say, those that lie between the plain and the obscure. But if one reads Hobbes at all closely—not only in *Leviathan*, but in *De Cive* and *Behemoth*—one finds some illumination.

Plain texts teach subjects their duty or narrate relatively simple tales. These Hobbes amassed, often in great quantities. But he left them relatively free of commentary or gloss. His readers are assured, for example, that there are even some "cleer texts" which "receive no controversie."[45] As examples of the simple tales, we find a great string of unadorned texts about Jewish history.[46] There is "plain" Scripture about Jesus' first coming and overall character.[47] And there is a brief narrative run-through of the life of Jesus as found in Matthew.[48]

But, principally, plain texts harbor those "easy places which teach men their duty."[49] Hobbes called attention to these easy places in Old and New Testament whenever he could; and these communicate a number of doctrines which bear on "simple obedience" to a sovereign power "as great, as possibly men can be imagined to make it."[50] The Scriptures tell us "without obscurity," for example, that salvation only requires belief in the single article of faith that Jesus is the Christ; *and* obedience to law.[51] (Indeed the latter, if "perfect," would suffice for salvation if it were not for original sin, which was itself "disobedience.")[52] Even Christ's teachings are sparse and plain, as recorded in Scripture: "Obey the law" is his principal message. "*Right, politie,* and *natural sciences,*" on the other hand, "are subjects concerning which Christ denies that it belongs to his office to give any precepts."[53] Christians are free to speculate on these latter doctrines, at least if they do not conflict with the command to obey. For, of course, "our Saviour . . . sayes Give to Caesar that which is Caesars."[54] Naturally, St. Paul's Epistle to the Romans, chapter 13—"the most quoted of all texts on the questions of political obligation throughout the seventeenth century"[55]—finds its way into Hobbes's interpretation of the plain political message of the Bible. In particular, Hobbes invoked it in chapter 42 of *Leviathan* amidst his assaults on Cardinal Bellarmine, whom he took to be the veritable high priest of Catholic resistance since he was the most powerful representative of claims for the autonomy of the church over against the sovereign.[56] However, Hobbes did not belabor Romans 13, having at the ready sufficient other atomes of Scripture with which to make the same point.

To papists, Presbyterians, Independents, and sectaries, Hobbes made Scripture plain. Therefore, on pain of their own salvation, they should not use Scripture for their personal or ecclesiastical ends, much less to counsel disobedience or resistance. The power of churchmen of any sort is utterly dependent upon the command of the sovereign; they have no independent power, including in matters of Biblical interpretation. They surely should not commit "the greatest, and main abuse of Scripture"; namely, to argue that the Kingdom of God is (with the superstitious papists) the "present church" or (with the enthusiastic sectaries) the time when the dead will "rise again at the last day" as Christ's elect.[57] The Kingdom of God, shown plainly in the Old Testament, was that literal kingdom over which God ruled directly by his covenant with Abraham. In the

New Testament, it is the promise that Christ will come "to reign actually and eternally . . . on Earth," whoever is there at the time to serve him. Boastful of its novelty, Hobbes drove this unobscure point home, with all its obedient conclusions about obedience.

> Because this doctrine (though proved out of places of Scripture not few, nor obscure) will appear to most men a novelty; I doe but propound it; maintaining nothing in this, or any other paradox of Religion; but attending the end of that dispute of the sword, concerning the Authority (not yet amongst my Countrymen decided,) by which all sorts of doctrine are to bee approved, or rejected; and whose commands, both in speech, and writing (whatsoever be the opinions of private men) must by all men, that mean to be protected by their Laws, be obeyed.[58]

The obscure passages Hobbes passed over in silence. That he did not single them out is probably no accident, for why call attention to them? There are already far too many interpreters who seek out "every obscure place of Scripture" and "praetermitting the easy places which teach them their duty, fall scanning only of the mysteries of religion."[59] As we shall see more clearly, Hobbes wanted to eliminate or redirect the mysteries—to submit them to "reason's inquisition," as he put it with regard to the ecclesiastical authority of the temporal sovereign.[60] An interesting exercise would be to peruse Hobbes's texts in this matter, in order to discover which books, chapters, or verses Hobbes left in obscurity. But one book is conspicuously absent throughout the greater part of Hobbes's discussion of Scripture, and that is Revelation or the Apocalypse.[61] Faced with Gog and Magog, the loosing of Satan, and the temptations of the whore of Babylon, we can perhaps readily understand why he who wanted to confirm reason by Scripture and to teach duty plainly would leave such stories and prophecies almost entirely out of account.

THE SCRIPTURE OF ATOMES

For all his silence on obscure texts of Scripture, and for all his amassing of those atomes of plain Scripture that command obedience, Hobbes in fact spent more time wrestling with passages of Holy Writ belonging to neither of these categories. The summary passage at the end of part 3 of *Leviathan* does not mention those many texts of

Scripture that Hobbes took great pains to interpret and that he admitted are "hard," "difficult," "allegorical," or "metaphorical."[62] Of these—and let us call them collectively the metaphorical ones—many revert to the plain meaning of obedience by the time Hobbes was done with them. But there are other metaphorical passages that deal with metaphysical questions. Hobbes interpreted these in such a way as to render them consistent with his materialism. Since these metaphorical passages are not discussed in Hobbes's political works before *Leviathan*—whereas plain obedient ones are—we may presume that they are those "Texts of Holy Scripture, alledged by me to other purpose than ordinarily they use to be by others."[63] Hobbes read out of, or into, them his offending new doctrines.

There is no little irony in this interpretative strategy, of course, since Hobbes is famous for expressing contempt for metaphor as an abuse of speech.[64] But this posture was always overly stiff because Hobbes himself was a master of metaphor. "*Leviathan* is itself a metaphor, while the argument supporting it is but an extended metaphor."[65] In the present context, then, what is most interesting is Hobbes's insinuation of materialism into the metaphorical texts of Scripture.

Chapter 34 presents a trinity of holy words—spirits, angels, and inspiration—whose interpretation turns on what Hobbes called his natural philosophy of body. His interpretative strategy is to show how these words, though often used metaphorically, in Scripture, are not inconsistent with the literal "truths" about body as disclosed to natural reason (which, again, is the "undoubted word of God"). This is no easy task, and Hobbes knew it. But instead of consigning spirits, angels, and inspiration to a silent obscurity, he knew that "it is necessary . . . to determine, out of the Bible, the meaning of such words, as by their ambiguity, may render what I am to inferre upon them, obscure, or disputable."[66] But in hopes of dispelling obscurity and avoiding dispute, Hobbes mobilized what we might call the materialist interpretation of Scripture.

"The World is . . . Corporeall."[67] Its substances are corporeal bodies; indeed, the philosophical notion of "substance" is meaningless without the notion of "corporeall body." "Incorporeall substance"—that Thomistic doctrine still lingering in Romish superstition—is self-contradictory. The words, Hobbes said, when "joined together, destroy one another."[68] Spirits, then, cannot be incorporeal substances, which is known to those who rationally and scientifically study causes. And a close reading of Scripture confirms this, Hobbes asserted. "Spirit," as discussed in Scripture, refers to many things, often metaphorically, among them a passion or wind or extraordinary understanding or life or (yet again) subordination to authority. But it does not refer to incorporeal substance—much less to ghosts, even holy ones. Genesis, Exodus, Judges, Samuel, Kings, Job, Ezekiel, Numbers, Deuteronomy, Romans, Matthew, Mark, Luke, and Acts are all made to deliver up their lines to show this is so. Hobbes concluded with the idea of the Holy Ghost not far from his mind: "How we came to translate *Spirits*, by the word *Ghosts*, which signifieth nothing, neither in heaven, nor earth, but the Imaginary inhabitants of mans brain, I examine not: but this I say, the word *Spirit* in the text signifieth no such thing; but either properly a reall *substance*, or Metaphorically, some extraordinary *ability* or *affection* of the Mind, or of the Body."[69]

Next, angels become messengers of any sort, including the air or winds which are themselves but "thin bodies."[70] They may also be images that "rise in the fancie in Dreams and visions." Hobbes confessed that once he believed that angels were "nothing but" these images. However, "many places of the New Testament" have "extorted from my feeble Reason, an acknowledgment, and beleefe that there be also Angels substantiall, and permanent."[71] But Scripture does not say that they are "no place." Wherever they are, they are bodies.

Inspiration meets its materialist interpretation as well. Against a backdrop of enthusiastic claims about God's elect having prophetic certainty of things now or to come, Hobbes said bluntly that inspiration is "nothing but the blowing into a man some thin and subtile aire, or wind, in such manner as a man filleth a bladder with his breath." He allowed that there are other uses of the word (beyond the hot air of religious enthusiasts). But they are all like that "easie metaphor, to signifie, that God enclined the spirit or mind of those Writers, to write that which should be usefull in teaching, reproving, correcting, and instructing man in the way of righteous living."[72] Lest we misunderstand what this "way" is, Hobbes later made it plain that "Righteousness is but the will to give to every one his owne, that is to say, the will to obey the Laws."[73] Thus, once we work through the metaphors, "inspiration," materially speaking, is air blown into a man; or, politically speaking, the godly inclination to those virtues associated with obedience.

Beyond spirits, angels, and inspiration, Hobbes found similar passages in Scripture whose metaphorical words require materialist interpretation. These, too, are novel and likely to offend, but Hobbes pressed them on his readers anyway. In the process, he proved to be a mortalist,[74] as well as a unitarian. The so-called and scripturally unwarranted trinity is really three persons—Moses, Jesus, and the Apostles—representing God.[75] He further stated that "there is no reason" to believe in transubstantiation: as if "after certain words spoken over a peece of bread, that presently God hath made it not bread, but a God, or a man, or both, and neverthelesse it looketh still as like bread as ever it did."[76] The lives of the saints turn out to be "but Old Wives tales."[77] And he found on the earth (wherever else metaphors might point) the ordinary site of so many scriptural referents: "As the kingdom of God, and Eternall life, so also Gods Enemies, and their Torments after Judgment, appear by the Scripture to have their place on Earth."[78] These religious views earned Hobbes the reputation of being a heretic—a charge he was particularly concerned to counter, in and out of print, late in life.[79] But he stuck to his views, nonetheless. Among other reasons, they were consistent with his general metaphysical commitments, which he claimed were the dictates of reason, and so, godly and true. Reason—and its scriptural confirmation—cannot suffer superstition and enthusiasm. The world, according to the man who referred to himself as "the little worm that is myself," is earthy and finite. It is subject to change and open to the scrutiny of our senses and our reason. It is composed of bodies, and these of smaller bodies, and these of yet smaller bodies, until at last we come to the smallest bodies of all, the atoms. Atoms are the stuff of matter, men, and worms, as well as of spirits, angels, and inspiration. Holy Writ about them is but the Scripture of Atomes.

THE SOVEREIGN READER

When all is said, we can see what Hobbes has done. He has interpreted Scripture in a systematic way, even if not quite in the way he summarized. He has shown, if he did not quite say, under which rules he has implicitly proceeded. These implicit rules can perhaps best be articulated in the form of commands, as Hobbes himself might have liked:

1. Deny nothing outright; save the word, even as it is made to convey some offending new doctrines.

2. Put Scripture in its place, at the end; let it confirm that which has come before and let it have the last word.

3. Divide the passages into three sorts: the plain, the metaphorical, and the obscure.

4. Conquer each with different strategies: pile up the plain ones that teach subjects their duties to their absolute sovereigns; interpret the metaphorical ones in a way consistent with the plain ones and/or with a materialist metaphysic; remain silent on the obscure ones.

5. Surrender all matters of interpretation—including these rules—to the sovereign should he (or it) command it.

These are Hobbes's rules; or, at least, they provide a better reconstruction of his practice of scriptural interpretation. One may well wonder why, since he was bold enough to advertise his offending new doctrines, he did not also own these rules as his. As with many other of Hobbes's pregnant silences, no definitive answer is possible. But perhaps it is a literary strategy of reassurance. Having put his Christian readers through the paces of part 3, and preparing them for the intellectual savaging of part 4, Hobbes suggested that all is really well, after all. His readers should be reassured that, although neither he nor anyone else can understand the full mysteries and even obscurities of Scripture, his reading nonetheless fits authorial purpose, the essential simplicity, and the main design of Holy Writ. Indeed, there are other literary strategies Hobbes employed. The epistle dedicatory prefixed to his (and most other) works has its own peculiar literary strategy. It seeks intellectual (if not more lucrative) patronage through humble submissions and sometimes obsequious praise. Good form requires praise for a great man at the outset; good form requires reassurance for the patient reader en route. Remember also that Hobbes himself knew of his own eloquence, even as he excoriated eloquence.[80] And, again, he was the master metaphorist against metaphor. The summary passage simply takes some license, a pardonable offense for an eloquent master of metaphor and literary form.

One would do better to wonder, not about Hobbes's license with the "main Designe" of Scripture, but about *Hobbes's* main design. In other words, what was Hobbes trying to do in interpreting Scripture the way he did? The answer to this must be cast in terms of *what* Hobbes intended to accomplish and *through whom* he hoped to accomplish it. In brief, Hobbes intended and hoped to reconstitute the language and community of his contemporaries[81]—that is, to teach obedience to English subjects and to enlighten enthusiastic and superstitious Christians in the ways of natural philosophy and reason.[82] Peace and truth—to use Hobbes's own evidently partisan terms—could not suffer those sword-wielders who would resist established sovereign power, or those crazed and benighted Christians who were gulled by too many mysteries and too much magic. Their language and their community needed a radical reconstitution.

Hobbes had to be read and believed for this reconstitution to come about. Lacking either pulpit or police, he had to persuade with his pen. Not unlike the Apostles themselves, Hobbes held "nothing of power, but of Perswasion."[83] The task was difficult, for he knew that he was trying to persuade those who might be disinclined to believe him. But to judge by the sheer scale of his literary production, he obviously thought himself up to the task. He wrote both to the sovereign and to a broader audience, to readers high and low.

To a possible sovereign Hobbes appealed directly in one of his most famous (if somewhat facetious) passages:

> I recover some hope, that one time or other, this writing of mine, may fall into the hands of a Soveraign, who will consider it himselfe, (for it is short, and I think clear,) without the help of any interested, or envious Interpreter; and by the exercise of entire Soveraignty, in protecting the Publique teaching of it, convert this Truth of Speculation, into the Utility of Practice.[84]

The mechanism of this public teaching is made perfectly clear by Hobbes: use the universities and let the teachings trickle down. It was no coincidence, of course, that he hated the dons and divines at Oxford and Cambridge; or that, in their turn, they hated him and had his books burned. In any case, his own "Discourse," as Hobbes says in the penultimate paragraph of *Leviathan*, may yet have its baptismal effect.

> It may be profitably printed, and more profitably taught in the Universities. . . . For seeing the Universities are the Fountains of Civill, and Morall Doctrine, from whence the Preachers, and the Gentry, drawing such water as they find, use to sprinkle the same (both from the Pulpit, and in their Conversation) upon the People, there ought certainly to be great care taken, to have it pure, both from the Venime of Heathen Politicians, and from the Incantations of Deceiving Spirits.[85]

Any judicious sovereign would have this done. Any sovereign, that is, who was dutifully concerned to protect the people in their property, to preserve order in the state, and to keep himself (or itself) in power would have the university and pulpit render the Scripture as plain and demystified as possible. He (or it) would, by command, make the Scripture teach duty and confirm reason. In fine, any sovereign worthy of the name would make Hobbes's reading of Scripture *the* canonical reading.

Now Hobbes was probably aware that no readily available sovereign—certainly neither Cromwell nor Charles II—was presently going to do this. He was, in any case, fully aware of an incredible tension in this feature of his politics of biblical interpretation. He wanted Scripture put last and divided and conquered in the way he showed it should be done. But the sovereign, on Hobbes's own account, can do with or to Scripture what he (or it) likes, including, for example, making Hobbes's reading of it a civil offense punishable by any number of horrors meted out against seventeenth-century heretics or accused unbelievers. (Hobbes himself seemed sufficiently sensitive to this. Thus, he pleaded that his own doctrines should not be—as he may have feared them to be—excluded or condemned. "Me thinks, the endeavour to advance the Civill Power, should not be by the Civill Power condemned."[86]) With some fear, then, Hobbes went ahead and published his offending new doctrines, Erastianism notwithstanding. He took his message directly to the people, or at least to them through their literate betters. To say that Hobbes went over the head of the sovereign to the people would be the wrong metaphor. Given the frontispiece to *Leviathan*, it would be more apt to say he plunged his message into the very body of that mortal god. In other words, Hobbes may have had a more direct route in mind in the matter of persuasion. The culture of disobedience and rebellion, of enthusiasm and superstition, may yet have been reconstituted by that greater community of readers *in whose assenting opinions sovereign power ultimately rested*. So Hobbes, unlike the deceitful Machiavelli,[87] put his work before a larger audience. We must presume he hoped to influence them thereby.

"Read thy self," Hobbes told his readers in the preface of *Leviathan*.[88] "Read my booke, and then Read thy self," he might better have told them. The transformative power of the word is the only power that wordsmiths have, and Hobbes was a powerful wordsmith. There is not only the demonstrative logic and the geometric form. There is also eloquence and metaphor and all the tools of rhetoric. There is sport and sarcasm, acerbic humor and earthy hilarity, all alongside the evocative terrors of a disordered life. The dreadful gloom of the puritan or the superstitious amazement of the papist are dispelled by Hobbes's alternating appeals to our natural reason or to our mortal fear of death. Hobbes's "ideal reader"[89] is one who has made it through *Leviathan* with its exercises in logic, civil science, the psychology of terror, and the Scripture of atomes. He or she is one who is willing to be and in fact has been cajoled, entertained, baited, subjected to novelty upon novelty, and pelted with countless atomes of Scripture. This ideal reader, in short, is the reader persuadable in the ways of truth and peace, as Hobbes understood them. Should Hobbes actually persuade readers he would have not only authored some new doctrines but created new vessels for them. To use his own imagery, he would have poured "New wine . . . into New Cask."[90]

TOLERATING THE TRUTH,
AND NOTHING BUT

In an intolerant world—one, say, where puritan hates papist, presbyter hates independent, and everyone hates heretics—a reconstitution of language and community could conceivably lead to a more tolerant society, or at least to one with a policy of civil toleration. Does Thomas Hobbes have such a policy in mind as part of his main design? Very few have been confident of answering this question affirmatively, whether or not they favored such a policy or wished Hobbes had. Reviving Leslie Stephen's view, Alan Ryan has recently made a cautious case for this reading of Hobbes's intent.[91] Richard Tuck has gone so far as to claim that *Leviathan* is itself "a defense of toleration."[92]

This interpretation counts a number of things in its favor. Our "beliefs, opinions, and interior cogitations" are free from the commands of anyone, including the sovereign, simply because we have no causal control over them.[93] They *must* be tolerated because we have no choice in the matter. It was the effect, if not the intent, of this line of reasoning to create enclaves of free thinking for philosophers or scientists, at least for those who kept the peace. In the tract on *Heresy*, Hobbes also argued (in part to clear himself from such charges) that heresy was originally conceived of as merely a private opinion that did not deserve punishment. More generally, Hobbes skeptically demolished the arguments of his clerical contemporaries who (with few exceptions) were against toleration. If logic ruled the contest of texts, much less the world itself, Hobbes's views might help serve toleration, if only because the effect of his writing would be against those against toleration. Taking a century and more at a glance, Hobbes certainly figures in the history of enlightened skepticism, whose eventual outcome was to make toleration a matter of principle.

Then, too, there is the important, if these days often overlooked, passage near the very end of *Leviathan*. Having for almost the last time blasted Catholic and Presbyterian doctrinaires as the principal architects of the kingdom of darkness—but reminding his readers that the civil wars had largely swept them aside anyway—Hobbes remarked:

> And so we are reduced to the Independency of the Primitive Christians to follow Paul, Cephas, or Apollos, every man as he liketh best: Which, if it be without contention, and without measuring the Doctrine of Christ, by our affection to the Person of his Minister, (the fault which the Apostle reprehended in the Corinthians,) is perhaps the best.

Hobbes then gives his reasons, among them the power of Scripture. "First, because there ought to be no Power over the Consciences of men, but of the Word it selfe, . . . and secondly, because it is unreasonable in them, who teach there is such danger in every little Errour, to require of a man endued with Reason of his own, to follow the Reason of any other man, or of the most voices of many other men."[94]

But, beginning even with Hobbes's next paragraph, the case for Hobbes as a defender of toleration is not further supported when we closely consider this passage or when we look one final time at Hobbes's account of scriptural interpretation more generally. The Independents and sectaries, of whom Hobbes spoke in the above passage, insist on and persist in "measuring the Doctrine of Christ"; and they had done so with "contention" to the point of civil war. *Behemoth* records again and for the last time Hobbes's oft-expressed judgments in this matter. Among the seven sorts of "seducers" of the people during the time of the Long Parliament were those who cried out for a "liberty of religion." They meet with Hobbes's characteristic accusations. "These were the enemies which rose against his Majesty from the private interpretation of the Scripture, exposed to every man's scanning in his mother-tongue."[95] He continued a few pages on: "This license of interpreting the Scripture was the cause of so many several sects . . . to the disturbance of the Commonwealth."[96] Earlier in *Leviathan*—and quite different from the tone of the Independency passage—Hobbes reminded his readers that "it is the Civill Soveraign that is to appoint Judges, and Interpreters of the

Canonical Scriptures," as well as to make "such Laws and Punishments, as may humble obstinate Libertines, and reduce them to union with the rest of the Church."[97] Since the reading of Scripture is not a purely private act but a public ceremony as well, Hobbes included it in the "Uniformity" of worship upon which he advised a sovereign to insist.[98] And anyway, toleration does not in turn breed more toleration. Indeed, as the English translation of *De Cive* puts the point, the "diversity of worshippers" actually causes intolerance, for they judge one another's worship as "uncomely, or impious."[99]

Amidst all the false and seditious doctrines, Hobbes called out for (if I may put it this way) toleration for the truth, and nothing but the truth. As he proclaimed in one of his many heated exchanges with Bramhall (an exchange marked once again by his fulminations against that "canting tribe" of Presbyterians and the "fractions of fractions of religion here in England"): "What use soever be made of truth, yet truth is truth, and now the question is not, what is fit to be preached, but what it true."[100] As we have seen, this means the "truth" of what Hobbes took to be reason, the doctrine of absolute obedience, and the Scripture of atomes. Needless to say, this would appear to entail a healthy dose of intolerance not only for intolerant clerics but for dissenters, sectarians, and enthusiasts, who in fact pressed from below their case for toleration of public expression and open worship. Indeed, Hobbes's "truth" might appear to entail a healthy dose of intolerance for everything except what John Locke would later call "the religion of Hobbes and Spinosa."[101] There were others in Hobbes's time who better deserved recognition in matters of toleration, especially William Walwyn, Richard Overton, John Lilburne, Roger Williams, or Gerrard Winstanley. There is not very much in *De Cive, Leviathan,* or *Behemoth* to place Hobbes in their company, or in the company of John Milton, whose passionate pleas for censureless publication surely make *Areopagitica* a genuine defense of toleration. Very little in any of Hobbes's writings place him in the company of the later Locke, whose arguments for the freedom of "indifferent" practices as well as belief surely make the *Letter concerning Toleration* a genuine defense of toleration. It is important, in the end, to recall that Hobbes was not writing *about* toleration, and such strains of it that we find in his work exist alongside more virulent strains of intoleration.

Let us give to Locke a final reflection. In my mind, he provides a startling contrast to Hobbes, not because his ideas are in every instance so different, but because in places they are so similar, even beyond the window of time that the 1660s and 1670s represent.

Given the circumscribed concerns of this essay, it bears observing that Locke, like Hobbes, feared those who would have "Scripture crumbled into verses."[102] He too purported to subscribe to a method of scriptural interpretation that relies upon authorial design, the whole text, and a plain reading.[103] But Locke would appear to actually interpret Scripture in terms of this stated method. This reading of Locke's method and practice, at any rate, would conform to the author of *A Paraphrase and Notes on the Epistles of St. Paul*, who "continued to read the same epistles over and over, and over again"; and who counseled "he that would understand St. Paul right, must understand his terms, in the sense he uses them, and not as they are appropriated, by each man's particular philosophy."[104] In the passage in which he referred with apparent horror to "the religion of Hobbes and Spinosa," Locke may well have had in mind one particular philosopher who had put forward and loudly advertised some bold new offensive doctrines in an attempt to engineer a mortal god. "Perhaps it would better become us to acknowledge our ignorance, than to talk such things boldly of the Holy One of Israel, and condemn others for not daring to be as unmannerly as ourselves."[105]

NOTES

This essay benefited from comments or criticisms supplied by Mary G. Dietz, Don Herzog, Jeffrey Isaac, Dana Chabot, Terence Ball, and (especially) Mark Goldie. I would also like to thank James Boyd White for his commentary at the Benjamin Evans Lippincott Symposium on the Political Philosophy of Hobbes at the University of Minnesota (spring 1988).

1. John Donne, *The First Anniversarie: An Anatomie of the World* (London, 1611), pp. 20–21.

2. Sir Robert Filmer, *Observations upon Aristotle's Politiques* (London, 1652). Quoted in David Wootton, ed., *Divine Right and Democracy* (Harmondsworth, Middlesex: Penguin, 1986), p. 113.

3. Thomas Hobbes, *Leviathan*, ed. C. B. Macpherson (Harmondsworth, Middlesex: Penguin, 1968), ch. 43, p. 626. All references to *Leviathan* will be to this edition.

4. Ibid., ch. 43, pp. 625–26.

5. Ibid., ch. 20, pp. 258–59.

6. *Behemoth*, vol. 6 in *The English Works of Thomas Hobbes*, ed. Sir William Molesworth, 11 Vols. (London: John Bohn, 1839–1845), p. 254. (All references to *Behemoth* will be to this volume.) Also see Hobbes's remarks on "intentionality . . . and other insignificant words" in *Leviathan,*, ch. 9, p. 101.

7. *Leviathan,* ch. 33, p. 423.

8. Ibid., ch. 33, p. 416.

9. Quoted in Wootton, *Divine Right and Democracy,* p. 232. Baxter speaks with special reference to the kingdom of Christ at the Second Coming.

10. For some exceptions not otherwise mentioned in this essay, see Gerard Reedy, *The Bible and Reason: Anglicans and Scripture in Late Seventeenth-Century England* (Philadelphia: University of Pennsylvania Press, 1985), ch. 2; Eldon J. Eisenach, *Two Worlds of Liberalism: Religion and Politics in Hobbes, Locke, and Mill* (Chicago: University of Chicago Press, 1981); Paul J. Johnson, "Hobbes Anglican Doctrine of Salvation," and Herbert W. Schneider, "The Piety of Hobbes," in *Thomas Hobbes in His Time,* ed. Ralph Ross, Herbert W. Schneider, and Theodore Waldman (Minneapolis: University of Minnesota Press, 1974); Patricia Springborg, "*Leviathan,* The Christian Commonwealth Incorporated," *Political Studies* 24 (1976): 171–83; and Joel Schwartz, "Hobbes and the Two Kingdoms of God," *Polity* 18 (1985): 7–24. There is, of course, a larger and related literature dealing with Hobbes's views on ecclesiastical authority, the church, the nature of God, and religion in general.

11. Basil Willey, *The Seventeenth Century Background* (Garden City, N.Y.: Doubleday & Company, 1953), pp. 79–80.

12. For discussion of the reception of Hobbes's ideas, see Samuel I. Mintz, *The Hunting of Leviathan* (Cambridge: Cambridge University Press, 1962), esp. pp. 37–38. Also see Mark Goldie, "The Reception of Hobbes," in *The Cambridge History of Early Modern Political Thought,* eds. J. H. Burns and Mark Goldie (Cambridge: Cambridge University Press, forthcoming), particularly for its theological debates.

13. David Johnston, *The Rhetoric of Leviathan: Thomas Hobbes and the Politics of Cultural Transformation* (Princeton, N.J.: Princeton University Press, 1986), p. 142. Johnston also refers to the principle that Scripture be read "according to reason," which is not mentioned in the summary passage.

14. Alan Ryan states that "the purpose of Hobbes's argument seems to be to drive scriptural considerations out of politics, in order to deprive the church of any independent political power." See his "Hobbes, Toleration, and the Inner Life," in *The Nature of Political Theory,* ed. David Miller and Larry Siedentop (Oxford: Clarendon Press, 1983), p. 203. As I hope to make clear, I agree with the judgment regarding the deprivation of churchmen of any independent political power. But should Hobbes's interpretation of Scripture prove successful with his readers, it could stay in the politics of "a truthful and peaceful" commonwealth. Indeed, it would help constitute such a commonwealth.

15. Most dramatically in the Review and Conclusion, *Leviathan,* p. 726.

16. Hobbes made this confession in his Latin autobiography, as translated by Benjamin Farrington in *The Rationalist Annual* (London: Watts and Co., 1958), p. 30.

17. *Leviathan,* Epistle Dedicatory, p. 76.

18. *Behemoth,* p. 174.

19. *Leviathan,* Review and Conclusion, p. 726.

20. See especially *Leviathan,* ch. 33.

21. *De Cive,* as translated (at least in part) by Hobbes as *Philosophical Rudiments concerning Government,* ed. Bernard Gert, *Man and Citizen* (Gloucester, Mass.: Peter Smith, 1978), p. 349, emphasis in original. For some skepticism

about Hobbes's unassisted translation or authorship of *Philosophical Rudiments*, see Richard Tuck, "Warrender's *De Cive*," *Political Studies* 33 (1985): 308–15.

22. *De Cive*, p. 385.

23. *Liberty, Necessity, and Chance*, in *English Works*, 5: 179.

24. *Behemoth*, p. 266.

25. Consider Basil Willey's judgment that "it was impracticable for Hobbes, as indeed it had proved for most people until the times of his modern disciples the Soviet rulers, to 'boot the Bible into the dustbin.' And yet it would have saved him a great deal of trouble and hypocrisy if he could have done so" (*The Seventeenth Century Background*, p. 120). Leo Strauss offers a similar judgment of Hobbes's "circumspection" in the matter of his allegedly atheistic beliefs, in *Natural Right and History* (Chicago: University of Chicago Press, 1953), p. 199.

26. This contrasts with the judgment of Howard Warrender who, in a work surprisingly less concerned with Scripture than one would have thought, states that "far from basing political obligation upon Christian Scripture, Hobbes is able to give the political sovereign such wide powers to interpret Scriptures because in his opinion, their significance is limited" (*The Political Philosophy of Hobbes: His Theory of Obligation* [Oxford: Clarendon Press, 1957], p. 228). Though I agree with Warrender's premise that Hobbes does not "base" obligation on Scripture, the conclusion does not follow. Indeed, I am inclined to say that, politically and rhetorically, the significance of Scripture is virtually unlimited! Conversely, F. C. Hood overstates the case about the source of Hobbes's doctrines when he claims that "Scripture was the only source of Hobbes's moral conviction." This flies in the face of what Hobbes said about morals being founded in reason (the "undoubted word of God" outside Scripture) and with what Hood himself says in a rather more Warrender-like moment: Hobbes's "odd interpretations of some texts need cause no surprise; in most cases he had little commitment to them" (*The Divine Politics of Thomas Hobbes* [Oxford: Clarendon Press, 1964], pp. 3–4).

27. *De Cive*, p. 291; *Leviathan*, ch. 31, p. 396.

28. *Leviathan*, ch. 32, p. 414. In *De Homine*, Hobbes also dated his era as a time when "miracles now having ceased." See Gert, ed. *Man and Citizen*, p. 72.

29. *Leviathan*, ch. 20, pp. 257–58.

30. *De Cive*, p. 237.

31. Ibid., p. 154.

32. *Leviathan*, ch. 22, p. 288.

33. Ibid., ch. 26, p. 319.

34. Ibid., ch. 26, p. 333.

35. Ibid., ch. 28, p. 362.

36. The language of "confirming" pervades Hobbes's discussion. For an early striking use, see *De Cive*, p. 154.

37. *Leviathan*, ch. 32, p. 411.

38. Ibid. Don Herzog points out that "may err" was mistakenly omitted in the Penguin edition. See his *Happy Slaves* (forthcoming), ch. 3, especially the concluding observations about Hobbes's "singularly eccentric interpretations of Scripture playing a 'central political role.'"

39. *De Cive*, p. 93; *Leviathan*, ch. 32, p. 409.

40. *De Cive*, p. 366.

41. For law, see *Leviathan*, ch. 26, p. 322. There is at least one rhetorical

flourish in *Behemoth* where we encounter texts of Scripture "so easy, as not to need interpretation" (p. 233).

42. *Leviathan*, Review and Conclusion, p. 728.

43. *De Cive*, p. 249.

44. *Leviathan*, ch. 43, p. 626.

45. Ibid., ch. 43, p. 617.

46. *De Cive*, pp. 318ff.

47. Ibid., pp. 333–34.

48. Ibid., pp. 377-78.

49. *Behemoth*, p. 232.

50. *Leviathan*, ch. 20, pp. 259–60.

51. Ibid., ch. 43, p. 615; cf. discussion of "other words, that are plain" (ch. 43, p. 620) and those "very evident places of Scripture" (ch. 38, p. 492) that speak to the requirements for salvation.

52. *De Cive*, p. 370. This is in a passage in which Hobbes complained, yet again, that "the holy Scriptures . . . by divers men are diversely understood." Also see *Leviathan*, ch. 43, p. 610.

53. *De Cive*, p. 345. Also see *Leviathan*, ch. 43, pp. 551–52.

54. *Leviathan*, ch. 20, p. 259, emphasis omitted.

55. Quentin Skinner, "Conquest and Consent: Thomas Hobbes and the Engagement Controversy," in *The Interregnum: The Quest for Settlement, 1646-1660*, ed. G. E. Aylmer (London: Macmillan, 1972), p. 83.

56. *Leviathan*, ch. 42, p. 589; cf. pp. 259, 516.

57. Ibid., ch. 44, p. 629.

58. Ibid., ch. 38, p. 484.

59. *Behemoth*, pp. 230, 232.

60. *De Cive*, p. 346.

61. Hobbes briefly mentioned the book of "Apocalypse" in *Leviathan* when discussing the metaphors for the word of God (ch. 36, p. 455) and for death and damnation (ch. 38, pp. 486, 490). For an account that emphasizes Hobbes's own apocalyptic moments, see J. G. A. Pocock, "Time, History, and Eschatology in the Thought of Thomas Hobbes," in *Politics, Language, and Time* (New York: Atheneum, 1973), pp. 148–201.

62. See, for example, *Leviathan*, ch. 34, p. 440; ch. 36, p. 453; ch. 38, pp. 486, 488, 490; ch. 42, p. 557; ch. 43, p. 620; and *Behemoth*, pp. 175, 230.

63. *Leviathan*, Epistle Dedicatory, p. 76.

64. Most famously in *Leviathan*, ch. 4, p. 102.

65. Sheldon Wolin, *Hobbes and the Epic Tradition of Political Theory* (Los Angeles: William Andrews Clark Memorial Library, 1970), p. 38.

66. *Leviathan*, ch. 34, p. 428.

67. Ibid., ch. 45, p. 659.

68. Ibid., ch. 34, p. 429.

69. Ibid., ch. 34, p. 433.

70. Ibid., ch. 34, p. 435.

71. Ibid., ch. 34, p. 440.

72. Ibid., ch. 34, pp. 440–41.

73. Ibid., ch. 43, p. 611.

74. Ibid., ch. 38, p. 483. Also see Hobbes's evasiveness when it comes to Matt. 10:28 in *Leviathan*, ch. 43, p. 610.

75. *Leviathan*, ch. 42, p. 522.

76. Ibid., ch. 37, p. 477.

77. Ibid., ch. 46, p. 702.

78. Ibid., ch. 38, p. 485.

79. See especially *An Historical Narration concerning Heresie, and the Punishment Thereof*, in *English Works*, 3: 385–408.

80. Though Hobbes frequently picked out the eloquence of certain authors and speakers as one of the causes of civil war, he confessed to his own "eloquence" in the Review and Conclusion to *Leviathan*, hoping that it "may stand very well together" with reason (p. 718).

81. In general, see James Boyd White, *When Words Lose Their Meaning: Constitutions and Reconstitutions in Language, Character, and Community* (Chicago: University of Chicago Press, 1984), esp. chs. 1, 10. For Hobbes, in particular, see Johnston, *The Rhetoric of Leviathan*, passim.

82. Hobbes's role in combating enthusiasm in the history of Enlightenment political science is mentioned in my "Political Science and the Enlightenment of Enthusiasm," *American Political Science Review* 82 (1988): 58.

83. *Leviathan*, ch. 43, p. 551.

84. Ibid., ch. 31, p. 408.

85. Ibid., Review and Conclusion, p. 728.

86. Ibid., Epistle Dedicatory, p. 75.

87. See Mary G. Dietz, "Trapping the Prince: Machiavelli and the Politics of Deception," *American Political Science Review* 80 (1986): 779.

88. *Leviathan*, Introduction, p. 82.

89. The phrase is White's, *When Words Lose Their Meaning*, p. 270.

90. *Leviathan*, Review and Conclusion, p. 726.

91. Ryan, "Hobbes, Toleration, and the Inner Life." This essay ends by "suggesting that the sense in which Hobbes has principled reasons for toleration must always and only be that he has epistemologically principled reasons, never morally principled reasons" (p. 217). Ryan makes an equally cautious but more contextual version of the same argument in "A More Tolerant Hobbes?" in *Justifying Toleration*, ed. Susan Mendus (Cambridge: Cambridge University Press, 1988). He shows how some of Hobbes's contemporaries were horrified by the prospects of the free thinking he represented and how Hobbes contributed over the long haul to various strands of modern doctrines of toleration. However, he also bids us to "not exaggerate" the case, for in the main Hobbes "was not writing about toleration but about the right of the civil sovereign to control the squabbling clergy" (p. 51).

92. See Richard Tuck's essay, "Hobbes and Locke on Toleration," in this volume, especially p. 165. Much else in the essay is quite compelling, especially the careful contextualization of the comparison between Hobbes and Locke. Yet, even then, I find more convincing Tuck's argument in another essay; namely, that Hobbes and the young Locke, as with Grotius and Lipsius before them, could combine in "so standard" a way "respect for the arguments of the sceptic, acceptance of a minimalist morality, and support for a potentially *in*tolerant state" (Richard Tuck, "Scepticism and Toleration in the Seventeenth Century," in Mendus, *Justifying Toleration*, p. 33, emphasis added).

93. "Internall Faith is in its own nature invisible, and consequently exempted from all humane jurisdiction" (*Leviathan*, ch. 43, p. 550); "The secret thoughts of a man run over all things, holy, prophane, clean, obscene, grave

and light, without shame, or blame; which verbal discourse cannot do" (*Leviathan*, ch. 8. p. 137).

94. *Leviathan*, ch. 47, p. 711. As Tuck observes, this passage was (conveniently?) omitted from the later Latin edition published after the Restoration.

95. *Behemoth*, p. 167. Compare this with Samuel Parker's judgment that Hobbes's doctrines had the same effect, as quoted in Tuck, "Hobbes and Locke," p. 21. This appears to be but one instance of the broader charge that Hobbes or Hobbism was committed to "libertinism." See Mintz, *The Hunting of Leviathan*, ch. 7.

96. *Behemoth*, p. 191. Also see his view that "the interpretation of a verse in the Hebrew, Greek, or Latin Bible is oftentimes the cause of civil war" (p. 343).

97. *Leviathan*, ch. 42, p. 576.

98. *Leviathan*, ch. 18, p. 233; ch. 30, p. 379; ch. 31, p. 405; ch. 42, pp. 545, 567.

99. *De Cive*, p. 304.

100. *Of Liberty and Necessity*, in *English Works*, 4:252.

101. John Locke, *Remarks upon Mr. Norris's Books*, in *The Works of John Locke*, 9 vols. (London, 1824), 9: 255.

102. In the preface to *A Paraphrase and Notes of the Epistles of St. Paul*, in *The Locke Reader*, ed. John W. Yolton (Cambridge: Cambridge University Press, 1977), p. 17.

103. John Locke, *The Reasonableness of Christianity* (Stanford, Calif.: Stanford University Press, 1958), esp. p. 25.

104. Locke, *Paraphrase and Notes*, in Yolton, *The Locke Reader*, p. 28.

105. Locke, *Remarks*, in *Works*, 9: 255-56.

The Contributors

DEBORAH BAUMGOLD is associate professor of political science at the University of Oregon. She is the author of *Hobbes's Political Theory* as well as articles on Hobbes and on philosophy of interpretation.

MARY G. DIETZ is associate professor of political science at the University of Minnesota. She is the author of *Between the Human and the Divine: The Political Thought of Simone Weil*, as well as articles on Machiavelli, Hannah Arendt, and feminist political thought.

JAMES FARR is associate professor of political science at the University of Minnesota, where he teaches political theory. He is coeditor of *Political Innovation and Conceptual Change* and *After Marx* and author of a number of articles in the philosophy of the social sciences and the history of political thought.

STEPHEN HOLMES is professor of political science and law at the University of Chicago. He is the author of *Benjamin Constant and the Making of Modern Liberalism*.

DAVID JOHNSTON is assistant professor of political science at Columbia University. He is the author of *The Rhetoric of Leviathan: Thomas Hobbes and the Politics of Cultural Transformation* and has published articles on Hobbes, compensatory justice, human agency, and other topics in political philosophy.

GORDON J. SCHOCHET is professor of political science at Rutgers University. He is the author of *Patriarchalism in Political Thought* and editor of *Life, Liberty and Property: Essays on Locke's Political Ideas.*

RICHARD TUCK is a Fellow of Jesus College, Cambridge, and the author of *Natural Rights Theories* and a number of articles on Hobbes and early modern political thought.

SHELDON S. WOLIN is professor of politics (emeritus), Princeton University. He is the author of *Politics and Vision, Hobbes and the Epic Tradition,* and *Presence of the Past: Essays on State and Constitution.*

Index

Absolutism, 13, 20, 24, 26, 33, 57
  as answer to multitude's clash of interests, 94–96
  in politics as parallel to absolutism in thought, 22
  in theological and scientific thinking, 18–19
  See also Monarchy, absolute; Sovereign; Sovereign power; Sovereignty
Acquisition as source of sovereign power, 58–59, 60–61, 63–64, 71n74, 72n23
Act, individual, obligation as consequence of, 58
Activities as intrinsically valuable for Plato, 41–42, 45
Act of Uniformity (1662), 155, 166
Acts of the Apostles, 178
Advantage seeking. *See* Opportunism
Aeschylus, 39
Agency, social, denial of, 83–84
Allegiance, 80–81, 88n38, 98–99, 117n68
  qualities needed to sustain, 92
  submission transformed into, 103
Ambition, 77, 96–97, 100, 106–7, 115n30, 132
  of elites, 82–83, 84, 95
  as immoderate love of political power, 76–77, 78, 87nn24, 28
Ambrose, 136
Anarchy, 67, 136, 142, 145–46, 150n48
Angels, 182, 183, 184
Anger, 40, 134

Anglicans, 128, 137, 150n51, 155, 160, 162–63, 168
  attitudes of on Conventicle Act and Act of Uniformity, 156–57
  comprehension schemes involving, 156–57, 158, 159
  use of *De Cive* rather than *Leviathan*, 166–67
Antidemocratic regime
  as favored by scientific and technical knowledge, 13–14
Antidisestablishmentarianism, 150n48
Apocalypse, 180, 193n61
Apostolic succession, 163
Apostles, the, 184
Appetites, 5, 45–48, 51
  Plato's view of, 46–47, 51
  See also Passions
Applause, irrational desire for, 132–33
Areopagitica (Milton), 190
"Are There Any Natural Rights?" (Hart), 73n45
Arian, Hobbes as an, 165
Aristocracy, 76, 111, 116n50, 118nn70, 72
Aristotelianism, 22
Aristotle, 25, 134, 143
  Hobbes's criticisms of, 131, 147n21
Arlington, earl of, 159, 167
Armies, 125, 133, 134, 146n4
  authority over, 138, 150n52
Arms, authority of, 137–38
Arrogance, 102, 106–7, 116n50

Hobbes on, 119n77, 157–60, 163–70, 188–91, 195nn91, 92
Locke on, 167–70, 190–91
Tönnies, Ferdinand, 87n14
Totalitarianism, 9–10
Traitor as a label, 128
Transubstantiation, 184
Treason as a label, 128
Trew Law of Free Monarchies, The (James I), 78–79
Trinity, 165
  as Moses, Jesus, and the Apostles, 184
Truth, 18, 22, 176, 177, 182, 190
  of geometry, 26–27
  in Hobbesian science, 20–21
  Plato on, 9–10, 11–13, 15
  Popper on, 9–10, 11–13
  reconstitution of language and community as necessary for, 185–86, 188
  relationship of to power, 12–13
Tuck, Richard, 188, 195n92
Tully, John, 154
Turgot Circle, 17
Two Treatises of Government (Locke), 153, 168, 169–70
Tyrannicide, 83
Tyranny, 16, 34n16, 42, 147n12, 147n21
  denunciation of, 126, 147n12
  as dislike, 25
  as label, 128–29
  of reason, 13
  right of resistance to, 79–80

Unconditionality
  of God, 24
  of sovereign, 84, 90n62
Unitarian, Hobbes as, 184
Universalist theories, 145, 152n77
Universal rule (in geometry), 26

Universal self-interest, 145
Universities
  as source of dangerous doctrines, 96–97, 100, 130–31
  use of to teach Hobbes's new doctrines, 78, 110–11, 151n67, 186–87
Utilitarianism, 2, 94–95, 119n77

Value, 41–43, 44, 48, 51, 126
Vanity, 132–34, 149n35
Veneration attached to names, 128
Vernacular, Bible in the, 142
Vice, 101, 126. *See also* Science of virtue and vice
Vilification, by use of labels, 128
Virtue, 11, 44, 48, 116n41, 126. *See also* Civic virtue; Science of virtue and vice

War of all against all, 59
Warrender, Howard, 2–3, 57, 71n7, 73n46, 193n26
"Was John Locke a Bourgeois Theorist?" (Isaac), 118n76
Watkins, J. W. N., 3, 115n36, 117n60
Wealth, 147nn13, 15
Wentworth, John (earl of Strafford), 127
Whigs, 82, 83, 84, 85, 169
Whole Duty of Man, The, (Hobbes), 150n51
Will, 27, 60, 67, 83, 183
  geometric figures generated by, 22, 27
  political obligation as product of, 57, 65, 69
Willey, Basil, 174, 193n25
Wood, Neal, 76
Word of God, 177–78
Worship, 117n60, 156, 167, 190
Worth. *See* Value
Wrath, 40, 134